STANDARD BASIC MATH AND APPLIED PLANT CALCULATIONS

Standard Basic Math and Applied Plant Calculations
STEPHEN M. ELONKA

Boiler Room Questions and Answers (2d ed., 1976)
ALEX HIGGINS AND STEPHEN M. ELONKA

Electrical Systems and Equipment for Industry
ARTHUR H. MOORE AND STEPHEN M. ELONKA

Standard Boiler Operators' Questions and Answers
STEPHEN M. ELONKA AND ANTHONY L. KOHAN

Standard Electronics Questions and Answers
STEPHEN M. ELONKA AND JULIAN L. BERNSTEIN
Volume I, Basic Electronics
Volume II, Industrial Applications

Standard Industrial Hydraulics Questions and Answers
STEPHEN M. ELONKA AND ORVILLE H. JOHNSON

Standard Instrumentation Questions and Answers
STEPHEN M. ELONKA AND ALONZO R. PARSONS
Volume I, Measuring Systems
Volume II, Control Systems

Standard Plant Operators' Manual (2d ed., 1975)
STEPHEN M. ELONKA

Standard Plant Operator's Questions and Answers
STEPHEN M. ELONKA AND JOSEPH F. ROBINSON
Volume I
Volume II

Standard Refrigeration and Air Conditioning Questions and Answers
(2d ed., 1973)
STEPHEN M. ELONKA AND QUAID W. MINICH

The Marmaduke Story
STEPHEN M. ELONKA

STANDARD BASIC MATH AND APPLIED PLANT CALCULATIONS

STEPHEN MICHAEL ELONKA

Contributing Editor, Power *magazine; Licensed Chief Marine Steam Engineer, Oceans, Unlimited Horsepower; Licensed as Regular Instructor of Vocational High School, New York State; Member, National Association of Power Engineers (life honorary); National Institute for the Uniform Licensing of Power Engineers, Inc., Honorary Chief Engineer; Author, "The Marmaduke Story"; Standard Plant Operators' Manual; Coauthor, "Standard Plant Operator's Questions and Answers," vols. I and II; "Standard Refrigeration and Air Conditioning Questions and Answers," "Standard Instrumentation Questions and Answers," vols. I and II; "Standard Electronics Questions and Answers," vols. I and II; "Standard Industrial Hydraulics Questions and Answers; "Standard Boiler Operators' Questions and Answers"; "Boiler Room Questions and Answers"; "Electrical Systems and Equipment for Industry"; "Handbook of Mechanical Packings"; "Plant Energy Systems"*

McGRAW-HILL BOOK COMPANY
New York   St. Louis   San Francisco   Auckland   Bogotá   Düsseldorf
Johannesburg   London   Madrid   Mexico   Montreal   New Delhi   Panama
Paris   São Paulo   Singapore   Sydney   Tokyo   Toronto

Library of Congress Cataloging in Publication Data

Elonka, Stephen Michael.
  Standard basic math and applied plant calculations.

  Includes index.
  1. Engineering mathematics.   2.   Power-plants—
Problems, exercises, etc.   I.   Title.
TA331.E46   620′.001′51   77-24884
ISBN 0-07-019297-9

234567890   MUBP   7654321098

The editors for this book were Tyler G. Hicks and Joseph Williams,
the designer was Naomi Auerbach, and the production supervisor
was Frank Bellantoni. It was set in Baskerville
by Progressive Typographers, Inc.

Printed by Murray Printing Company and bound by The Book Press.

Dedicated to
Philip W. Swain, *Power* editor from 1921 to 1954

CONTENTS

PREFACE

Why another math book when there are *hundreds* in print today? Because this volume is *unique*; because it presents *free-hand* calculations and *mental estimating* methods for the first time. Also, the *basics* of math are presented in an easy-to-understand style. Thus, this book is written to help *everyone,* whether a high school, trade school, technical institute, or college engineering student; stationary and marine engineers boning up for their license examinations; degreed engineers cramming for their professional engineer's certificate; or *anyone* having trouble with math in *any* field. In short, it is intended to best serve the needs of those seeking to brush up on basic tools and/or preparing for a licensing exam.

From my experience in teaching fourth-year high school students and cadet midshipmen at King's Point, I know the many areas of weakness that even bright students have with mathematics. *Today* this holds true more than ever. This volume will help the reader to perform calculations *quicker* with *fewer* errors. It is a review of mathematics the reader may have forgotten or never learned in the first place.

In addition to the many mathematical short-cuts explained in plain talk and illustrated in detail, most chapters have an assortment of *typical* on-the-job plant problems (a total of 90) on various subjects that *all* energy-system engineers (especially) should understand. Of major importance today for conserving energy are the numerous problems on combustion.

The *basic* content of this volume is due to the imaginative mathematical thinking of Phil Swain, editor of *Power* magazine for 33 years, with whom I was privileged to work from 1947 until he retired. The *typical* plant calculations covered are those which *Power* editors have been answering for plant engineers since the earliest days of the magazine. For more detailed information on each problem, the end of each chapter lists one or more reference books in the *Standard* series published by McGraw-Hill Book Company.

And, for the *first* time, this volume contains a complete chapter on metric conversion factors, in addition to a handy *metric conversion table,* with all the *new* metric unit *prefixes* to provide a fast and easy means of conversion from one system of notation to another.

In acknowledgment, I'm deeply grateful to Tyler G. Hicks, editor in chief of the "Standard Handbook of Engineering Calculations," for suggesting that I prepare this volume for publication as a *first* book for all those interested in mechanics, science, or engineering.

My thanks also go to my old friend Dr. Herbert M. Neuhaus of Santa Monica, California, for checking the electrical calculations in Chapter 13. And also to Automatic Electric Sales Corporation (subsidiary of General Telephone & Electronics) for allowing me to publish the 24 pages of metric conversion factors, which includes their new and highly valuable metric unit prefixes.

Stephen Michael Elonka

STANDARD BASIC MATH AND APPLIED PLANT CALCULATIONS

1

SHORT CUTS TO MATH

"What you don't use, you *lose*." We'll sail through this refresher course in math to bring back all the things you learned in school (but probably forgot), with one *great* difference: you'll be making your calculations *faster* because of the many shortcuts you are going to learn in this chapter.

Adding, subtracting, multiplying, and dividing are the commonest and most important operations of engineering mathematics. Let's start with addition.

ADDITION

Addition uses up a lot of hours in an engineer's lifetime. Learning how to save many of these hours, while gaining sureness, is certainly worth study and drill.

Below is an addition of two numbers as commonly set down:

$$26.13$$
$$\underline{415.38}$$
Total 441.51

Here 3 plus 8 is 11. Put down 1 and carry 1. Then, 1 plus 1 plus 3 is 5, etc. This is the usual procedure, and we can't suggest any improvement.

In contrast, try first the customary way of adding a long column of figures:

$$
\begin{array}{r}
26.13 \\
415.38 \\
260.41 \\
22.85 \\
191.06 \\
205.43 \\
88.55 \\
739.11 \\
\underline{263.05} \\
\text{Total } 2211.97
\end{array}
$$

Following the usual procedure, we added the digits in the last column to get 37. We set down the 7 in the last place of the sum and added the 3 to the sum of the digits in the next to the last column, and so on.

This is neither the fastest nor the surest way to add such a column. The longer the column the greater the chance of error. If the check is made on the final sum only, an error discovered in this sum will require repeating the *entire* adding operation.

This Is Faster

To avoid this, subtotal each column of digits separately and check each of these subtotals before adding them to give the grand total. Then check the grand total by readding the subtotals only.

Here it is, worked out:

$$
\begin{array}{r}
26.13 \\
415.38 \\
260.41 \\
22.85 \\
191.06 \\
205.43 \\
88.55 \\
739.11 \\
\underline{263.05} \\
.37 \\
2.6 \\
39. \\
37 \\
\underline{18 \quad\quad} \\
\text{Total } 2211.97
\end{array}
$$

First add the single columns working *down.* Then, to check, add them reading *up* to reduce the chance of repeating former errors. At this point put check marks opposite each subtotal as a reminder that it is correct. Then add the subtotals, first reading *down,* then reading *up* as a check.

This principle can be carried a lot further. Suppose an engineer is working out any long series of computations, each of which depends on the one before. A mistake in any step throws out all subsequent steps. To avoid wasting time working on wrong figures be sure to check each step before proceeding to the next step.

Mental Addition

Skill in "mental arithmetic" is cherished not only by school children but even more by chief engineers and bank presidents.

For engineers exact and approximate mental arithmetic are equally important. This lesson will stick to exact addition done without writing down any totals or subtotals.

For a starter consider this column, which has single-digit figures:

$$
\begin{array}{r}
2 \\
8 \\
7 \\
4 \\
9 \\
3 \\
2 \\
\underline{5} \\
\text{Total } 40
\end{array}
$$

Instead of reading 2 and 8 is 10, plus 7 is 17, plus 4 is 21, we simply read (silently or out loud): 2, 10, 17, 21, 30, 33, 35, 40. The expert generally skips some of these steps, chiefly by noting combinations that make 10, such as 1 and 9, 2 and 8, 3 and 7, etc. Thus he sees at a glance that the sum of the first three numbers is 17. He may see the 4 and 9 as 13, which added to 17 is obviously 30. Then the 3, 2 and 5 come together in his mind as a 10 to bring the total to 40.

When adding single digits it is often convenient to think of adding 9 as adding 10 and subtracting 1 and of adding 8 as adding 10 and subtracting 2, and so on.

All this is pretty well known, but many good engineers and good mathematicians don't get the maximum speed and sureness in mentally adding columns of figures containing two or more digits.

Take the following sum:

$$
\begin{array}{r}
26 \\
45 \\
33 \\
72 \\
94 \\
16 \\
58 \\
15 \\
24
\end{array}
$$

Most people find that it takes some concentration to add 26 to 45 and get 71 surely, and so on. To make the job much easier and surer add each of these two-digit numbers in two steps. First add the units place, then the tens place.

You might read it this way: 26 plus 5 is 31, plus 40 is 71, and so on. Better yet, merely recite: 26, 31, 71, 74, 104, 106, 176, 180, 270, 276, 286, 294, 344, 349, 359, 363, 383, total.

BETTER WAY TO MULTIPLY

Multiplication may be exact or approximate. Allowing for the value of a person's time, approximate multiplication is often smarter engineering than the exact variety. This is particularly true where the exactness in figuring is wasted either because it greatly exceeds the accuracy of the data or because the figuring is far too finespun for the given problem.

To reverse an old adage, "never use a man to do a boy's work." Also don't measure firewood with a micrometer or figure the volume of a roof tank to the thousandth part of a gallon.

Certain rules of arithmetic won't work except for exact multiplications. For example, here's the usual one for placing the decimal point in the product of two decimals.

Rule: *First multiply the two numbers as whole numbers. The given product has as many decimal places as are in the two numbers combined.*

EXAMPLE: Multiply 24.3 by 0.0613. First, $243 \times 613 = 148,959$.

The decimal places in two numbers multiplied total 5, so the correct product is 1.48959.

Now it's clear that this rule won't work unless the multiplication is complete to the last digit. That's why it won't work with a slide rule or other approximate multiplication methods.

To avoid this limitation we recommend discarding this rule and placing the decimal point by inspection, that is, by common sense. For example, here we are multiplying 20 plus by $^1/_{20}$ plus, so the answer must be a little more than 1. The only possibility is 1.48959. Likewise if the product were read on the slide rule as 1490 the same procedure would give 1.490.

Checking Multiplications

When checking an operation in arithmetic try to do the job some new way to avoid repeating the same mistakes. For example, if you add a column of figures reading *down* from the top, why not check reading *up* from the bottom?

Also, when checking a multiplication, don't merely repeat the original operation. It is much safer to reverse the numbers and re-multiply, like this:

PROBLEM: What is 462 × 893? ─────────────────────

$$
\begin{array}{r}
462 \\
893 \\
\hline
1386 \\
4158 \\
3696 \\
\hline
412566
\end{array}
\qquad
\begin{array}{r}
893 \\
462 \\
\hline
1786 \\
5358 \\
3572 \\
\hline
412566
\end{array}
$$

With the operations thus completely changed, duplication of a wrong product is much less likely than if the first multiplication were merely repeated.

Significant Figures

Here we stress the practical importance of significant figures (SF), noting that 3 or 4 SF are satisfactory for most engineering problems and that often 2 SF are good enough.

Strangely enough, practical engineers, educated on the job, have often been the greatest offenders in such matters. Boiler efficiencies crudely determined have been reported to 6 or 7 SF, like this: 76.8432%, an indicated precision far beyond the capacity of the world's finest testing laboratories. It isn't sensible.

When two or three numbers are multiplied to give an area or volume, each number introduces its own percentage error into the product. That is, if two of three numbers to be multiplied are correct and one in error by 3%, the product will be 3% wrong.

If all three numbers are in error, the errors may add up or partly cancel. Most often the net percentage error of the product is somewhat greater than the largest percentage error in one of the individual numbers.

Take a case where a sheet of metal is measured with a micrometer at 0.016 in. to the nearest thousandth. The right thickness might be anywhere from 0.0155 to 0.0165 in. Now 0.0165 differs from 0.016 by about 3%. Suppose the other dimensions of the sheet are measured, correctly to 0.01 in., as 43.02 and 25.43 in.

In working out the volume of this sheet it is a waste of time either to record or use the final 2 and 3. If you drop the 2 and use 43.0, the resulting error is only $1/20$%. The error from dropping the 3 and using 25.4 is only about $1/10$%. These errors are unimportant when the thickness figure may throw the volume off by 3%.

In this case, then, write

$$\text{Volume} = 43.0 \times 25.4 \times 0.016$$

At each stage drop all figures beyond 3 SF as useless. Then

$$\begin{array}{r} 254 \\ \underline{43} \\ 762 \\ \underline{1016} \\ 109 \quad \text{to 3 SF} \end{array}$$

Point off to 1090. Next, multiply 1090 by 0.016:

$$\begin{array}{r} 109 \\ \underline{16} \\ 654 \\ \underline{109} \\ 174 \quad \text{to 3 SF} \end{array}$$

Point off to 17.4 cu in. Considering the 3% possible error in thickness, the true volume here may range anywhere from about 17.0 to 18.0.

If carefully used, the lower (CD) scales of a 10-in. slide rule give an error of about $^1/_{10}$% in multiplying two numbers and a somewhat higher error when several numbers are multiplied. The slide rule is recommended where this error is not objectionable, which is true for most practical engineering calculations.

Suppose the following numbers are to be multiplied longhand *dependably* to 3 SF: 0.0024632 × 25.41 × 465.132.

To play safe, write each number and operation to 4 SF. Neglecting decimal points, we then have 2463 × 2541 × 4651.

First	2463	Then	6258
	2541		4651
	2463		6258
	9852		31290
	12315		37548
	4926		25032
	6258		2910

The answer must approximate $^1/_{500}$ × 25 × 500, so it will be about 25. Accordingly write 29.10 as the final product. This is dependable to 29.1.

MULTIPLICATION AND DIVISION HINTS ─────────────

We have seen that when two or more numbers are multiplied, a given percentage error in one produces the same percentage error in the product. This holds for division, also. A certain percentage error in either divisor or dividend creates the same percentage error in the quotient. The number with the largest percentage error dominates the situation, making it useless to have much greater accuracy in the other figure.

Let's apply this idea to a sheet of metal. The sheet is $8^3/_8$ in. wide and 0.028 in. thick (to the nearest thousandth). What length contains 10 cu in. of metal? Note that the thickness is dependable to only 2 SF, so carry all factors and results to 3 SF only. To 3 SF

$$8.38 \times 0.028 = 0.235 \quad \text{and} \quad \frac{10}{0.235} = 42.5 \text{ in.}$$

While this is written to 3 SF, for "good luck," it is not dependable beyond 2 SF (simply 42 or 43 in.).

In engineering it is often necessary to carry out a string of multiplications or divisions or a combination of both. While such operations are generally best handled by computers, slide rules, or logarithms, these conveniences may not be at hand when the computations must be made. People working such problems longhand can waste a lot of time fussing with decimal points and excessive significant figures. An example shows how to avoid such waste.

EXAMPLE: What is the value of $3.1416 \times 8^{3}/_{8} \times 8^{3}/_{8} \times 42.1 \div 42.3 \div 4658$, if the $8^{3}/_{8}$ is not dependable beyond $^{1}/_{32}$ in.? In that case, the product may easily be in error by at least 1%, so that anything beyond 4 SF is a waste of time. Therefore, carry all numbers and operations (up to the last) to 4 SF only.

The problem then reads: what equals $3.142 \times 8.375 \times 8.375 \times 42.1 \div 42.3 \div 4658$? Discarding decimal places, this becomes $3142 \times 8375 \times 8375 \times 421 \div 423 \div 4658 = ?$

Continuing to neglect decimal points, and sticking to 4 SF, we get

$$3142 \times 8375 = 2631$$
$$2631 \times 8375 = 2203$$
$$2203 \times 421 = 9275$$
$$9275 \div 423 = 2193$$
$$2193 \div 4658 = 4708$$

To locate the decimal point by inspection, set down the original problem in roughly approximate form but with correct decimal places, thus:

$$\frac{3 \times 8 \times 8 \times 40}{40 \times 4000} = \frac{3 \times 8}{500} = \frac{24}{500} = 0.05 \text{ (about)}$$

Therefore the answer, to 3 SF, is 0.048.

Convenient Reciprocals

Everybody knows the following short way to divide a number by 5: just multiply by 2 and divide by 10:

$$\frac{1452}{5} = ?$$

$$1452 \times 2 = 2904$$

$$\frac{2904}{10} = 290.4 \quad Ans.$$

Again, to divide a number by 25, multiply by 4 and divide by 100:

$$\frac{2630}{25} = ?$$

$$2630 \times 4 = 10,520$$

$$\frac{10,520}{100} = 105.2 \quad Ans.$$

Similarly, to multiply a number by 25, divide it by 4 and multiply by 100:

$$4328 \times 25 = ?$$

$$\frac{4328}{4} = 1082$$

$$1082 \times 100 = 108,200 \quad Ans.$$

In the same way, $3\frac{1}{3}$ or $33\frac{1}{3}$ can be paired with 3, $16\frac{2}{3}$ with 6, and 125 or $12\frac{1}{2}\%$ with 8.

Note that the two numbers of each such pair multiplied together give some power of 10, such as 1 or 10 or 100 or 1000, etc. Note, also, that one number of the pair is a "hard" number to handle in multiplication or division and the other a relatively "easy" number.

This is more clearly shown in Table 1-1. Any number on the "easy" side, multiplied by any corresponding number on the "hard" side gives some power of 10. With suitable adjustment of decimal points, opposite numbers are reciprocals. We then get the following timesaving rules.

Rule 1: *To multiply by any listed "hard" number, divide by any corresponding "easy" number, and then adjust the decimal point by inspection.*

Rule 2: *To divide by any listed "hard" number, multiply by any corresponding "easy" number, and then adjust the decimal point by inspection.*

Note that here, as in other problems involving multiplication and division, it is often convenient to omit all decimal points until the

TABLE 1-1   Paired Numbers: Reciprocals

"Hard" number	"Easy" reciprocal	"Hard" number	"Easy" reciprocal	"Hard" number	"Easy" reciprocal
$1/2$	0.2	0.5	2	5	20
$1/3$	0.3	$31/3$	3	$331/3$	30
$1/4$	0.4	0.25	4	2.5	40
$1/6$	0.6	$12/3$	6	$162/3$	60
$1/8$	0.8	1.25	8	12.5	80
$1/12$	0.12	$0.831/3$	1.2	$81/3$	12

NOTE: Decimal points are disregarded, as explained in text.

final answer is reached. At that stage the decimal point is easily located by inspection and common sense.

PROBLEM: What is $16^2/3\%$ of $2.40?
SOLUTION:

$$\frac{240}{6} = 40 = \$0.40 \quad Ans.$$

PROBLEM: Divide 614 by $1^1/4$.
SOLUTION: $614 \times 8 = 4912$. By inspection, 491.2 is the answer.

MORE SHORTCUTS

To multiply a number by 9, multiply by 10, then subtract the original number.

EXAMPLE: $2783 \times 9 = ?$

$$\begin{array}{r} 27,830 \\ \underline{2,783} \\ 25,047 \quad Ans. \end{array}$$

Rule: *Where two numbers to be multiplied are respectively above and below the same multiple of 10 by the same amount, their product equals the square of this multiple of 10 minus the square of the difference between either number and the multiple of 10.*

EXAMPLE: $998 \times 1002 = ?$
Here the multiple of 10 is 1000, the difference is 2, and the square of the difference is 4. Then

$$1000 \times 1000 = 1,000,000$$
$$1,000,000 - 4 = 999,996 \quad Ans.$$

EXAMPLE: $97 \times 103 = ?$

Here the multiple of 10 is 100, the difference 3, and its square 9. Then

$$100 \times 100 = 10,000$$
$$10,000 - 9 = 9991 \quad Ans.$$

EXAMPLE: $880 \times 1120 = ?$

The multiple of 10 is 1000.

$$1000 \times 1000 = 1,000,000$$
$$120 \times 120 = 14,400$$
$$1,000,000 - 14,400 = 985,600 \quad Ans.$$

EXAMPLE: $53 \times 47 = ?$

The multiple of 10 is 50.

$$50 \times 50 = 2500$$
$$3 \times 3 = 9$$
$$2500 - 9 = 2491 \quad Ans.$$

OTHER EXAMPLES:

$$23 \times 17 = ?$$
$$20 \times 20 = 400 \qquad 400 - 9 = 391 \quad Ans.$$
$$24 \times 16 = ?$$
$$20 \times 20 = 400 \qquad 400 - 16 = 384 \quad Ans.$$

Rule: *Where a number is multiplied by a two-digit number, it may happen that dividing the two-digit number by 2 or by 3 will change it into a one-digit number. In that case it may be convenient to divide the two-digit number by 2 or 3 and multiply the other number by the same factor.*

EXAMPLE: $37 \times 18 = ?$

Here half of 18 is 9. So we can say

$$37 \times 18 = 74 \times 9 = 666 \quad Ans.$$

EXAMPLE:

$$25 \times 27 = 75 \times 9 = 675 \quad Ans.$$

Here is a variation of the same idea:

$$49 \times 22 = 98 \times 11 = 980 + 98 = 1078$$

Rule: *You can divide one of the numbers by any factor if the other number is then multiplied by the same factor.*

If you use a little ingenuity, you will find many opportunities of applying this idea.

EXAMPLE: $3^1/_3 \times 42 = ?$
Apply a factor of 3:

$$10 \times 14 = 140 \quad Ans.$$

EXAMPLE: $24 \times 16^2/_3 = ?$
Apply a factor of 6:

$$4 \times 100 = 400 \quad Ans.$$

EXAMPLE: $125 \times 1616 = ?$
Apply a factor of 8:

$$1000 \times 202 = 202{,}000 \quad Ans.$$

Rule: *To add two fractions each having a numerator of 1, add the denominators to get the numerator of the answer. Multiply the denominators to get the denominator of the answer.* Thus

$$^1/_2 + ^1/_3 = ^5/_6$$
$$^1/_3 + ^1/_5 = ^8/_{15}$$
$$^1/_7 + ^1/_{12} = ^{19}/_{84}$$

Rule: *To subtract a smaller fraction from a larger, where both have numerators of 1, subtract the smaller denominator from the large denominator to get the numerator of the answer. Multiply the denominators to get the denominator of the answer.* Thus

$$^1/_3 - ^1/_7 = ^4/_{21}$$
$$^1/_2 - ^1/_3 = ^1/_6$$
$$^1/_7 - ^1/_{15} = ^8/_{105}$$

A special case of the foregoing occurs when the denominators of the fractions differ by 1. In that case the foregoing rule comes down to the following rule.

Rule: *The numerator of the answer is 1, and the denominator is the product of the denominators.* Thus

$$^1/_2 - {^1/_3} = {^1/_6}$$
$$^1/_3 - {^1/_4} = {^1/_{12}}$$
$$^1/_4 - {^1/_5} = {^1/_{20}}$$

Where one group of digits in a multiplier is a factor of another group of digits in the same multiplier, shortcuts may be possible. These are best explained by examples.

EXAMPLE: $614 \times 287 = ?$

Here note that 28 is 4×7. Then we have

$$
\begin{array}{r}
614 \\
287 \\
\hline
4298 \\
17192 \\
\hline
176218 \quad Ans.
\end{array}
$$

Since 28 is 4 times 7, the line 17192 is obtained by multiplying 4298 (itself a product of 614 and 7) by 4.

EXAMPLE: $3172 \times 2814 = ?$

Here the 28 is double the 14, so the problem is worked out like this:

$$
\begin{array}{r}
3172 \\
2814 \\
\hline
12688 \\
3172 \\
\hline
44408 \\
88816 \\
\hline
8926008 \quad Ans.
\end{array}
$$

Rule: *A mixed number is a whole number plus a fraction. Where each of two mixed numbers to be multiplied is a whole number plus $^1/_2$, the product is half the sum of the whole numbers plus the product of the whole numbers plus $^1/_4$.*

EXAMPLE: $\qquad 4^1/_2 \times 6^1/_2 = ?$

Take $4 + 6 = 10$

$$
\begin{array}{rr}
\text{Half of } 10 = & 5 \\
4 \times 6 = & 24 \\
\text{Add } ^1/_4 & \underline{^1/_4} \\
& 29^1/_4 \quad Ans.
\end{array}
$$

EXAMPLE: $15^1/_2 \times 8^1/_2 =$?

Take $15 + 8 = 23$

$$\begin{aligned}
\text{Half of } 23 &= \quad 11^1/_2 \\
15 \times 8 &= 120 \\
\text{Add } ^1/_4 &\quad \underline{\quad ^1/_4} \\
&\quad 131^3/_4 \quad Ans.
\end{aligned}$$

FRACTIONS CAN BE FUN ————————————————

The value of a fraction remains unchanged when numerator and denominator are multiplied or divided by the same number. Thus $^3/_7 = ^6/_{14} = ^9/_{21}$, etc., and $^{12}/_{48} = ^4/_{16} = ^2/_8 = ^1/_4$.

Several fractions having the same denominator can be added and subtracted by merely adding or subtracting their numerators. The original denominator remains unchanged:

$$^4/_{17} + ^3/_{17} - ^2/_{17} = ^5/_{17}$$

To turn $5^7/_8$ (a mixed number) into a simple fraction, multiply the 5 by the 8 to get 40. This figure 40 plus 7 is 47, and the final fraction is $^{47}/_8$. Actually this comes from the two rules already stated:

$$5^7/_8 = 5 + ^7/_8 = ^5/_1 + ^7/_8 = ^{40}/_8 + ^7/_8 = ^{47}/_8$$

Working this simple sum shows the trick in adding fractions. Change the fractions without changing their values until all have the same denominator. Then add by the rule already given.

EXAMPLE:

$$^7/_2 + ^5/_{12} + ^7/_{16} + ^7/_5 + ^4/_{15} = ?$$

The common denominator chosen must be one into which any of the individual denominators will divide evenly. The most obvious number to use would be $2 \times 12 \times 16 \times 5 \times 15 = 28,800$. This will work out all right, but the number is needlessly large and clumsy, so it is worth looking for the smallest number that is divisible by all the separate denominators, the number commonly called the *least common denominator* (lcd).

The first step is to factor each denominator, in the following way:

$$2 = 2$$
$$12 = 2 \times 2 \times 3$$
$$16 = 2 \times 2 \times 2 \times 2$$
$$5 = 5$$
$$15 = 3 \times 5$$

From these figures it is clear that the least common denominator must be a number that can be divided by any of the existing denominators. This means that it must contain each factor the largest number of times that factor occurs in any of the individual denominators.

For example, 2 must appear as a factor at least 4 times because it appears 4 times in 16. The factors 3 and 5 never appear more than once each in any single denominator, so the least common denominator will contain one 3 and one 5. Then the lcd is

$$2 \times 2 \times 2 \times 2 \times 3 \times 5 = 240$$

The next step, is to multiply the numerator and denominator of each fraction by a number that will make the denominator 240:

$$^7/_2 = {}^7/_2 \times {}^{120}/_{120} = {}^{840}/_{240}$$
$$^5/_{12} = {}^5/_{12} \times {}^{20}/_{20} = {}^{100}/_{240}$$
$$^7/_{16} = {}^7/_{16} \times {}^{15}/_{15} = {}^{105}/_{240}$$
$$^7/_5 = {}^7/_5 \times {}^{48}/_{48} = {}^{336}/_{240}$$
$$^4/_{15} = {}^4/_{15} \times {}^{16}/_{16} = {}^{64}/_{240}$$

Add the numerators:

$$840 + 100 + 105 + 336 + 64 = 1445$$

The sum of the fractions is

$$^{1445}/_{240} = 6^5/_{240} = 6^1/_{48}$$

It frequently happens that fractions and decimals must be added. Sometimes the decimals can be conveniently converted into fractions as a preliminary to this addition. Generally it is more convenient to convert the fractions into decimals.

In doing this you must face the fact that many common fractions cannot be converted exactly into decimals. In engineering this is no real objection, because exact solutions of actual problems are neither necessary nor possible. One reason is that formulas are oversimplified and imperfect. More important, the measurements supplying the data are always more or less in error. It will always be impossible to get exact measurements.

Therefore when fractions are converted into decimals for addition to other decimals, you must make up your mind what degree of accuracy is needed and justified by the data. From this you establish the number of decimal places. Find value of

$$1.326 \text{ in.} + \frac{7}{16} \text{ in.} + 2\frac{5}{8} \text{ in.} + \frac{5}{6} \text{ in.} + \frac{4}{7} \text{ in.}$$

Here it is known, say, that accuracy beyond the hundredth part of an inch is neither possible nor needed. Computations, however, will be carried one place farther, to the thousandth of an inch, to avoid piling up errors. Then

$$
\begin{array}{r}
1.326 \\
0.438 \\
2.625 \\
0.833 \\
\underline{0.571} \\
5.793
\end{array}
$$

Multiplying and dividing fractions is easier than adding or subtracting. *To multiply, multiply numerators to get the numerator of the product and multiply denominators to get the denominator of the product. To divide, invert the divisor and multiply.* Thus

$$\frac{3}{7} \times \frac{4}{9} = \frac{12}{63} = \frac{4}{21}$$

$$\frac{7/16}{3/10} = \frac{7}{16} \times \frac{10}{3} = \frac{70}{48} = \frac{35}{24}$$

Next work out a problem combining several multiplications and divisions and involving both decimals and common fractions:

$$24.6 \div \frac{17}{64} \div 0.026 \times \frac{24}{33} \div \frac{53}{12}$$

First convert all mixed numbers to simple fractions and all decimal fractions to common fractions:

$$\frac{246}{10} \div \frac{17}{64} \div \frac{26}{1000} \times \frac{24}{33} \div \frac{53}{12}$$

Next invert for division:

$$\frac{246}{10} \times \frac{64}{17} \times \frac{1000}{26} \times \frac{24}{33} \times \frac{12}{53}$$

This equals

$$\frac{246 \times 64 \times 1000 \times 24 \times 12}{10 \times 17 \times 26 \times 33 \times 53}$$

which cancels down to

$$\frac{246 \times 64 \times 100 \times 24 \times 2}{17 \times 13 \times 11 \times 53}$$

To save labor decide at this point how many significant figures are justified. Let's say it is 4 SF in the intermediate steps. Then the fraction reduces to 586.5, in which the first three digits are dependable.

MORE SIGNIFICANT FIGURES _____

Because of the importance of significant figures in all engineering work, let's review this subject with new examples and additional hints on the use of powers of 10.

The idea, taught in most public schools, that carrying computed results to a certain number of decimal places ensures a certain grade of precision is entirely false. In fact, carrying the result to only two decimal places may keep the error less than 0.001% in one case. In another, using four decimal places instead of five may introduce an error of 5%.

To get to first base in computations the engineer must put aside this decimal places nonsense and start thinking in terms that have some practical meaning, preferably significant figures. A certain number of them, unlike decimal places, represent a certain general order of percentage accuracy, whether the quantity is large or small.

To find the number of significant figures count all digits (including zeros) starting with the first digit that is not a zero. Then
   2346.23 has 6 SF
   2346.230 has 7 SF
   0.000012 has 2 SF
   496,302 has 6 SF
   496,302.4 has 7 SF
   1000.003 has 7 SF
   1000.0 has 5 SF

The only exception to this rule for counting the SF occurs where the number has no digits after the decimal point and where, *at the same time,* one or more digits *immediately* preceding the decimal point are ciphers.

There is a very practical reason for this. You can round the number 0.2843 to 0.28 if you wish to give only 2 SF, but you can't round off 2843 to read 28. You have to add the two zeros in place of the 43, so the number reads 2800 when rounded to 2 SF.

But suppose the 2800 should just happen to be the true value. Seeing 2800, a person not familiar with the derivation could not tell whether this mark actually stood for 2800, whether it was a 2-SF rounding of some number like 2835, or a 3-SF rounding of, say, 2804. This confusion will not occur where you report 2800 in your own computations. You will then know whether it represents 2800 or a rounding of 2835 or 2804.

Professional mathematicians (and engineers to an increasing degree) are very fussy about the number of significant figures. They look upon the man who uses 5 SF where nothing beyond 3 SF could have any possible meaning as a sort of unconscious liar, pretending to a precision that does not exist.

A scientific researcher will generally put down only as many significant figures as the accuracy of his experimental measurements can justify. Thus if a physicist reports a specific gravity as 1.0324, he means that the quality of his measurements makes him reasonably certain that the value is more than 1.032 and less than 1.033, say. If, knowing this situation, he should report the specific gravity as 1.03243, just because his arithmetic brought that answer from his measurements, he would feel that he should be "read out of the club" for false pretensions of precision.

We have noted that the significant figures of a number like 2800 may not be clear to the person who did not compute it. The professional mathematician gets around this confusion by habitually using powers of 10. In this system

$$10^2 = 100 \qquad 10^{-1} = 0.1$$
$$10^3 = 1000 \qquad 10^{-2} = 0.01$$
$$10^4 = 10,000 \qquad 10^{-3} = 0.001$$

and so on.

With these tools the mathematician can always make clear the number of significant figures. If you really mean 2800, you write it 2800. If you mean a number between 2000 and 3000 of which the first two digits are 28, you write it 28×10^2. If you mean a number between 2000 and 3000 of which the first three digits are 280, you write 280×10 or 28.0×10^2.

Here is another comparison of the two ways of representing numbers. This reports the number 5781.3 to various numbers of significant figures:

SF	Usual	Powers of 10
5	5781.3	5.7813×10^3
4	5781	5.781×10^3
3	5780	5.78×10^3
2	5800	5.8×10^3
1	6000	6×10^3

To see the effect of abridging numbers where the closest digit dropped is 5 (the worst possible case), first test the following set of numbers: 1.5, 1.05, 1.005, 1.0005, 1.00005, etc. Chopping off the 5 in each case will result in the following errors:

Original number	Final number	Final SF	Approximate error, %
1.5	1	1	50
1.05	1.0	2	5
1.005	1.00	3	0.5
1.0005	1.000	4	0.05

These are the worst possible errors from dropping digits. For a series like 9.5, 9.95, 9.995, 9.9995, etc., the error would run only one-tenth that just figured for 1.5, 1.05, 1.005, and 1.0005, respectively.

The upshot of all this is that it very rarely pays to go beyond 5 SF in engineering work. Most often 4 SF are enough, and there are many practical problems where 3 SF or even 2 SF are entirely satisfactory.

Many engineers, for example, always multiply the diameter of a circle by 3.1416 to get the circumference although 5 SF is needlessly precise for the run of practical applications. If 3.14 (3 SF) is used, the resulting error in the computed circumference of a 3-in. boiler tube will be less than 0.005 in. because $0.0016 \times 3 = 0.0048$.

RATIO, WHAT IS IT? ─────────────────────

A ratio is a quantity *comparison* obtained by dividing one quantity by another. It is nothing more than a quotient of two like quantities.

How does a foot compare with a yard? For a fair comparison both must be in the same units. Feet are most convenient. How then does 1 ft compare with 3 ft? As 1 is to 3 is the correct answer. The ratio is 1 to 3, and it may be expressed in any of the following ways:

$$\text{Ratio} = 1 \text{ to } 3 = 1 : 3 = 1 \div 3 = {}^1\!/_3 = 0.333 = 33.3\%$$

All mean the same thing.

Since a ratio is always a quotient, it isn't surprising that engineers often assume erroneously that any quotient is a ratio. Strictly speaking, a quotient is not a true ratio unless both quantities are simple numbers or quantities expressed in the same units.

For example, it would give a wrong idea to say that the ratio of 16 oz to 8 lb is 2. Certainly 16 oz is not twice as much as 8 lb. The proper comparison is of 16 oz with 128 oz. The correct ratio is

$$16 \text{ to } 128 = 1 \text{ to } 8 = 1 : 8 = {}^1\!/_8 = 0.125 = 12.5\%$$

A true ratio compares like things—days with days, one numerical count with another (say, a count of adults with a count of total population), dollars with dollars, pounds with pounds.

AND PROPORTION? ─────────────────────

Although proportion loosely means a ratio, its true meaning is different. In proportion we say that one ratio equals another.

For example it may be true or assumed in a certain factory that work turned out is proportional to number of workers employed. This simply means that the ratio of pieces turned out on one day to pieces turned out on another equals the ratio of workers on the first day to those on the other.

Suppose 16 workers turn out 88 pieces. How many pieces will 21 workers produce? Call this unknown number P. Then P is to 88 as 21 is to 16:

$$\frac{P}{88} = \frac{21}{16}$$

The first step in solving this equation for P is to clear the fractions. Multiplying each denominator by the opposite numerator gives $P \times 16 = 88 \times 21$. Dividing both sides of the equation by 16 gives

$$P = 88 \times \frac{21}{16} = 115.5$$

Therefore 21 workers will turn out 115.5 pieces.

Some prefer the old-fashioned setup for this proportion:

$$P : 88 : : 21 : 16$$

read P is to 88 as 21 is to 16.

The first rule in solving such a proportion is this: *The product of the means equals the product of the extremes.* The means are the two inside numbers, and the extremes are the two outside numbers. Thus

$$P \times 16 = 88 \times 21$$

As before, this reduces to $P = 115.5$ pieces turned out in the factory.

PERCENTAGE NO PROBLEM _____

A percentage is a ratio expressed as parts per 100. The ratio of 1 to 5 is $\frac{1}{5}$ or 0.2, but it is easier for most of us to picture 20% than 0.2 part out of 1. By constant practice both engineers and businessmen have gained skill in picturing percentages.

To get a percentage merely multiply the corresponding ratio by 100. Thus a ratio of 0.3 is 30%.

In business and engineering many different quantities must often be expressed as a percentage of a single base. For example, various costs and receipts of a business may be expressed as percentages of the gross receipts. In the same way, all losses in boiler operation may be expressed as a percentage of the heat in the fuel fired.

To make many such computations from a single base, it may be quicker to multiply than to divide. A case in point is Table 1-2, showing numbers and corresponding percentages. Here it is assumed that 163 represents 100% for some operation. The number

TABLE 1-2 Percentages from Single Base*

Number	%
141	86.4
86	52.7
132	80.9
196	120.1
182	111.5
125	76.6
94	57.6
137	84.0
28	17.2

* Assume that 163 represents 100%

of performances in the first column is expressed (column 2) as percentages of 100. The usual procedure is to divide the number in the first column by 163 then multiply by 100. When the column is long and multiplication is easier than division, prepare a multiplying constant, 100 divided by the base number. Here the constant is $100 \div 163$ is 0.6135. If this is written 0.613, the resulting error is about 5 parts in 613, or about 0.1%, which is assumed to be all right for the case in the table. Then all we do is to multiply each number in the first column by 0.613 to get the corresponding percentage for the second column.

This procedure is particularly convenient with either computing machines or a slide rule. With a slide rule, the entire series of calculations can be completed with a single setting of the sliding scale. With a computing machine the multiplier can be set up and remain unchanged until computations are completed.

Percentage vs. Points

Often we must deal with percentage of percentages. When boiler efficiency increases, say, from 76 to 81%, what is the percentage gain in efficiency? Some would say 5%, but this is not correct. Gain in efficiency is 5 points. Percentage gain is $5 \div 76 = 6.6\%$. What is the fuel saving here? It isn't 5%, nor is it 6.6%.

Without going into the theory, fuel saving when efficiency is increased is equal to the point gain in efficiency times 100 divided by the higher or lower efficiency. Here it is 5 × 100 ÷ 81 = 6.2%.

DECIMAL PLACES ─────────────────────────────

For generations arithmetic teachers have been giving pupils the idea that the operations of arithmetic should be carried to some stated number of decimal places determined by custom or the teacher. The pupil generally ends up with the vague idea that two decimal places is rough, three decimal places fairly close, and four decimal places quite accurate. All of which is not true.

The best way to prove that these decimal place "standards" are nonsense is to test them out for extreme cases. See where we land if we assume that four decimal places is about right for any job of careful computation. Let's apply this notion to two numbers, 1000.00155 and 0.00105. Written to four decimal places, they become 1000.0016 and 0.0011. The error is 1 part in 20,000,000 for the first number and 1 part in 20 for the second number. Both figures are carried to four decimal places, but one is a million times more precise than the other.

Except in rare instances, merely setting down a number like 1000.00155 in an engineering report marks its writer as a greenhorn with numbers. On the other hand writing 0.00105 as 0.0011 would often be inexcusably rough.

The first step toward practicality in applying arithmetic to real problems is to stop thinking how many decimal places and start thinking in one of the three following measures of precision in numbers:

    1. Precise to 1 part in _____

    2. Precise to _____ percent

    3. Carry to _____ SF

Thus, when you are computing, you should say to yourself, "I shall put down enough digits for the error from omitting further digits not to exceed 1 part in _____ or _____ percent, or I shall carry results to _____ SF."

Suppose a number is 10.05, and we write it 10.0. The resulting error is 5 parts in 1000, or 1 part in 200. It is also 1/2 percent.

With one exception to be explained later, the number of significant figures in any number as written is merely the total number of digits written down, *starting with the first digit that is not a zero.* Thus

Number	SF
235.46	5
2.3546	5
0.0046	2
15	2
35.0000	6
1.006	4

The only exception to this rule is where there are no digits (not even zeros) after the decimal point, and where one or more digits immediately left of the decimal point are zeros. Thus 23,400 might have either 3, 4, or 5 SF. However, 23,403 definitely has 5 SF, and 23,400.0 definitely has 6 SF. More about this later.

For practice assume that the following quantities are to be abridged to various specified numbers of SF

$$6253.462$$
$$4.86346$$
$$0.0943165$$
$$0.000443968$$

Then the abridged numbers are found to be as follows:

SF	Abridged number
5	6253.5
	4.8635
	0.094317
	0.0044397
4	6254
	4.864
	0.09432
	0.004440

Continuing to reduce the number of significant figures, we have:

SF	Abridged number
3	6250
	4.86
	0.943
	0.00444
2	6300
	4.9
	0.94
	0.0044
1	6000
	5
	0.9
	0.004

From the foregoing we know that the number 6250 really has 3 SF because the 0 does not represent the actual value of the fourth digit but is merely inserted to make the number come out in thousands rather than in hundreds. A person who did not know the source of 6250 would say that it had at least 3 SF and possibly 4 (on the chance that 0 might happen to be the true value of the fourth digit).

In the same way anyone seeing the number 6000 without knowing its derivation, might take it to be a round number with 1 SF, but it could conceivably have 2, 3, or even 4 SF.

POWERS OF 10

Mathematicians have their own way of making the situation clear in such cases. They rewrite the numbers previously given as 6.2535×10^3, 6.254×10^3, 6.25×10^3, 6.2×10^3 and 6×10^3. Here 10^3 (10 to the third power) merely means that the decimal point is to be moved *three places to the right*. The four numbers are obviously carried to 4, 3, 2, and 1 SF.

Generally, engineers are dealing with their own computations and will know whether a written 6300 actually means 6300 (4 SF) or is merely 6354 rounded to 2 SF.

EASY SQUARE ROOT

This square-root method is simple. Here is the rule to remember:

1. Move the decimal point left or right (as necessary) in jumps of *two places* at a time until a number between 1 and 100 is obtained.

2. By inspection find the *whole number* (no decimal places) closest to the desired square root. Call this the *first root*.

3. Divide the first root into the number and carry the result to *one decimal place only*. Call this *the first quotient*.

4. Average the first quotient and the first root to *one decimal place only*. Call this *the second root*.

5. Divide original number by second root. Carry result to *four decimal places* and call it *second quotient*.

6. Average second root and second quotient. Carry result to 3 *decimal places*. (Table 1-3 has been carried to 4 places to show more clearly what the error is.) This will be the square root of the number obtained in step 1. Its error will not exceed 0.003.

TABLE 1-3   Steps in Figuring Square Root for 41 examples from 1.1 to 97.0

Number	First root	First quotient	Average second root	Second quotient	Average final root	Exact square root to 4 decimal places	Error less than 1/3 %	1/10 %	1/50 %	1/200 %
1.1	1	1.1	1.0	1.1	1.0500	1.0488	*			
1.2	1	1.2	1.1	1.0909	1.0954	1.0954				*
1.3	1	1.3	1.2	1.0833	1.1416	1.1402	*			
1.4	1	1.4	1.2	1.1667	1.1833	1.1832			*	
1.6	1	1.6	1.3	1.2308	1.2654	1.2649		*		
1.8	1	1.8	1.4	1.2857	1.3428	1.3416		*		
2.0	1	2.0	1.5	1.3333	1.4166	1.4142	*			
2.2	1	2.2	1.6	1.3750	1.4875	1.4832	*			
2.4	2	1.2	1.6	1.5000	1.5500	1.5492		*		
2.6	2	1.3	1.6	1.6250	1.6125	1.6125				*
2.8	2	1.4	1.7	1.6471	1.6735	1.6733			*	
3.0	2	1.5	1.7	1.7647	1.7323	1.7321			*	
3.5	2	1.8	1.8	1.9444	1.8722	1.8708	*			
4.0	2	2	2	2	2	2				*
4.5	2	2.2	2.1	2.1429	2.1214	2.1213				*
5.0	2	2.5	2.2	2.2727	2.2363	2.2361			*	
5.5	2	2.8	2.4	2.2917	2.3458	2.3452		*		
6.0	2	3.0	2.5	2.4000	2.4500	2.4495		*		
6.5	3	2.2	2.6	2.5000	2.5500	2.5495			*	
7.0	3	2.3	2.7	2.5925	2.6463	2.6458			*	
7.5	3	2.5	2.7	2.7778	2.7389	2.7386			*	
8.0	3	2.7	2.9	2.7586	2.8293	2.8284		*		
8.5	3	2.8	2.9	2.9310	2.9155	2.9155				*
9.0	3	3	3	3	3	3				*
9.5	3	3.2	3.1	3.0645	3.0823	3.0822				*
10.0	3	3.3	3.1	3.2258	3.1629	3.1623			*	
11.0	3	3.7	3.3	3.3333	3.3166	3.3166				*
13.0	4	3.2	3.6	3.6111	3.6056	3.6056				*
15.0	4	3.8	3.9	3.8461	3.8730	3.8730				*
19.0	4	4.8	4.4	4.3182	4.3591	4.3589				*
23.0	5	4.6	4.8	4.7917	4.7958	4.7958				*
27.0	5	5.4	5.2	5.1923	5.1961	5.1962				*
35.0	6	5.8	5.9	5.9322	5.9161	5.9161				*
45.0	7	6.4	6.7	6.7164	6.7082	6.7082				*
55.0	7	7.9	7.4	7.4324	7.4162	7.4162				*
65.0	8	8.1	8.0	8.1250	8.0625	8.0623				*
75.0	9	8.3	8.6	8.7209	8.6604	8.6603				*
85.0	9	9.4	9.2	9.2391	9.2195	9.2195				*
93.0	10	9.3	9.6	9.6875	9.6437	9.6437				*
95.0	10	9.5	9.7	9.7938	9.7469	9.7468				*
97.0	10	9.7	9.8	9.8980	9.8490	9.8489				*

7. Note how many *double* places the decimal point was moved in step 1. Move it back *the same number of single places* in the opposite direction.

EXAMPLE: The steps below are numbered from 1 to 7 as in the rule above:

1. To get the square root of 263,400, first move the decimal point two double steps left to give 26.34.

2. Since 5 squared is 25 and 6 squared is 36, select 5 (the closest) as the first root.

3. Dividing 26.34 by 5 *to one decimal place* gives 5.2, the *first quotient.*

4. Averaging 5 and 5.2 *to one decimal place* gives 5.1. This is the *second root.*

5. Dividing 26.34 by 5.1 to four decimal places gives 5.1647. This is the second quotient.

6. Averaging 5.1 and 5.1647 to three decimal places gives 5.132. This is the square root of 26.34.

7. Moving the decimal point two single steps right gives 513.2. This is the correct square root of 263,400 to the first decimal place.

Mathematicians will recognize this as a method of successive approximation. But even people trained in computation may need the warning to carry to the exact number of places listed in the rule. To use more places wastes time and is not necessary to achieve the indicated accuracy.

Table 1-3 shows the actual error of this method for 41 examples covering the range from 1.1 to 97.0. In no case does the error exceed $\frac{1}{3}$%. Most results are much closer than that.

QUICK APPROXIMATIONS

Arithmetical shortcuts shown so far in this chapter are all exact. Equally useful to the engineer in many cases are shortcuts that give a reasonably close approximate answer in a few seconds. They can be especially helpful when a rough answer must be obtained in a hurry and no slide rule or other mathematical aid is at hand.

When numbers to be multiplied or divided fall close to 1, 10, 100, 1000, etc., or to 0.1, 0.01, 0.001, etc., certain shortcuts are easily applied. Take a case where several numbers are to be multiplied and each falls within 10% of one of these powers of 10. This means that each number considered lies in one of the following groups:

0.9 to 1.1	0.09 to 0.11
9 to 11	0.009 to 0.011
90 to 110	0.0009 to 0.0011
900 to 1100	etc.

Note by what percentage each number to be multiplied exceeds or falls short of the nearest power of 10. For example, the number 92 falls short of 100 by 8%; the number 0.00105 exceeds 0.001 by 5%; the number 957,000 falls short of 1,000,000 by 4.3%, etc.

Here is the rule for the approximate multiplication of a string of numbers of this sort: *Replace the actual numbers by the nearest powers of 10 and multiply. Get the algebraic sum of the individual percentage variations. Apply this as a correction to the product of the powers of 10 to get the desired product.*

EXAMPLE: Multiply (approximately)

$$106.2 \times 0.943 \times 0.00102 \times 9860$$

The product of the nearest powers of 10 is

$$100 \times 1 \times 0.001 \times 10,000 = 1000$$

Get the algebraic sum of the percentage variations as follows:

	%	
Number	Over	Under
106.2	6.2	
0.943		5.7
0.00102	2.0	
9860		1.4
Total	8.2	7.1
Net	1.1	

Therefore, the final product is 1000 increased by 1.1%, or 1011. Working the problem in the conventional way, we find the correct product to 4 SF to be 1007. Here, the error is 0.4%. This procedure is a great timesaver.

A modification can be used where most but not all of the numbers to be multiplied fall within 10% of some power of 10. *In that case multiply the fitting numbers by this shortcut method. Then complete multiplication of the remaining numbers by usual methods.*

EXAMPLE: $46 \times 108.3 \times 9.72 \times 1.035 = ?$

First work out $108.3 \times 9.72 \times 1.035$. Multiplying powers of 10 gives

$$100 \times 10 \times 1 = 1000$$

Figure the percentage variations:

Number	Over	Under
108.3	8.3	
9.72		2.8
1.035	3.5	
Total	11.8	2.8
Net	9.0	

So

$$108.3 \times 9.72 \times 1.035 = 1000 + 90 = 1090 \text{ (approx)}$$

By ordinary multiplication to 3 SF, $1090 \times 46 = 50{,}100$. In this case, the exact answer to 5 SF is 50,118.

The engineer who would like to know just how far to trust such methods can soon find out by a little easy experimentation, using no numbers except 11 and 9, since these correspond to the worst possible cases, 10% over and 10% under.

Suppose there are two numbers, each 10% over:

	Exact	Rule	Error, %
11×11	121	120	-0.8

Suppose there are two numbers, each 10% under:

	Exact	Rule	Error, %
9×9	81	80	-1.2

Suppose there are two numbers, one 10% over and one 10% under:

	Exact	Rule	Error, %
9×11	99	100	$+1$

This demonstrates that when there are two numbers, the only way to get an error above 1% is to have both numbers *under* by nearly the full 10% limit we have assumed.

Moreover, the 10% limit was arbitrarily chosen to make the rule cover a fair proportion of engineering problems. By closing in the limit to 5%, or less, a much higher degree of accuracy is assured.

The following examples show the maximum possible error for two and three numbers where none differs from the nearest power of 10 by more than 5%:

Number	Exact	Rule	Error %
1.05 × 1.05	1.102	1.10	0.2
1.05 × 1.05 × 1.05	1.158	1.15	0.7
0.95 × 0.95	0.902	0.90	0.2
0.95 × 0.95 × 0.95	0.857	0.85	0.8

Approximate Division

A similar rule applies to division where both numbers fall within 10% or some other specified small percentage of powers of 10. However, instead of using a separate rule for division, the following rule will cover any combination of multiplication and division. *First write the problem in the form of a fraction. Then solve the fraction in powers of 10 and apply a net percentage correction as before. The only difference is that the "overs" and "unders" are reversed for any numbers in the denominator.* These are marked * in the following example:

EXAMPLE: $92.6 \times 1.03 \div 0.982 \times 923 \div 1.083 = ?$
   First rewrite as a fraction

$$\frac{92.6 \times 1.03 \times 923}{0.982 \times 1.083}$$

Solve for powers of 10

$$\frac{100 \times 1 \times 1000}{1 \times 1} = 100,000$$

The next step is to figure the percentage variation, reversing the overs and unders for numbers in the denominator (*):

Number	% Over	% Under
92.6		7.4
1.03	3.0	
923		7.7
982	1.8*	
1.083		8.3*
Total	4.8	23.4
Net		18.6

Finally, reduce 100,000 by 18.6 to give 81,400. Here the exact answer is 82,777, so the error is 1.6%.

LOGARITHMS SAVE TIME _____

Logarithms were invented many years ago as a shortcut to save time in multiplication and division primarily, and secondarily in such operations as powers and roots.

Logs substitute addition for multiplication, subtraction for division, multiplication for powers, and division for roots.

The ordinary slide rule, which is laid out from tables of logarithms, performs almost any operation you can perform with log tables, but the accuracy of a slide rule is limited by its length. With close reading the lower scales of an ordinary 10-in. slide rule cannot be read closer than 0.1%. This is near enough for many engineering problems. Where closer figuring is required, you must use longhand figuring, a computing machine, or a table of logarithms.

Here we explain simply what logs are and how they are used for the ordinary operations of multiplying, dividing, finding powers, and extracting roots.

In higher mathematics logs have various bases, but in ordinary work, unless otherwise specified, the base is always assumed to be 10. That will be assumed in this book.

Definition

The log of any number is simply the power to which 10 must be raised to give that number. Thus to get 1000 you have to cube 10 and raise it to the third power. That is $10 \times 10 \times 10 = 1000$. Therefore the log of 1000 is 3. We write it $\log 1000 = 3$.

In the same way $\log 100 = 2$, $\log 10,000 = 4$, $\log 10,000,000 = 7$, and so on.

The logarithm of 1 is 0. For any number less than 1 the logarithm is negative, or a minus quantity. Sticking to the powers of 10 and running down from large numbers through 1 to smaller numbers, we find that the logs follow in a consistent series, as shown at the left in Table 1-4.

We won't attempt to explain the meaning of negative powers except to note, for example, that 10 to the -4 power is 0.0001, so $\log 0.0001 = -4$.

Inspecting Table 1-4, we get the following rule for the logs of the

TABLE 1-4   Simple Table of Logarithms

Large numbers through 1 to smaller numbers		Four-place logs of whole numbers 1 to 10	
Power of 10	log	number	log
10,000	4	1	0.0000
1,000	3	2	.3010
100	2	3	.4771
10	1	4	.6021
1	0	5	.6990
0.1	−1	6	.7782
0.01	−2	7	.8451
0.001	−3	8	.9031
0.0001	−4	9	.9542
0.00001	−5	10	1.0000

powers of 10: *The log of 1 is 0. If the number is 10 or more, the log is equal to the number of zeros. If the number is 0.1 or less, the log is 1 more than the number of zeros between the decimal point and the 1.*

Here is the rule for multiplying any two numbers: *The sum of the logs of two or more numbers is the log of their product.*

PROBLEM: $10 \times 1000 \times 0.01 \times 100 = ?$

$$\text{Sum of logs} = 1 + 3 - 2 + 2 = 4$$

Therefore the product must be the number whose log is 4. This must be 1 followed by four zeros, or 10,000.

Here is the rule for division: *To divide a first number by a second, subtract the log of the second from the log of the first. The difference is the log of the quotient.*

PROBLEM: $1000 \div 10 = ?$

$$\log 1000 - \log 10 = 3 - 1 = 2 = \log 100$$

Therefore

$$\frac{1000}{10} = 100$$

PROBLEM: $0.01 \div 0.001 = ?$

$$\log 0.01 - \log 0.001 = -2 - (-3) = -2 + 3 = 1$$

The number whose log is 1 is 10. Therefore

$$\frac{0.01}{0.001} = 10$$

Granting that these computations are easy, the reader may well ask what use they are, since all these operations with the powers of 10 are perfectly easy without logs. The answer is that this is the best way to begin to understand logs.

For the next step in understanding note Table 1-5 of four-place logs of the whole numbers from 1 to 10.

Test this with a few simple computations.

PROBLEM: $2 \times 3 = ?$

$$
\begin{aligned}
\log 2 &= 0.3010 \\
+\log 3 &= \underline{0.4771} \\
\text{Sum} \quad &\; 0.7781 = \log 6 \text{ (almost)}
\end{aligned}
$$

The product is 6. Note that the operation does not necessarily give the exact answer. Logarithms always involve some error, but it can be made as small as desired by using log tables with more decimal places. A five-place log table is accurate enough for almost any engineering computation, but astronomers, for example, sometimes use seven- and eight-place tables for their ultraprecise computations.

PROBLEM: $8 \div 4 = ?$

$$
\begin{aligned}
\log 8 &= 0.9030 \\
-\log 4 &= \underline{0.6021} \\
\text{Difference} \quad &\; 0.3009 = \log 2 \text{ (almost)}
\end{aligned}
$$

The quotient is 2.

Finding Logarithms

Table 1-5 is a standard four-place table (four decimal places) of logs from 1 to 10 by hundredths. For example, the log of 7.32 is 0.8645, and the log of 1.86 is 0.2695.

PROBLEM: What is log 3.276?

TABLE 1-5 Four-place Common Logarithms of Numbers

No.	0	1	2	3	4
1.0	0.0000	0043	0086	0128	0170
1.1	0414	0453	0492	0531	0569
1.2	0792	0828	0864	0899	0934
1.3	1139	1173	1206	1239	1271
1.4	1461	1492	1523	1553	1584
1.5	1761	1790	1818	1847	1875
1.6	2041	2068	2095	2122	2148
1.7	2304	2330	2355	2380	2405
1.8	2553	2577	2601	2625	2648
1.9	2788	2810	2833	2856	2878
2.0	3010	3032	3054	3075	3096
2.1	3222	3243	3263	3284	3304
2.2	3424	3444	3464	3483	3502
2.3	3617	3636	3655	3674	3692
2.4	3802	3820	3838	3856	3874
2.5	3979	3997	4014	4031	4048
2.6	4150	4166	4183	4200	4216
2.7	4314	4330	4346	4362	4378
2.8	4472	4487	4502	4518	4533
2.9	4624	4639	4654	4669	4683
3.0	4771	4786	4800	4814	4829
3.1	4914	4928	4942	4955	4969
3.2	5052	5065	5079	5092	5105
3.3	5185	5198	5211	5224	5237
3.4	5315	5328	5340	5353	5366
3.5	5441	5453	5465	5478	5490
3.6	5563	5575	5587	5599	5611
3.7	5682	5694	5705	5717	5729
3.8	5798	5809	5821	5832	5843
3.9	59⊤1	5922	5933	5944	5955
4.0	6021	6031	6042	6053	6064
4.1	6128	6138	6149	6160	6170
4.2	6232	6243	6253	6263	6274
4.3	6335	6345	6355	6365	6375
4.4	6435	6444	6454	6464	6474
4.5	6532	6542	6551	6561	6571
4.6	6628	6637	6646	6656	6665
4.7	6721	6730	6739	6749	6758
4.8	6812	6821	6830	6839	6848
4.9	6902	6911	6920	6928	6937
5.0	0.6990	6998	7007	7016	7024
5.1	7076	7084	7093	7101	7110
5.2	7160	7168	7⊤77	7185	7193
5.3	7243	7251	7259	7267	7275
5.4	7324	7332	7340	7348	7356

5	6	7	8	9	Ave. diff.
0212	0253	0294	0334	0374	42
0607	0645	0682	0719	0755	38
0969	1004	1038	1072	1106	35
1303	1335	1367	1399	1430	32
1614	1644	1673	1703	1732	30
1903	1931	1959	1987	2014	28
2175	2201	2227	2253	2279	26
2430	2455	2480	2504	2529	25
2672	2695	2718	2742	2765	23
2900	2923	2945	2967	2989	22
3118	3139	3160	3181	3201	21
3324	3345	3365	3385	3404	20
3522	3541	3560	3579	3598	19
3711	3729	3747	3766	3784	18
3892	3909	3927	3945	3962	17
4065	4082	4099	4116	4133	
4232	4249	4265	4281	4298	16
4393	4409	4425	4440	4456	
4548	4564	4579	4594	4609	15
4698	4713	4728	4742	4757	
4843	4857	4871	4886	4900	14
4983	4997	5011	5024	5038	
5119	5132	5145	5159	5172	13
5250	5263	5276	5289	5302	
5378	5391	5403	5416	5428	
5502	5515	5527	5539	5551	12
5623	5635	5647	5658	5670	
5740	5752	5763	5775	5786	
5855	5866	5877	5888	5899	11
5966	5977	5988	5999	6010	
6075	6085	6096	6107	6117	
6180	6191	6201	6212	6222	10
6284	6294	6304	6314	6325	
6385	6395	6405	6415	6425	
6484	6493	6503	6513	6522	
6580	6590	6599	6609	6618	
6675	6684	6693	6702	6712	
6767	6776	6785	6794	6803	9
6857	6866	6875	6884	6893	
6946	6955	6964	6972	6981	
7033	7042	7050	7059	7067	9
7118	7126	7135	7143	7152	8
7202	7210	7218	7226	7235	
7284	7292	7300	7308	7316	
7364	7372	7380	7388	7396	

TABLE 1-5 (*Continued*)

No.	0	1	2	3	4
5.5	7404	7412	7419	7427	7435
5.6	7482	7490	7497	7505	7513
5.7	7559	7566	7574	7582	7589
5.8	7634	7642	7649	7657	7664
5.9	7709	7716	7723	7731	7738
6.0	7782	7789	7796	7803	7810
6.1	7853	7860	7868	7875	7882
6.2	7924	7931	7938	7945	7952
6.3	7993	8000	8007	8014	8021
6.4	8062	8069	8075	8082	8069
6.5	8129	8136	8142	8149	8156
6.6	8195	8202	8209	8215	8222
6.7	8261	8267	8274	8280	8287
6.8	8325	8331	8338	8344	8351
6.9	8388	8395	8401	8407	8414
7.0	8451	8457	8463	8470	8476
7.1	8513	8519	8525	8531	8537
7.2	8573	8579	8585	8591	8597
7.3	8633	8639	8645	8651	8657
7.4	8692	8698	8704	8710	8716
7.5	8751	8756	8762	8768	8774
7.6	8808	8814	8820	8825	8831
7.7	8865	8871	8876	8882	8887
7.8	8921	8927	8932	8938	8943
7.9	8976	8982	8987	8993	8998
8.0	9031	9036	9042	9047	9053
8.1	9085	9090	9096	9101	9106
8.2	9138	9143	9149	9154	9159
8.3	9191	9196	9201	9206	9212
8.4	9243	9248	9253	9258	9263
8.5	9294	9299	9304	9309	9315
8.6	9345	9350	9355	9360	9365
8.7	9395	9400	9405	9410	9415
8.8	9445	9450	9455	9460	9465
8.9	9494	9499	9504	9509	9513
9.0	9542	9547	9552	9557	9562
9.1	9590	9595	9600	9605	9609
9.2	9638	9643	9647	9652	9657
9.3	9685	9689	9694	9699	9703
9.4	9731	9736	9741	9745	9750
9.5	9777	9782	9786	9791	9795
9.6	9823	9827	9832	9836	9841
9.7	9868	9872	9877	9881	9886
9.8	9912	9917	9921	9926	9930
9.9	9956	9961	9965	9969	9974

5	6	7	8	9	Ave. diff.
7443	7451	7459	7466	7474	
7520	7528	7536	7543	7551	
7597	7604	7612	7619	7627	
7672	7679	7686	7694	7701	7
7745	7752	7760	7767	7774	
7818	7825	7832	7839	7846	
7889	7896	7903	7910	7917	
7959	7966	7973	7980	7987	
8028	8035	8041	8048	8055	
8096	8102	8109	8116	8122	
8162	8169	8176	8182	8189	
8228	8235	8241	8248	8254	
8293	8299	8306	8312	8319	6
8357	8363	8370	8376	8382	
8420	8426	8432	8439	8445	
8482	8488	8494	8500	8506	
8543	8549	8555	8561	8567	
8603	8609	8615	8621	8627	
8663	8669	8675	8681	8686	
8722	8727	8733	8739	8745	
8779	8785	8791	8797	8802	
8837	8842	8848	8854	8859	
8893	8899	8904	8910	8915	
8949	8954	8960	8965	8971	
9004	9009	9015	9020	9025	5
9058	9063	9069	9074	9079	
9112	9117	9122	9128	9133	
9165	9170	9175	9180	9186	
9217	9222	9227	9232	9238	
9269	9274	9279	9284	9289	
9320	9325	9330	9335	9340	
9370	9375	9380	9385	9390	
9420	9425	9430	9435	9440	
9469	9474	9479	9484	9489	
9518	9523	9528	9533	9538	
9566	9571	9576	9581	9586	
9614	9619	9624	9628	9633	
9661	9666	9671	9675	9680	
9708	9713	9717	9722	9727	
9754	9759	9764	9768	9773	
9800	9805	9809	9814	9818	
9845	9850	9854	9859	9863	
9890	9894	9899	9903	9908	
9934	9939	9943	9948	9952	
9978	9983	9987	9991	9996	

Here it is necessary to interpolate, that is, find a value between two adjacent values in the table. We have

$$\log 3.28 = 0.5159$$
$$\log 3.27 = \underline{0.5145}$$
$$\text{Difference } 0.0014$$

It is clear that log 3.276 must be

$$0.5145 + 0.6 \times 0014 = 0.5145 + 0.0008 = 0.5153$$

The reverse process uses interpolation to find the number which has a given log.

PROBLEM: Of what number is 0.7799 the log?

$$\log 6.03 = 0.7803$$
$$\log \underline{6.02} = \underline{0.7796}$$
$$\text{Difference } 0.01 \quad 0.0007$$

Note that $0.7799 - 0.7796 = 0.0003$, so the number must be $6.02 + \frac{3}{7} \times 0.01$. The nearest single-place decimal to $\frac{3}{7}$ is 0.4, so the correct number is 6.024.

The same table serves for any number larger than 10. Thus log $32,760 = ?$ As noted, log $3.276 = 0.5153$. Now 32,760 is $3.276 \times 10,000$, so log 32,760 is

$$0.5153 + \log 10,000 = 0.5153 + 4 = 4.5153$$

Here is the rule for the logs of numbers greater than 10: *Point off to make a number between 1 and 10 and read its log from Table 1-5. Before the decimal point in the log put a number that is 1 less than the number of digits before the decimal point in the given number.*

In the case of a number less than 1, take the log from the table in the manner just indicated. Then place before the decimal point of the log a number 1 more than the number of zeros between the decimal point of the number and the first digit not a zero. Put a minus sign over the number before the decimal point.

PROBLEM: What is log 0.000654?

$$\log 6.54 = 0.8156$$

The number 0.000654 has three zeros between the decimal point and the first digit is not a zero, so the log is $\overline{4}.8156$. The minus sign over the 4 indicates that the 4 is minus while the part of the log after the point is plus. The meaning and use are explained on p. 39.

Logs to Multiply and Divide.

The rule is: *Add logs to multiply, subtract to divide.*

PROBLEM: $2.856 \times 8531 = ?$

SOLUTION:

Number	Log	
2.856	0.4558	
8531	3.9310	
Sum	4.3868	= log of 24,370

Therefore $2.856 \times 8531 = 24{,}370$.

This answer is not exact, but you can always find a log table with enough places to give any required degree of precision.

PROBLEM: $72.16 \times 0.04137 = ?$

SOLUTION:

Number	Log	
72.16	1.8583	
.04137	$\bar{2}.6167$	
Algebraic sum	0.4750	= log of 2.985

So $72.16 \times 0.04137 = 2.985$

PROBLEM: $0.003216 \div 0.5215 = ?$

SOLUTION:

Number	Log	
0.003216	$\bar{3}.5073$	
0.5215	$\bar{1}.7172$	
Algebraic difference	$\bar{3}.7901$	= log of 0.006167

Here the algebraic difference was

$$0.5073 - 3 + 1 - 0.7172 = -2.2099 = \bar{3}.7901$$

PROBLEM: $253.2 \times 14.6 \times 0.0146 \div 82.3 \div 539.3 = ?$

SOLUTION:

Number	Logs to add	Logs to subtract
253.2	2.4034	
14.6	1.1644	
0.0146	$\bar{2}.1644$	
82.3		1.9154
539.3		2.7318
	1.7322	4.6472
	-4.6472	
	$\bar{3}.0850$	= log of 0.001216

Logs for Powers and Roots

Suppose we want to square 2.345. That is merely the product of 2.345 and 2.345, so we add the logs thus:

Number	Log
2.345	0.3702
2.345	0.3702
Sum	0.7404 = log of 5.500

The square of 2.345, to the accuracy of our four-place log tables, is 5.500.

Again, the cube of 2.345 would be 2.345 × 2.345 × 2.345, and we could proceed to add up the three logs. However, it's easier just to multiply by 3 like this:

$$\log 2.345^3 = 3 \times \log 2.345 = 3 \times 0.3702 = 1.1106$$

This is the log of 12.9, so $2.345^3 = 12.9$.

It is true that the log of *any* number to *any* power is merely the index of the power multiplied by the number's log. This holds even where the power is not a whole number, and it brings us to a class of problems where logs are essential because there is no other way to get the answer.

EXAMPLE: When air is compressed or expanded in a cylinder without friction and without transferring heat to or from the cylinder walls, the ratio of absolute pressures equals the volume ratio raised to the 1.4 power.

Consider the case of a perfect compressor in which the volume at start of compression is 5 times the volume at end of compression. What is the final absolute pressure?

Since the volume ratio is 5, the pressure ratio is $5^{1.4}$, that is, 5 to the 1.4 power. Since log 5 is 0.6990, 1.4 × 0.6990 = 0.9786, the log of 9.52. This means that final absolute pressure is 9.52 × 14.7, where 14.7 psia is the absolute pressure of the atmosphere. The psia final pressure is 139.9 psia, or 125.2 psig.

Getting roots is just as easy. Divide the log of the number by the index of the root to get the log of the root.

PROBLEM: What is the fifth root of 17.06?

$$\log 17.06 = 1.2320$$

This divided by 5 is 0.2464, which is the log of 1.764. Therefore the fifth power of 17.06 is 1.764.

SUGGESTED READING

Hicks, Tyler G: "Standard Handbook of Engineering Calculations," McGraw-Hill Book Company, New York, 1972. (Has 1000 calculation procedures accompanied by worked-out numerical examples and about 4000 related calculation procedures.)

2

PUTTING MATH TO WORK

Here we start with freehand figuring and go on to practical geometry and mental estimating of engineering problems to help you arrive at answers in the *easiest* and *quickest* possible time. Not only are these methods of calculating *easier* for solving on-the-job plant problems, but they are also helpful for *quickly* calculating the many problems in various grades of engineering license examination.

FREEHAND FIGURING

The main trick in freehand figuring is to round out the actual numbers involved into numbers easy to handle. At the same time, errors made in one direction can be partly compensated by deliberate errors in the other direction.

In this connection when two numbers are to be multiplied, note that the answer will not be greatly changed if one number is increased by a certain small percentage and the other is decreased by approximately the same percentage.

PROBLEM: $48 \times 104 = ?$ Change both in opposite direction about 4%. Then $50 \times 100 = 5000$; so $48 \times 104 = 5000$, approximately. (The exact answer is 4992.)

PROBLEM: $27 \times 225 = ?$ The approximate answer is $30 \times 200 = 6000$. (The exact answer is 6075.)

Here's a similar rule for division: *The answer in division will not be greatly in error if both numbers are increased or both decreased by about the same percent.* In this case, the percent of change need not be small.

PROBLEM: $296 \div 39 = ?$ Approximately, $300 \div 40 = 30 \div 4 = 7.5$. (The exact answer is 7.59.)

PROBLEM: $935 \div 108 \times ?$ Knock both down about 6 to 8%.
Then $860 \div 100 = 8.6$ (approx). (The exact answer is 8.66.)

PROBLEM: $146 \div 93 = ?$ Jack both up about 8%. Then $160 \div 100 = 1.6$ (approx). (The exact answer is 1.57.)

A Special Case

If all the numbers involved are close to powers of 10, approximate multiplication and division can be reduced to simple addition and subtraction. This applies where all numbers involved are within 10%, say, of 1 or 10 or 100, or 0.1 or 0.01, etc.

No matter where the actual decimal point is, think of each number as 1, plus or minus 0.01, 0.02, 0.03, 0.04, 0.05, 0.06, 0.07, etc. To multiply a string of such numbers find the *net excess* over 1, or the *net deficit* below 1. The answer (except for decimal place) is merely 1 plus this net excess, or minus this net deficit. All this will be clear from examples.

PROBLEM: $96.2 \times 103 = ?$ Shifting decimal points gives $0.96 \times 1.03 = ?$ The 0.96 has a deficit of 0.04 and the 1.03 an excess of 0.03 leaving a net deficit of 0.01. The product is then 0.99. Correcting the decimal place, we have $96.2 \times 103 = 9900$, approximately. (The exact answer is 9908.6.)

PROBLEM: $0.0105 \times 103,000 \times 94 \times .097 = ?$ Write it $1.05 \times 1.03 \times 0.94 \times 0.97 = ?$ The computation $5 + 3 - 6 - 3$ shows a net deficit of 1. So the approximate product is 0.99, or 9900 corrected for the decimal place. (The exact answer is 9861.1.)

Where one number is divided by another, the same rule applies after reversing the sign of the excess or deficit in the divisor.

PROBLEM: $106 \div 9.8 = ?$ Write it $1.06 \div 0.98 = ?$ The 1.06 has a surplus of 0.06. The deficit of 0.98 is 0.02. Reverse it to give a surplus of 0.02, and add this to 0.06 to give 0.08. Then the approximate answer is 1.08, or 10.8 corrected for the decimal place. (The exact answer is 10.8.)

PROBLEM: $938 \div 1020 = ?$ Write it $0.94 \div 1.02 = ?$ The 0.94 has a deficit of 0.06. The 0.02 surplus of 1.02 reverses to a 0.02 deficit. The net deficit is 0.08. Therefore, $938 \div 1020 = 0.92$, approximately. (The exact answer is 0.9196.)

MORE ABOUT FREEHAND FIGURING _____

Thus far, you learned that approximate mental arithmetic—freehand figuring—is really an art, one in which most top-flight engineers and scientists are expert. The idea is to get a rough answer quickly for preliminary estimates and similar uses without benefit of slide rule, reference books, or even pencil and paper.

The errors involved in cutting a lot of corners may range from 1 or 2% up to 10%, or even higher. The expert in practical math knows when 10% is close enough for his purposes. He also knows when he must be within 1% to be safe, or even within 0.1%. Being too accurate for the purpose in hand marks the tyro with figures.

Here's a sample of wasted accuracy. You want to buy a piece of rope to wrap five times around a 6-ft tank, with a bit to spare. The diameter of the centerline of the rope coils is the tank diameter plus the rope diameter. Some would add these, then multiply by 5 and by 3.1416 like this:

$$6 + 0.04 = 6.04 \qquad 6.04 \times 3.1416 \times 5 = 94.88 \text{ ft.}$$

Considering the purpose, this operation doesn't make much sense. Why not forget the trifling rope diameter? And why not take 3 as the value of pi here? Then the rope length needed will be about $5 \times 6 \times 3 = 90$ ft. To be on the safe side you buy 100 ft.

School teachers do a lot of harm when they teach boys and girls to use 3.1416 as pi for all occasions. Even worse is the figure $3^1/_7$, taught in some schools. I could write a book about what's wrong with $3^1/_7$. Pi should be 3.1416, 3.141, 3.1, or just 3, according to the accuracy needed for the particular job.

NUMBERS TO REMEMBER _____

As handy tools for freehand figuring always keep a few approximate constants in your head. Pick them to meet your own needs. According to books, the area of a circle is 0.7854 times the square of the diameter. This is nothing but 3.1416 divided by 4. To put it another way, the area of a circle is 78.54% of the area of the square it fits in.

Here again it would be very foolish to use 0.7854 for all occasions. Much of the time 0.78 is close enough, and it happens every now and then that the purpose at hand is served if the area of the circle is taken as either three-quarters of the square or eight-tenths of the square, whichever is easier to use.

EXAMPLE: Find the approximate area of a 60-ft-diameter circle. The square is 3600 sq ft. Three-quarters of 3600 is 2700. Call it 2800 sq ft. (The exact answer is 2827.44 sq ft.)

EXAMPLE: Find the approximate area of a 50-ft-diameter circle. The square is 2500. Then $2500 \times 0.8 = \frac{1}{4} \times 8000 = 2000$ sq ft, approximate area of 50-ft circle. (The exact answer is 1963.5 sq ft.)

Since engineers work a lot with water and common metals it is convenient to remember the constants in Table 2-1.

Now for some more free-swinging practice problems.

PROBLEM: How many gallons in a hogshead if the height is 5 ft, center diameter 5 ft, and top and bottom diameters 4 ft?

SOLUTION: Take the average diameter as 4.5 ft. The first step is to

TABLE 2-1   Constants of Water and Common Metals

	Close	Rough
Water:		
cu in. per gal	231	230
Weight of 1 cu ft, lb	62.4	62 or 60
Volume of 1 cu ft, gal	7.5	
Weight of 1 cu in, lb:		
Cast iron	0.26	0.25
Steel	0.28	0.3
Brass	0.31	0.3
Copper	0.32	0.3

square this diameter. Roughly $4.5 \times 4.5 = 4 \times 5 = 20$ sq ft. Three-quarters of 20 is 15, the approximate area of an average section of the hogshead.

The volume, then, is $5 \times 15 = 75$ cu ft. The capacity in gallons is about $75 \times 7.5 =$ about $80 \times 7 = 560$ gal. (The exact answer is 596.4 gal.)

The statement that $4.5 \times 4.5 = 4 \times 5$ involves little error. We find that 4×5 is 20 while 4.5×4.5 is 20.25, only 1% higher.

The rule is this: *The product of a number by itself can be replaced by the product of two numbers, one slightly higher than the original number and the other the same amount lower.*

EXAMPLE: What is the area of a plot 212 ft square? Roughly $212 \times 212 = 200 \times 224 = 44{,}800$, say 45,000 sq ft. The exact area is 44,944 sq ft.

The same idea operates in reverse. Instead of moving the two numbers apart, they can be moved together. Here is the rule: *If two numbers are nearly equal (say within 25%), their product is about the same as the square of their average.*

EXAMPLE: What is the area of a table top 3.5×4.5 ft? A square table of the same average dimension would be $4 \times 4 = 16$ sq ft. The exact area of a 3.5×4.5 table is 15.75 sq ft (Fig. 2-1).

Here we must sound a note of warning. Don't try to apply this

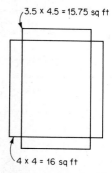

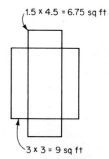

FIG. 2-1 A square table of some average side lengths has about the same surface as a rectangular table.

FIG. 2-2 The relation in Fig. 2-1 doesn't hold for this long, thin rectangle.

method if the two dimensions differ widely. Take the case of a table 1.5 × 4.5 ft, 3 times as long as it is wide. Here the average squared would be 3 × 3 = 9 sq ft, whereas the actual area of a 1.5 × 4.5 table is 6.75 sq ft (Fig. 2-2).

On the other hand, this shortcut never gives an error of more than 1% if the two dimensions differ by not more than 20%.

PROOF BY TRIAL: Find the exact and approximate area of a plot 90 × 110 ft. The true area is 9900. The approximate area = 100 × 100 = 10,000 sq ft, which is an error of 1%.

Handy Examples

Here goes for more practice in fast and furious arithmetic *to be done without touching pencil or paper.*

Let's start with problems involving cylinders (pipes, wires, tanks, rods). The volume of a cylinder is the length times the area of the cross-sectional circle. The circle area is diameter squared times 0.785. In this work never carry this beyond 0.78, and whenever safe and more convenient substitute 0.80 or 0.75.

EXAMPLE: Estimate the weight of a $1^3/_8$-in. round brass rod, 17 ft long (Fig. 2-3a).

Since $1^3/_8$ is 1.375, you may be tempted to square 1.375, but don't do it. Here it's easier to work with $1^3/_8$ when you see that $1^3/_8$ squared is $^{121}/_{64}$—a little less than 2.

Since 2 is a little high, multiply it by 0.75 (a little low) to get the approximate section area, 1.5 sq in.

The 17-ft length is about 200 in., so the approximate volume is 200 × 1.5 = 300 cu in. When the unit weight of brass is taken as 0.3 lb per cu in., the total weight of the rod is about 90 lb. (The exact answer is 96.93 lb.)

EXAMPLE: Estimate the weight of a 250-ft length of no. 16 bare copper wire (Fig. 2-3b).

The diameter of no. 16 is 51 mils. Call it 0.050 in. or $^1/_{20}$ in. Then the diameter squared is $^1/_{400}$. This times 0.8 is 0.002 sq in.

To get the number of inches in 250 ft divide 12 by 4 and multiply by 1000. The answer is 3000 in. Then 3000 × 0.002 = 6 cu in. At 0.3 lb per cu in., the wire weighs about 2 lb. (The exact answer is 1.92 lb.)

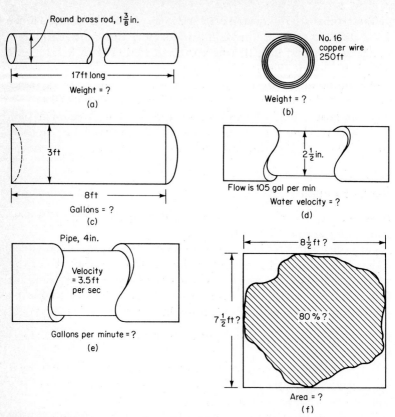

FIG. 2-3 Finding answers to these six problems can be done mentally after a little practice.

EXAMPLE: What is the gallon capacity of a cylindrical tank 3 ft in diameter and 8 ft long in the straight part if one head is concave and the other convex (Fig. 2-3c)?

The convex and concave heads just cancel, so the capacity is the same as that of a flat-headed tank, 8 ft long. The diameter squared is 9. This times 0.8 is 7.2. Call it 7 sq ft. Then $7 \times 8 = 56$ cu ft.

Gallons capacity = 56×7.5. Note that 7.5 is three-quarters of 10, so cut one-quarter off 56 to get 42, and multiply this by 10 to get 420 gal. (The exact answer is 424.11 gal.)

EXAMPLE: What is the velocity of water in a $2^1/_2$-in. pipe delivering 105 gal per min (Fig. 2-3d)?

Since 1 gal = 231 cu in., delivery is about 230 × 100 = 23,000 cu in. per min. This is about 24,000 ÷ 60 = 400 cu in. per sec.

The square of 2½ is about 2 × 3 = 6. This times 0.8 is 4.8. Call it 5 sq in. Then the water velocity is 400 ÷ 5 = 80 in. per sec, or 80 ÷ 12 = about 6 or 7 ft per sec. (The exact answer is 7.2 ft per sec.)

EXAMPLE: How many gallons per minute will be delivered by a 4-in. pipe if the water velocity is 3.5 ft per sec (Fig. 2-3e)?

The section area is 4 × 4 × ¾ = about 12 sq in. The distance the water flows per minute is 3.5 × 60 = 7 × 30 = 210 ft. Cubic inches delivered per minute = 12 × 12 × 210 = 144 × 210 = about 150 × 200 = 30,000.

Since 1 gal = 231 cu in., the answer is 30,000 ÷ 231 = about 3000 ÷ 24 = 1000 ÷ 8 = 125 gpm. (The exact answer is 130.9 gpm.)

EXAMPLE: Approximate the area of the irregular shape in Fig. 2-3f if the estimated length is about 8.5 ft and the estimated width about 7.5 ft, and the shape seems to fill about 80% of the rectangle.

The approximate area is 0.8 × 8.5 × 7.5 = about 0.8 × 8 × 8 = about 50 sq ft. (The exact answer is 51 sq ft.)

Instant Answer for Steel

If you're good at estimating sizes, you won't need a measuring rule or a weighing scale to come close to the true weight of a steel shaft, square bar, or steel plate. Just memorize the figures on the sketch in Fig. 2-4. Then do the rest in your head.

EXAMPLE: 8 ft of 1-in. round will weigh 8 × 10 ÷ 4 = 20 lb. Also 9 ft of 1-in. square rod will weigh 9 × 10 ÷ 3 = 30 lb.

EXAMPLE: Suppose a steel plate 3 ft × 8 ft is ¾ in. thick. Since ¾ is ⁶/₈, the weight per square foot is 6 × 5 = 30 lb. Total weight = 3 × 8 × 30 = 720 lb.

Weights of rods larger than 1 in. go up in proportion to the square of the size. Thus a 3-in. square will weigh 3 × 3 = 9 times as much as 1-in. square, or 9 × 10 ÷ 3 = 30 lb per foot. In same way a 5-in. round shaft weighs 5 × 5 × ¹⁰/₄ = 62 lb per foot.

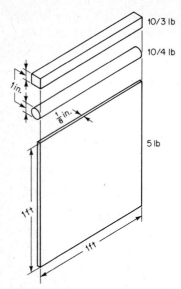

FIG. 2-4 Estimate the weight of these shapes mentally.

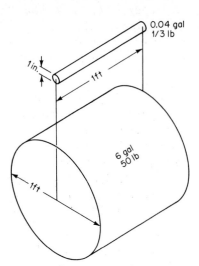

FIG. 2-5 The contents of cylinders must often be estimated mentally.

For Water

In pipes and round tanks water always takes the shape of a cylinder. If you know (Fig. 2-5) the weight or gallonage of a standard cylinder of water 1 ft long and 1 in. or 1 ft in diameter, it will be easy to figure the weight or gallon capacity of any pipe or round tank.

Just remember that capacity goes up as the *square* of the diameter. Thus a 4-in. pipe will hold $4 \times 4 = 16$ times as much water as a 1-in. pipe. Then 1 ft of 4-in. pipe will hold $16 \times 0.04 = 0.64$ gal, or $16 \times \frac{1}{3} = 5.3$ lb of water.

For large tanks it will be more convenient to measure diameter in feet. For example, a 20-ft diameter tank will hold $20 \times 20 = 400$ times as much per foot of length as a 1-ft-diameter tank. This comes to $400 \times 6 = 2400$ gal per foot of length. Thus total content of a 20-ft round tank 15 ft high will be $2400 \times 15 = 36,000$ gal.

WARNING: Figures given are rounded for quick mental arithmetic, so results are not exact and should not be used for precise work.

BACK TO SQUARE ROOT _____

A circle is 3.1416 times the radius squared. This is just another way of stating the rule just given and less convenient for an engineer because he measures the diameter much more often than he measures the radius (Fig. 2-6*a*).

The school-day formula is pictured in Fig. 2-6*b*. It is the same as saying that the area of a circle equals that of 3.1416 "quarter squares." Each square has the radius for a side. Now note that if you divide 3.1416 by 4, you get 0.7854, which is simply 78.54 percent.

Figure 2-6*c* shows that the volume of a flat-ended tank is the length times 78.54% of the square the end fits. And that is 78.54% of the square of the diameter.

If the tank has a convex head (Fig. 2-6*d*), include only two-thirds of its length in the length of the tank. For the same reason deduct two-thirds length of a concave head.

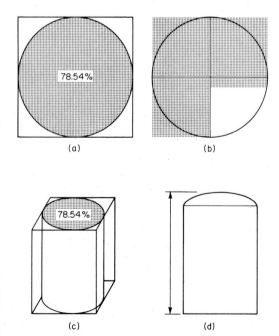

FIG. 2-6 Areas and volumes of tanks can be estimated without calculations.

EXAMPLE: What is the cubical content of a tank of 50 in. diameter with one flat end and one convex end if the straight part is 70 in. long and the convex head 15 in. long?

The equivalent length is $70 + (^2/_3 \times 15) = 80$ in. The cross-sectional area is $50 \times 50 \times 0.7854 = 1963$ sq in. Volume = $1963 \times 80 = 157,000$ cu in. Capacity is about $157,000 \div 231 = 675$ gal. (The exact answer is 680 gal.)

PROBLEM: What diameter circle will have an area of 72 sq in? *To get the diameter divide by 0.785 and then take the square root.*

SOLUTION: Dividing 72 by 0.785 gives 91.7. Table 2-2 shows that the square root is 9.57 in., which is also the diameter.

Square-Root Shortcut

In Chap. 1 we learned how to get square roots without tables or slide rule. The following rule applies only to numbers between 1 and 100:

1. By inspection set down the square root *to the nearest whole number only.* This will fall between 1 and 10.

TABLE 2-2   Square Roots

No.	Root	No.	Root	No.	Root	No.	Root	No.	Root	No.	Root	No.	Root	No.	Root	No.	Root
1.0	1.000	2.0	1.414	3.0	1.732	4.0	2.000	5.0	2.236	6.0	2.449	7.0	2.646	8.0	2.828	9.0	3.000
1.1	1.049	2.1	1.449	3.1	1.761	4.1	2.025	5.1	2.258	6.1	2.470	7.1	2.665	8.1	2.846	9.1	3.017
1.2	1.095	2.2	1.483	3.2	1.789	4.2	2.049	5.2	2.280	6.2	2.490	7.2	2.683	8.2	2.864	9.2	3.033
1.3	1.140	2.3	1.517	3.3	1.817	4.3	2.074	5.3	2.302	6.3	2.510	7.3	2.702	8.3	2.881	9.3	3.050
1.4	1.183	2.4	1.549	3.4	1.844	4.4	2.098	5.4	2.324	6.4	2.530	7.4	2.720	8.4	2.898	9.4	3.066
1.5	1.225	2.5	1.581	3.5	1.871	4.5	2.121	5.5	2.345	6.5	2.550	7.5	2.739	8.5	2.915	9.5	3.082
1.6	1.265	2.6	1.612	3.6	1.897	4.6	2.145	5.6	2.366	6.6	2.569	7.6	2.757	8.6	2.933	9.6	3.098
1.7	1.304	2.7	1.643	3.7	1.924	4.7	2.168	5.7	2.387	6.7	2.588	7.7	2.775	8.7	2.950	9.7	3.114
1.8	1.342	2.8	1.673	3.8	1.949	4.8	2.191	5.8	2.408	6.8	2.608	7.8	2.793	8.8	2.966	9.8	3.130
1.9	1.378	2.9	1.703	3.9	1.975	4.9	2.214	5.9	2.429	6.9	2.627	7.9	2.811	8.9	2.983	9.9	3.146

No.	Root	No.	Root	No.	Root	No.	Root	No.	Root	No.	Root	No.	Root	No.	Root	No.	Root
10	3.162	20	4.472	30	5.477	40	6.325	50	7.071	60	7.746	70	8.367	80	8.944	90	9.487
11	3.317	21	4.583	31	5.568	41	6.403	51	7.141	61	7.810	71	8.426	81	9.000	91	9.539
12	3.464	22	4.690	32	5.657	42	6.481	52	7.211	62	7.874	72	8.485	82	9.055	92	9.592
13	3.606	23	4.796	33	5.745	43	6.557	53	7.280	63	7.937	73	8.544	83	9.110	93	9.644
14	3.742	24	4.899	34	5.831	44	6.633	54	7.348	64	8.000	74	8.602	84	9.165	94	9.695
15	3.873	25	5.000	35	5.916	45	6.708	55	7.416	65	8.062	75	8.660	85	9.220	95	9.747
16	4.000	26	5.099	36	6.000	46	6.782	56	7.483	66	8.124	76	8.718	86	9.274	96	9.798
17	4.123	27	5.196	37	6.083	47	6.856	57	7.550	67	8.185	77	8.775	87	9.327	97	9.849
18	4.243	28	5.292	38	6.164	48	6.928	58	7.616	68	8.246	78	8.832	88	9.381	98	9.899
19	4.359	29	5.385	39	6.245	49	7.000	59	7.681	69	8.307	79	8.888	89	9.434	99	9.950

2. Divide this into the original number and carry the answer (quotient) to *one decimal place only.*

3. Average the original whole-number square root and this quotient to *one decimal place only* and call this average the *approximate square root.*

4. Divide the original number by the approx square root and carry the quotient to *three decimal places.*

5. Average this latest quotient and the approx square root to three decimals and call this the *exact square root.*

Except for an occasional number between 1 and 3, the "exact" root thus obtained will never be in error by more than 1 in the third decimal place.

PROBLEM: Find the square root of 11.

SOLUTION: The nearest whole-number root is 3. Then $11 \div 3 = 3.6$. The average of 3 and 3.6 is 3.3 = approximate root. Then $11 \div 3.3 = 3.333$. The average of 3.3 and 3.333 is 3.317 = "exact" square root of 11.

PROBLEM: Find the square root of 42.62. The nearest whole-number root = 6.

$$\frac{42.62}{6} = 7.1 + \text{av. of 6 and } 7.1 = 6.5 = \text{approx root}$$

$$\frac{42.62}{6.5} = 6.557 \text{ av. } 6.5 \text{ and}$$

$$6.557 = 6.528 = \text{"exact" square root.}$$

Numbers 1 to 3

For any numbers between 3 and 100 this rule will never give an error of more than 1 in the third decimal place. Between 1 and 3 the error may sometimes be slightly greater. For example, the square root of 2 by this rule would be 1.416 instead of 1.414.

Where you want high accuracy in the square root of numbers between 1 and 3, insert the following step between step 3 and step 4 in the rule already given:

Next, divide the number by the approximate square root obtained in step 3 and carry the quotient to *two decimal places only.* Average this quotient and the approximate square root of 3 *to two decimal places* and use the average as a *corrected approximate square root* in step 4.

PROBLEM: What is the square root of 2.304?
The nearest whole number = 1 (use 2 if you prefer)

$$\frac{2.304}{1} = 2.3$$

Av. of 1 and 2.3 = 1.6

$$\frac{2.304}{1.6} = 1.44$$

Av. 1.6 and 1.44 = 1.52

$$\frac{2.304}{1.52} = 1.516$$

Av. of 1.52 and 1.516 = 1.518 = "exact" square root

Numbers beyond Range

For numbers greater than 99 or less than 1 move the decimal point left or right two digits at a step until the number is in the range. Then take the square root by the rule already given.

Finally move the decimal point in the opposite direction a single digit for each two digits moved in the original number.

PROBLEM: Find the square root of 23,000. Moving the point *two double steps* to the *left* gives 2.3. The square root of 2.3 is 1.517. Move the point back *two single steps* to the *right* to get 151.7 as the square root of 23,000.

PROBLEM: Find the square root of 0.000032. Move the point three double steps to the right to get 32. The square root of 32 is 5.657. Then move the point left three *single* steps to get 0.005657 as the square root of 0.000032.

PROBLEM: The bunker pictured in Fig. 2-7a is level full of coal running 50 cu ft per ton. The heat value of the coal is 13,800 Btu (British thermal units) per lb. Two boilers are operating steadily on this coal. Each is producing 3000 lb of steam per hr at a 1.15 factor of evaporation and an efficiency of 65%. How many hours will the coal in the bunker run the boilers?

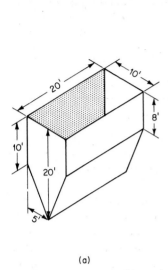

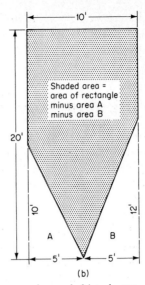

Shaded area = area of rectangle minus area A minus area B

(a)   (b)

FIG. 2-7 The volumes of irregular shapes may be needed in a hurry.

SOLUTION: First draw the end view of the bunker and fill in all the indicated dimensions by common sense (Fig. 2-7*b*). Note that the end is a 10 × 20 ft rectangle minus the two bottom triangles.

$$\text{Triangle } A = 5 \times 10 \times \tfrac{1}{2} = 25 \text{ sq ft}$$
$$\text{Triangle } B = 5 \times 12 \times \tfrac{1}{2} = \underline{30 \text{ sq ft}}$$
$$55 \text{ sq ft}$$

$$\text{Net area} = (10 \times 20) - 55 = 145 \text{ sq ft}$$
$$\text{Volume} = 145 \times 20 = 2900 \text{ cu ft}$$

$$\text{Weight coal} = \frac{2900}{50} = 58 \text{ tons} = 116{,}000 \text{ lb}$$

Now turn to the boiler part of it. "Standard" steam absorbs 970 Btu per lb. At a 1.15 factor of evaporation each pound absorbs 970 × 1.15 = 1115 Btu. The combined hourly heat output of two furnaces will be 2 × 3000 × 1115 = 6,690,000 Btu.

Every pound of coal burned will deliver 0.65 × 13,800 = 8970 Btu to boilers, so the hourly coal required will be

$$\frac{6{,}690{,}000}{8970} = 745.8 \text{ lb}$$

Then the *total* number of hours that the boilers will run from coal in the bunker is

$$\frac{116,000}{745.8} = 155.5 \text{ hours}$$

HOW TO USE RIGHT TRIANGLES _____

More than 2000 years ago, a Greek named Pythagoras proved by exact logic (repeated in every high-school geometry book) that if you build up squares on the three sides of any right triangle, the area of the square on the hypotenuse equals the sum of the squares on the two legs.

Test this yourself by drawing a right triangle, measuring the sides, and then squaring the numbers. Or, if you want, you can cut actual squares out of cardboard or sheet metal and weigh them.

One famous combination (Fig. 2-8) has legs equaling 3 and 4. The hypotenuse will measure 5. You can lay out this 3-4-5 right triangle in any unit—inches, centimeters, feet, yards, miles, etc.

Also it will work for any three numbers in the ratio of 3-4-5, for example, 30-40-50, 6-8-10, 9-12-15, and 12-16-20.

Conversely, if the sides of a right triangle are in the proportion 3-4-5, the angle between the 3 leg and the 4 leg will always be a right angle. This gives an easy way to lay out a right angle with nothing but a tape to work with.

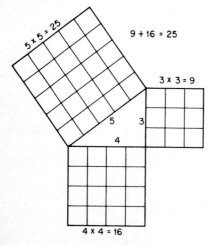

FIG. 2-8 The sum of squares on legs of a right triangle equals the square of the hypotenuse.

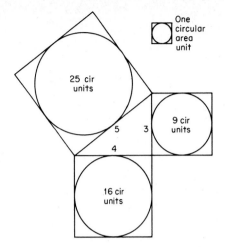

FIG. 2-9 The area of the big circle equals the sum of the areas of the other two circles.

Figure 2-9 shows that circles can be added in the same way. Any circle is 87.5% of the square it fits in, so the area of the big circle must be the sum of the two small circles.

In Fig. 2-10 we add up several circles. First add up A and B, as already explained in Fig. 2-9. Take a and b as the two legs of the

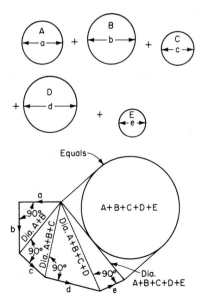

FIG. 2-10 A large circle has the combined area of all the small circles.

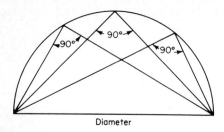

FIG. 2-11 Any angle drawn this way in a semicircle will come out a right angle.

first triangle. Then the hypotenuse is the diameter of a circle whose area is the sum of *A* and *B*.

The next step is to take this and *c* as the legs of a new right triangle. The hypotenuse of this second triangle will be the diameter of a circle whose area is *A + B + C*.

Keep on this way until you get the final big circle, the sum of all the small ones.

When dealing with pipe it isn't necessary to *draw* any circles. Just lay off the inside diameters as *a, b, c,* etc., and measure the final diameter.

Figure 2-11 pictures another fundamental fact that has many practical uses. Any angle drawn as shown in a semicircle will be a right angle. Try it!

Figure 2-12 shows how to test a machined part that is supposed to be a true half circle in section. If the machinist's square always touches at *A, B,* and *C,* the half shell is true.

WARNING: Don't tilt the square. Also note that even if the curve is truly circular, this won't work if the curve is more or less than exactly half a circle.

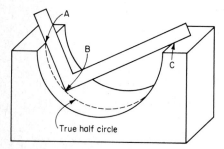

FIG. 2-12 If the half circle is true, the machinist's square will always touch as shown.

VECTORS SAVE TIME

You might say that a vector is always going somewhere. It's a quantity that has a direction. The quantity 2 miles isn't a vector because it has no direction, but 2 miles *north* is a vector. In the same way a force of 2 lb is not a vector, but 2 lb force *in a specified direction* is a vector.

It's easy to see that an arrow is the natural symbol for a vector. The arrow points in the direction of the action, and the length of the arrow represents the amount of the action, which may be a *distance,* a *velocity,* a *force* or something else.

Here's a sample problem with distance vectors (Fig. 2-13). You start from your house and walk 4 miles straight north. That is a vector, or arrow, 4 units long and pointing north. Then you walk 3 miles east, another arrow tacked onto the end of the first. Finally you walk south 1 mile, adding a third vector arrow as shown.

What is the result of all this wandering? Merely that you got from where you started to where you arrived, an achievement represented by an arrow running straight from start to finish. That vector is the *resultant* or *vector sum* of the others.

Next try an experiment. Walk the same distances and directions as before but change the order of the legs. Go 1 mile south, then 3 east, then 4 north and draw the arrows end to end for this itinerary. Again draw the *resultant* arrow from where you started to where you finished.

No matter what the order of steps, your resultant (accomplishment) always ends up as a northeast trip of 4.2 miles.

Now you can see the rule for adding vector arrows. Move them around over the paper any way you want (never changing their direction). Place them end to end in any order so as to form a

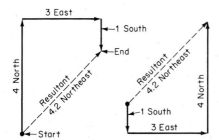

FIG. 2-13 To add vectors merely place the arrows head to tail. The dotted arrow drawn from the start of the first arrow to the tip of the last is the resultant.

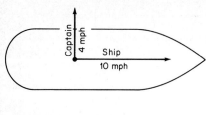

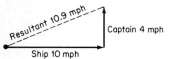

FIG. 2-14 Simple example of speed in two directions to find the resultant velocity.

one-way path. Then draw a line from the beginning of the first arrow to the end of the last. This is the resultant, or net effect, of all the vectors combined, both in direction and amount. This rule holds true whether the vectors show distance, speed, force, or something else.

Figure 2-14 is a simple example of velocity. While the ship is sailing due north at 10 mph, the captain walks west briskly across the deck at 4 mph. Clearly his speed over the bottom is greater than 4 mph, and even greater than 10 mph, but it can't be as much as 14 mph because he isn't walking north.

To find what's happening add the 10-mph north vector to the 4-mph west vector, as pictured, to get one that scales 10.9 mph about north-northwest.

Vectors work just as well for forces, where several push or pull in various directions on the same point. In Fig. 2-15 the chains supporting the 1000-lb weight are unequal. What is the load on each?

Here it is important to note that the point where the three chains meet is in equilibrium, so the net force on this point is zero. That is merely another way of saying that the vectors representing the tensions in *A*, *B*, and *C* add up to zero.

For the resultant to be zero, the end of the last arrow must land at the beginning of the first, closing the triangle. You know vector *A*, so draw it (lower left, Fig. 2-15). The amounts of *B* and *C* are not known, but their directions are. We also know that *C* must pass through the start of *A* and *B* through the arrow point of *A*.

So draw the direction lines of *B* and *C* as indicated. Where they cross must be the tip of *B* and the start of *C*, so the triangle can be

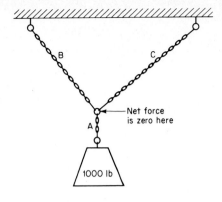

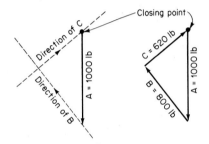

FIG. 2-15 Vectors used for forces of several pushes or pulls in various directions on the same point.

completed as shown at lower right. Tension scales 800 lb in chain *B* and 620 lb in *C*.

Three Forces in Balance

Perhaps the most important use of vectors is for figuring out forces balancing at a point. Whenever two or more wires, ropes, cables, chains, or struts come together at a point in a stable structure or rig, the forces at that point must balance out, that is, add up to zero (as *vectors*). They must form a closed triangle, the tip of the last arrow falling on the start of the first, so that the resultant is zero.

In the usual case three forces act on the point. One is completely known in amount and direction. The other two are known in direction because a force always acts along the line of the rope or strut. Also, in the case of a rope or other flexible member, the force is always a *pull; you can't push on a rope.*

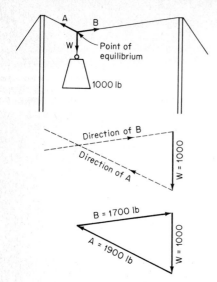

FIG. 2-16 The point where the loads connect is in equilibrium under three forces.

Weight on Cable

Suppose a 1000-lb weight is hung on a slack cable, which then takes the position shown in Fig. 2-16, top. The point where the weight hits the cable is in balance under three forces, the 1000-lb downward pull of the weight and the two unknown pulls acting in known directions A and B.

The problem is to draw a triangle for these three forces. First draw the downward vector for the 1000-lb weight and through its two ends draw the direction lines for A and B. Where they cross fixes the left corner of the triangle, which can then be completed as shown in Fig. 2-16. Note that the arrows all track around in the same sense (very important). Scale A and B as about 1900 and 1700 lb, respectively.

Everybody knows that the rope tension is greater when a weight is hung on a taut rope than on a slack rope. Test this by repeating the problem just given using a rope with less sag.

Jib-Crane Problem

Figure 2-17 can represent an actual jib crane or an equivalent rig in which the boom is merely a timber butted against the wall with a

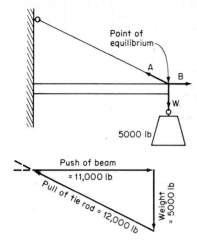

Point of
equilibrium

A
B

W.

5000 lb

Push of beam
= 11,000 lb

Pull of tie rod = 12,000 lb

Weight
= 5000 lb

FIG. 2-17 The point of equilibrium is at the top outer end of
boom. Three balancing forces
are acting downward.

support below to keep it from slipping down. The load on this support is the small weight of the inner end of the boom and does not
enter into problem.

The three forces in balance at the intersection at the top outer
end of the boom are the 5000-lb weight straight down, the tension
in A acting upward toward the left along the line of the tie rod, and
the force of the strut pushing straight out horizontally to the right.
Make the arrow triangle as before, keeping the arrows tracking
around in the same sense. The tie-rod pull scales 12,000 lb, and the
boom thrust is 11,000 lb.

ROD STRONGER THAN TUBE? _____

Whether you bend it or twist it, the solid rod is both stronger and
stiffer than a tube of the same material and of the same outside
diameter.

To pin down the argument, we looked up the standard formulas
and figured out just how strong a tube is (in bending) compared
with a solid rod of the same outside diameter. Figure 2-18 shows
what happens when you drill out the solid rod to various hole
diameters. Hole size is shown as decimal fractions of the outside
diameter.

All the pieces are shown as cantilever beams projecting the same

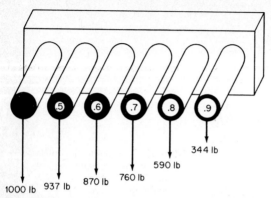

FIG. 2-18 Loads indicate relative strength and stiffness.
A solid rod is stronger than a tube of the same diameter.

distance from a wall. If the material and outside diameter are such that 1000 lb is the safe load at the end of the solid rod, the safe load for the tubes is as shown in Fig. 2-18.

The thick tube at the left (hole equals half the outside diameter) shows up fairly well, only 6.3% less than the solid rod, but the loss of strength becomes serious as the walls are thinned down. By the time the inside diameter is up to nine-tenths of the outside, the strength is down 65.6% to a load of 344 lb. This last is only one-third as strong as rod.

It happens that stiffness holds in the same proportion as strength (for tubes of the same outside diameter only). So the tube with the 0.5 hole is 93.7% as stiff as the rod, and the 0.9 hole tube 34.4% as stiff.

To express stiffness another way, all the beams will show the same deflection (depression at the ends) if loaded as shown in Fig. 2-18.

For shafts under torsion the formulas are different, but here also the solid rod is stronger and stiffer *for the same outside diameter.*

If this is so, somebody will ask: Why do we use tubes so often for beams, ships' shafts, machine parts, etc.? The answer is already on your tongue. *For a given weight of metal* the tube is much stronger and much stiffer than a solid rod.

For illustration we figured out what would happen if you took the metal in a 1-in. rod and made it into a 2-in. (OD) tube. The tube walls would be 0.134 thick. In bending, this tube figures 3.5 times as strong as the rod and 7 times as stiff.

WHY ARE BEAMS STRONG?

Figure 2-19 is an exaggerated sketch of a cantilever (overhanging) beam with a 1000-lb load at the free end, 12 ft from the supporting wall. The *bending moment* (leverage or torque) at the wall is $12 \times 1000 = 12,000$ lb-ft.

In this kind of beam the bending moment is always greater at the wall than at any other section. So if the cantilever beam has a uniform cross section (as with standard wooden beams and rolled-steel shapes) the only section you need to figure for safety is that at the wall. If the beam is strong enough at the wall, it is overstrong everywhere else.

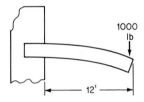

FIG. 2-19 The bending moment at the wall is $1000 \times 12 = 12,000$ lb-ft.

The beam resists the bending effect of the load by setting up an equal and opposite internal bending moment. Figure 2-20 shows how. As the beam bends, the top gets convex and the bottom concave. The centerline (neutral axis) does not change its length and therefore carries no load, but the top or convex side is stretched (tension) and the bottom or concave side shortened (compression). The lever arm of this compression or tension is the distance between these outside layers.

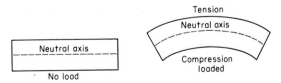

FIG. 2-20 When a beam is bent, the top fibers stretch under tension and the bottom ones shorten under compression.

It follows logically that the strength of a given beam section (its ability to resist bending) depends mainly on three qualities: (1) the amount of material in the top and bottom sections, (2) how far apart these masses are, and (3) how well the material can withstand a high unit stress.

It's easy to see from this why an I beam is so strong. First, it is made of a strong material (steel). And most of this section area is in the top and bottom flanges, while the thin web serves mainly to hold them as far apart as practical.

Everybody knows that a wood 2 × 4 stands bending better on edge than when laid flat. This is just one of many demonstrations of the rule that increasing beam depth is more helpful than increasing the width. This can be tested with three boards, as in Figs. 2-21 and 2-22.

If you place the three side by side, the load-carrying ability goes up in exact proportion. Three boards carry 3 times the load of one board. You get the same result if you place the three boards in layers like a cake (Fig. 2-22). The three-layer board still carries only 3 times the load of the one layer. Now glue the planks together and you get a whopping big dividend for your trouble. Acting now like a solid beam, the double plank becomes 4 times as strong as the single and the triple plank 9 times as strong.

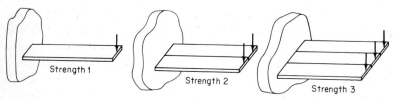

Strength 1

Strength 2

Strength 3

FIG. 2-21 The strength of a beam is directly proportional to its width. Two planks laid side by side take twice as much load, and three planks support triple the load.

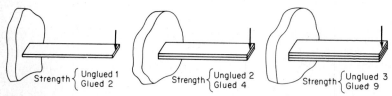

Strength { Unglued 1
          { Glued 2

Strength { Unglued 2
          { Glued 4

Strength { Unglued 3
          { Glued 9

FIG. 2-22 Strength is also proportional to the square of the depth. Three separate beams piled on top of each other can take a triple load. Glued together, they take 9 times the load.

The gluing forces the top plank to stretch and the bottom to compress. Being far apart, they can now buck a heavy bending load.

This leads to a simple rule: *The bending strength of a rectangular beam section is directly proportional to the width and also proportional to the square of the depth.*

With a 2 × 4 laid flat, the depth is 2 and the width 4 (assuming full dimensions, not the customary dimensions of planed lumber). Then the strength laid flat is proportional to 4 × 2 × 2 = 16. But place the beam on edge so that the width is 2 and depth is 4 and the strength is proportional to 2 × 4 × 4 = 32, twice as much as when laid flat.

BENDING MOMENTS

When a matter is important we say it is *momentous* or *of great moment*, and when we pull hard on the end of a long wrench, our pull has a lot of *moment*. In engineering the moment or *torque* (they're the same thing) is the product of force by lever arm. So in Fig. 2-23 the moment of the wrench is 20 × 70 = 1400 lb-in.

The "Weakest Link"

If the beam has the same section throughout its whole length, you need test only where bending moment is greatest. (A beam, like a chain, is no stronger than its weakest point.) So there are three things to know: (1) Where is the bending moment greatest? (2) What is the moment at that point? (3) What is the ability of that section to withstand bending?

Consider the cantilever beam in Fig. 2-24. The bending moment is greatest at the wall and is 60 × 1000 = 60,000 lb-in. To avoid

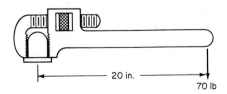

FIG. 2-23 The moment of 70-lb pull at 20 in. lever arm is 70 × 20 = 1400 lb-in.

20 in.

70 lb

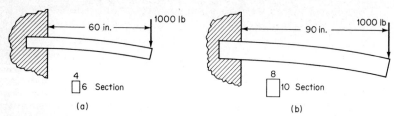

FIG. 2-24 The moment (*a*) 60,000 lb-in. and (*b*) 90,000 lb-in. The section modulus is (*a*) 24 and (*b*) 133. The unit stress is (*a*) 2500 and (*b*) 677 lb per sq in. Beam (*b*) is much safer than beam (*a*).

breaking, the beam section at the wall must set up an internal bucking moment of 60,000 lb-in.

Just as *external* moment is the product of two factors (force times lever arm), the equal and opposite *internal* moment is the product of *unit stress* and *section modulus*.

Unit Stress

Unit stress is maximum tensile or compressive stress in pounds per square inch in top or bottom fibers.

Section Modulus

The resistance of the *shape,* as distinct from the resistance of the *material,* is called the section modulus. For a rectangular cross section this modulus is width times depth squared divided by 6.

Then for Fig. 2-24*a*, the section modulus is $4 \times 6 \times 6 \div 6 = 24$. Moment = $24 \times$ unit stress = 60,000, or unit stress = $60,000 \div 24 = 2500$ psi. This would not be a satisfactory safety margin for a beam of long-leaf pine with an ultimate flexural strength of only about 5700 psi.

The beam in Fig. 2-24*b* is much safer. Here moment is $90 \times 1000 = 90,000$ lb-in. (greater by one-half), but the section modulus is $8 \times 10 \times 10 \div 6 = 133$ (almost 6 times as great). So the unit stress is only $90,000 \div 133 = 677$ psi.

Simple Beam Stronger

Now let's consider a so-called *simple beam,* loaded at the center (Fig. 2-25). In any simple beam with a concentrated load (whether in the center or not) the greatest moment is always at the load.

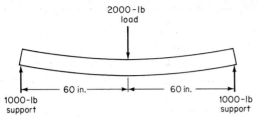

FIG. 2-25 The moment of the center of this simple beam is ¼ × 120 × 2000 = 60,000 lb-in, the same as the cantilever beam in Fig. 2-24a.

Here the load is 2000 lb, so the thrust of each support is 1000 lb. To figure the bending moment at load merely take this point as a fulcrum. Then the moment produced by the 1000-lb upward thrust of either support times the 60-in. lever arm is 1000 × 60 = 60,000 lb-in.

Note that this is the same as for a cantilever of half length and half load (Fig. 2-24a). In other words, a center-loaded simple beam is 4 times as strong as an end-loaded cantilever beam of the same section and length.

Formula for Simple Beam

The maximum bending moment of a center-loaded simple beam is ¼ × length × load. Figure 2-26 shows how the simple beam can be viewed as two cantilever beams of half length with half load. Just invert the forces and imagine a 120-in. beam balanced on a center support and carrying a 1000-lb load at each end, like a seesaw. Each half acts like a 60-in. cantilever beam with a 1000-lb end load.

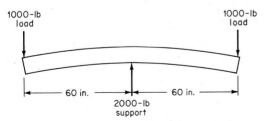

FIG. 2-26 Inverting the forces of Fig. 2-25 shows why the moment is the same as for the cantilever in Fig. 2-24a of half length and half load.

DATA AND FORMULAS _____

Now let's sum up what we have learned about beams so far. First are three definitions of terms as used here:

Stress here means the biggest tensile or compressive unit stress (pounds per square inch) in the extreme top and bottom fibers of the beam.

Moment means bending moment (pound-inches) at the point under consideration.

Modulus means section modulus for the given beam shape, a factor that depends on its form and area.

The Danger Point

A beam, like a chain, is no stronger than its most stressed point. So if the beam has a uniform sawed or rolled section, as usual, all you need test for safety is the danger point, the point where the moment is greatest. If the beam is strong enough at the danger point, it will be overstrong everywhere else. We have defined the three variables, *stress, moment,* and *modulus.* Here are the formulas:

$$\text{Moment} = \text{stress} \times \text{modulus}$$
$$\text{Stress} = \frac{\text{moment}}{\text{modulus}}$$
$$\text{Modulus} = \frac{\text{moment}}{\text{stress}}$$

Table 2-3 shows how to figure maximum moment for four common beam cases. It also gives modulus for standard light I beams and modulus formulas for sections of rectangular, round or tubular shape, also the safe stresses for structural steel and ordinary timber under normal conditions and steady loads.

For more data consult handbooks.

PROBLEM: What depth of light standard I beam would carry safely a steady 5000-lb load hung from middle of a 10-ft (120-in.) span?

$$\text{Moment} = \frac{1}{4} \times 120 \times 5000 = 150,000 \text{ lb-in.}$$
$$\text{Safe stress} = 20,000 \text{ psi}$$
$$\text{Modulus} = \frac{\text{moment}}{\text{stress}} = \frac{150,000}{20,000} = 7.5$$

**TABLE 2-3   How to Figure Maximum Moment
for Four Common Beam Problems**

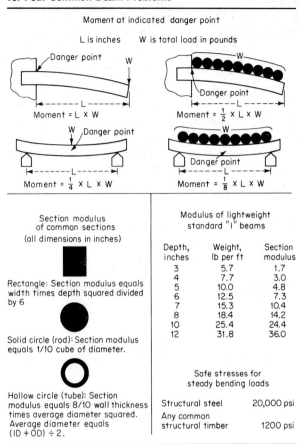

Moment at indicated danger point

L is inches   W is total load in pounds

Moment = L × W

Moment = $\frac{1}{2}$ × L × W

Moment = $\frac{1}{4}$ × L × W

Moment = $\frac{1}{8}$ × L × W

Section modulus of common sections (all dimensions in inches)	Modulus of lightweight standard "I" beams		
	Depth, inches	Weight, lb per ft	Section modulus
Rectangle: Section modulus equals width times depth squared divided by 6	3	5.7	1.7
	4	7.7	3.0
	5	10.0	4.8
	6	12.5	7.3
	7	15.3	10.4
Solid circle (rod): Section modulus equals 1/10 cube of diameter.	8	18.4	14.2
	10	25.4	24.4
	12	31.8	36.0

	Safe stresses for steady bending loads	
Hollow circle (tube): Section modulus equals 8/10 wall thickness times average diameter squared. Average diameter equals (ID + OD) ÷ 2.	Structural steel	20,000 psi
	Any common structural timber	1200 psi

A 7-in. light standard beam weighing 15.3 lb per ft with a section modulus of 10.4 is amply safe.

PROBLEM: A 4-in. standard-weight steel pipe is to be used as a beam bridging a 4-ft (48-in.) gap and carrying a block and fall at the center. What is the safe load using the conservative stress value of 10,000 psi?

Average pipe diameter = 4.25 in.

Wall thickness = 0.24 in.

Modulus = $0.8 \times 0.24 \times 4.25 \times 4.25 = 3.46$

Safe moment = $3.46 \times 10,000 = 34,600$ in.-lb

Moment = $\frac{1}{4} \times$ load $\times 48 = 12 \times$ load

$$\text{Load} = \frac{\text{moment}}{12} = \frac{34,600}{12} = 2880 \text{ lb}$$

WARNING: With beams of medium length you won't get into trouble figuring strength by the formulas given, but they may be dangerous for very stubby or very slender beams. You'd better not use these formulas for beams *shorter* than twice their depth, for wooden beams that run longer than eight depths without side bracing, or for steel I beams longer than 10 ft without side bracing.

SUGGESTED READING _____

Elonka, Stephen M., and Anthony L. Kohan: "Standard Boiler Operators' Questions and Answers," McGraw-Hill Book Company, New York, 1969. (Has 51 calculations and formulas.)

Elonka, Stephen M., and Joseph F. Robinson; "Standard Plant Operators' Questions and Answers," vols. I and II, McGraw-Hill Book Company, New York, 1959. (Has 126 calculations and formulas.)

3

BASIC POWER FACTS

Before learning to calculate the great variety of plant problems necessary for more efficient operation, a thorough understanding of force, work, power, torque, speed, leverage, centrifugal force, rotation, etc., is necessary. Here we briefly review these basic tools of engineering mathematics and illustrate them in great detail with 45 figures.

FORCE, WORK, AND POWER

Force is a push or pull. Engineers generally measure force in pounds or tons.

Work is done when a force acts on a moving body. The amount of work, in foot-pounds, is the product of the pounds push or pull by the number of feet the object moves in the direction of the force.

Power is the rate of doing work, generally measured in foot-pounds per minute, foot-pounds per second, horsepower, or kilowatts.

To get either of the first two measures of power, divide the foot-pounds of work by the minutes or seconds required to do the work.

One horsepower is equivalent to doing work at the rate of 550 ft-lb per sec or 33,000 ft-lb per min; 1 kW = 1.33 hp.

FORCE EXPLAINED

In Fig. 3-1*a* the force of gravity acts straight down 40 lb on the weight and is balanced by the 40-lb upward pull of the supporting cord. When a body is standing still or moving in a straight line at constant speed, the forces on the body always balance.

Figure 3-1*b* has a 10-lb force applied to push the block to the right, which is balanced by an equal friction force pushing on the block to the left. In this case the block is not lifted, so its 40-lb weight doesn't enter in.

Many forces act on the elements of a structure, such as the jib crane (Fig. 3-1*c*). At *A*, for example, the load pulls straight down 1 ton, the tie rod pulls more than 1 ton up left on a slant, and the beam thrusts out horizontally to the right, also with a force over 1 ton. These forces balance at *A*.

WORK PICTURE

A common case of work is lifting a weight straight up. When the 40-lb weight Fig. 3-2*a* is lifted 4 ft, the work done is 4 × 40 = 160

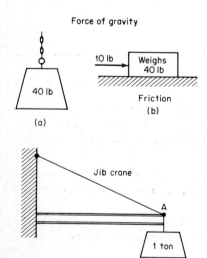

FIG. 3-1 Force is a push or pull, usually measured in pounds or tons.

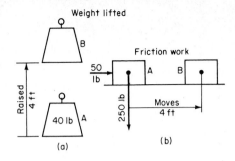

Weight lifted

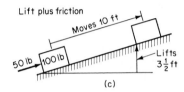

Lift plus friction

FIG. 3-2 Work takes place when a force acts on a moving body and is measured in foot-pounds.

ft-lb. But note that work is not always weight times distance. In Fig. 3-2b, for example, we don't consider the 250-lb weight but only the 50-lb push and the 4-ft movement in the direction of the push. Work here is $50 \times 4 = 200$ ft-lb.

Sliding a block up an inclined plane (Fig. 3-2c) combines lift work and friction work. Total work is $50 \times 10 = 500$ ft-lb. The lifting fraction is $3^{1}/_{2} \times 100 = 350$ ft-lb.

Figuring Power

In Fig. 3-3a the net lift on the elevator car is $8000 - 6500 = 1500$ lb, so the power absorbed in lifting is $1500 \times 800 = 1,200,000$ ft-lb per min, or

$$\frac{1,200,000}{33,000} = 36.4 \text{ hp}$$

Actually more motor power than this would be needed to allow for friction losses. In Fig. 3-3b the rope pull would be 1000 lb if there were no friction. Here the actual work input is

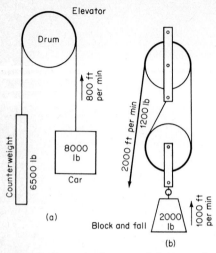

FIG. 3-3 Power is the rate of doing work, measured in foot-pounds per minute, foot-pounds per second, horsepower, or kilowatts.

$$1200 \times 2000 = 2,400,000 \text{ ft-lb per min}$$

and the useful work is

$$2000 \times 1000 = 2,000,000 \text{ ft-lb per min}$$

We have figured power as force times distance divided by time. We can get the same result by changing the order of these operations to distance divided by time multiplied by force. To put this another way, 1 hp is 1 lb acting at 550 ft per sec or 33,000 ft per min.

Then we have these rules: *Horsepower is pounds force times speed in feet per second divided by 550, or horsepower is pounds force times speed in feet per minute divided by 33,000.* Lifting a 400-lb weight 900 ft per min requires

$$400 \times \frac{900}{33,000} = \text{about 11 hp (plus power for friction)}$$

TORQUE AND SPEED

Power is usually delivered through rotating parts rather than in a straight-line push. In either case horsepower is the force in pounds

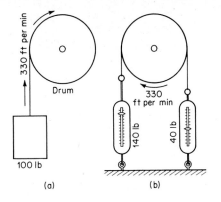

FIG. 3-4 (*a*) The difference between 1 hp doing useful work and (*b*) 1 hp delivered as heat.

times the distance through which it acts in 1 min divided by 33,000, because 1 hp is 33,000 ft-lb per min.

Figure 3-4*a* shows a hoisting drum turning with a rim speed of 330 ft per min, winding up a weight of 100 lb at the same speed. Work done is

$$330 \times 100 = 33{,}000 \text{ ft-lb per min} = 1 \text{ hp}$$

Now look at Fig. 3-4*b*. The two spring balances pull on the leather-strap brake. The net drag on the drum surface is

$$140 - 40 = 100 \text{ lb}$$

The surface moves 330 ft in 1 min, so the work done is

$$330 \times 100 = 33{,}000 \text{ ft-lb per min}$$

Again this is 1 hp, but the power is delivered as heat (friction) rather than as useful work.

Torque

Now let's consider torque and the relation of torque and rotative speed to power delivered. Torque is nothing but twisting effort measured as the product of the pull by the length of the lever arm of the pull (Fig. 3-5).

The lever arm may be measured in feet, in which case the torque is in foot-pounds. Often it is more convenient to measure the lever arm in inches, in which case the product of lever arm in inches by the force in pounds gives the torque in inch-pounds.

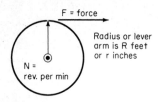

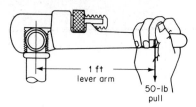

FIG. 3-5 Rim speed is 6.283 × R × N.

FIG. 3-6 Here torque is 50 ft-lb or 600 in.-lb.

For example, in Fig. 3-6, if man pulls 50 lb at a point 12 in. from the center of the fitting, the torque is $1 \times 50 = 50$ ft-lb or $12 \times 50 = 600$ in.-lb.

Torque and Power

Suppose (Fig. 3-5) that we have the radius of a wheel and the rotative speed in revolutions per minute (rpm). In 1 revolution every point on the rim moves $2 \times 3.1416 \times R$ ft, where the R is the radius in feet. This is $6.283 \times R$ ft per revolution.

If N is the rotative speed in rpm, the distance traveled by the rim in 1 min will be $6.28 \times R \times N$ ft. If the force at the rim is called F, the horsepower will be $6.28 \times R \times N \times F \div 33,000$. Note that this boils down to $R \times N \times F \div 5250$. Now $R \times N$ is nothing but the torque in foot-pounds. Call this T. Then horsepower is $T \times N \div 5250$.

If the radius is measured in inches, the product of radius and force is the torque in inch-pounds (call it t) and horsepower will be $t \times N \div 63,000$. For convenient reference the torque-speed-power formulas are repeated on page 79. Let's apply these to the 1-hp motor generator set pictured in Fig. 3-7. The set runs at 1750 rpm. Find the torque. Then $t = 63,000 \div 1750 = 36$ in.-lb.

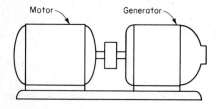

FIG. 3-7 The motor-generator set runs at 1750 rpm; 36 in.-lb = 1 hp.

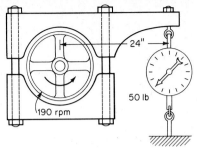

FIG. 3-8 Prony brake measures brake horsepower.

24 X 50 X 190 ÷ 63,000 = 3.6 hp

It may be worth remembering that when any machine shaft delivering 1 hp is running at the common electrical speed of 1750 rpm, the torque or twist in the shaft equals a 1-lb pull at the end of a wrench 1 yd long.

Figure 3-8 shows a prony brake measuring the power of a small engine. Here torque $t = 24 \times 50 = 1200$ in.-lb. At 190 rpm the brake power is $190 \times 1200 \div 63,000 = 3.6$ hp.

FORMULAS FOR ROTARY POWER

R = radius of torque arm, ft
r = radius of torque arm, in.
F = force at end of torque arm, lb
$T = R \times F$ = torque, ft-lb
$t = r \times F$ = torque, in.-lb
N = rotative speed, rpm
P = horsepower

Then

$$P = \frac{T \times N}{5250}$$

$$P = \frac{t \times N}{63,000}$$

Force Multipliers

How do we multiply force? Here are some common ways.

EXAMPLE: The force-multiplication factor for a lever (Fig. 3-9) is the

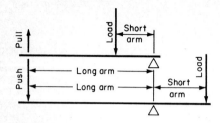

FIG. 3-9 The lever has many uses in industry.

length of the long (input) arm divided by the length of the short (output) arm. If you pull 3 ft from the fulcrum and the load is 1 ft from the fulcrum, you can lift 3 times the amount you pull.

In the usual case of a lever and certain other devices pictured, friction would waste only a small percentage of the applied energy. At the other extreme, friction might use up more than half the power in the case of a wedge or a screw jack. Of course the actual percentage wasted will depend on lubrication and many other factors.

It's easy to figure force multiplication factor for any special case if you remember that (neglecting friction) *the work you get out of any such machine equals the work you put in.*

That's another way of saying *what you lose in distance you can make up in force.* In every device that multiplies force the applied force must move a greater distance than the delivered load. The force-multiplication factor is merely the movement of the applied force divided by the movement of the load.

In short, if you have to push the handle 4 in. to lift the load 1 in., the machine will then multiply force by 4.

Where the motion is continuous and rotary, you can substitute torque for force and rpm for speed. Thus, in pulley or gear drive, if the driving shaft rotates 4 times as fast as the driven shaft, the delivered torque will be 4 times the input torque.

With the worm and gear wheel, count how many times the worm must rotate to cause one complete rotation of the wheel. That number is the multiplication factor.

RULES TO REMEMBER

Lever (Fig. 3-9):   With the pull on the long arm and the load on the short arm, the multiplication factor is the long arm divided by the short arm.

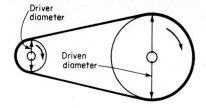

FIG. 3-10 The pulley and pinion is another lever.

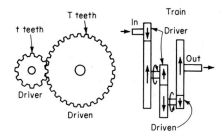

FIG. 3-11 Gear and pinion and gear train.

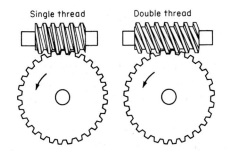

FIG. 3-12 Worm and worm gear provide leverage.

Pulley (Fig. 3-10):   The factor is the diameter of the driven pulley divided by the diameter of the driver.

Spur gear (Fig. 3-11):   The factor is the number of teeth on the driven gear divided by the number of teeth on the driver. For a gear train, apply this rule to each meshing pair. The factor for the whole train is the product of the factors of all the pairs.

Worm and gear (Fig. 3-12):   The factor is the number of teeth on the gear in a single-threaded work. For double thread, divide this factor by 2. For triple thread, divide it by 3.

Inclined plane (Fig. 3-13):   The figure illustrates how many inches the object moves in the direction of applied pull for each inch of rise. The ratio is the multiplication factor. Usually the pull is applied (as pictured) in the slant direction, which is the most ef-

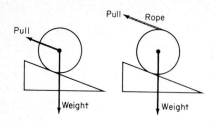

FIG. 3-13 Inclined plane and weight.

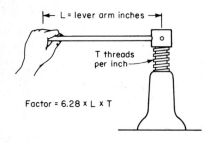

FIG. 3-14 Screw jack lifts heavy weights.

fective. The scheme pictured at the right (often used in handling barrels and heavy pipe) gives a factor double that for direct push or pull.

Screw jack (Fig. 3-14):   The factor is the distance your hand moves to raise the screw 1 in. This is $2 \times 3.14 = 6.28$ times the lever arm multiplied by the number of threads per inch. But beware of very high friction.

Wedge (Fig. 3-15):   The factor is the distance the wedge advances for every inch of additional separation of the parts being wedged. This equals the length of the wedge divided by its width.

It's worth remembering that force-multiplying devices can be divided into two main classes: (1) those which maintain a constant multiplication factor and (2) those in which the factor changes.

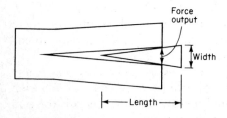

FIG. 3-15 Wedge has great force output.

Class 1 includes lever, pulley, gear, inclined plane, wedge, screw jack, hydraulic jack, and block and fall. For any gadget of this class, just figure how many inches the applied force must move to move the load 1 in. That number will be the force-multiplication factor.

Class 2 includes the toggle, the taut wire, and the cam. Here the method just described won't give a dependable value of the multiplication factor because the factor keeps changing as the device moves. An exact answer requires a bit of math, but you can find the approximate factor on the drawing board.

Just draw the device to scale in the desired position. Then redraw it, moved slightly. Scale off the movement of the output end and of the input end. Divide the input movement by the output movement to get the approximate force-multiplication factor.

The smaller the movement, the more exact the method will be up to the point where the movements are too small to measure accurately.

Toggle (Fig. 3-16): The multiplication factor keeps increasing as the toggle position approaches a straight line. For any given position, the factor is b divided by $2a$ in Fig. 3-16. Thus, if b is 10 in. and offset a is 1 in., the multiplication factor is $10 \div 2 = 5$.

Taut wire (Fig. 3-17): This is a toggle in reverse. Here again, the multiplication factor is b divided by $2a$. The tighter the wire, rope, or chain, the greater the load that can be lifted by bowstringing it, as shown.

Hydraulic jack (Fig. 3-18): The multiplication factor is proportional to the number of times the cross-sectional area of the small plunger shown goes into that of big plunger. To get the same

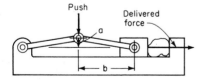

FIG. 3-16 Toggle applied to do work in machine.

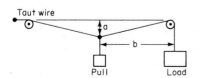

FIG. 3-17 Taut wire and bowstringing.

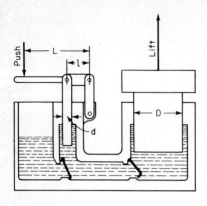

FIG. 3-18 A hydraulic jack is a great force multiplier.

result quicker, divide D by d, then square. Thus, if D is 5 and d is 1 in., $D \div d = 5$. This squared is 25, so the lift is 25 times the force on the small plunger. In Fig. 3-18 the force is further increased by the leverage of the handle, $L \div I$. In the problem just worked, if L were 3 times I, the total multiplication factor would be $3 \times 25 = 75$.

Cam (Fig. 3-19):   A cam can be designed to produce any desired pattern of movement, and so the multiplication factor can change in any desired way. To figure the factor for a given position, put the cam in that position and give the handle a small movement. By test (or by sketch on the drawing board), see how much the handle must be moved to give the jaw a small movement (say $1/8$ in.). Then the multiplication factor is the movement of the handle divided by the movement of jaw.

Block and fall (Fig. 3-20):   For Fig. 3-20a, showing a single pair, the multiplication factor equals the number of strands of

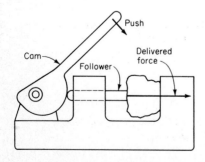

FIG. 3-19 Cam produces various moments.

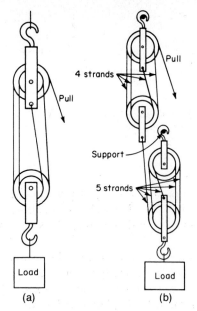

FIG. 3-20 Block and fall reeved for lifting various loads.

rope running to the block that carries the load. Here the number is 4. In Fig. 3-20*b* the factor for the upper block and fall is 4, and that for the lower is 5. For the combination it is $4 \times 5 = 20$.

FIGURING LEVERAGE

Figure 3-21 shows a man's hand pushing down on a crowbar to lift a rock. The hand is 4 times as far from the fulcrum as is the rock being lifted, so the mechanical advantage is 4 to 1. In short, neglecting friction (which would be small here) a 100-lb push lifts a 400-lb rock.

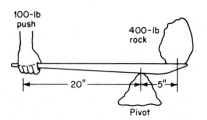

FIG. 3-21 Here the mechanical advantage is 4 to 1.

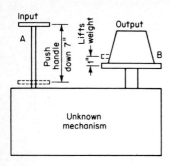

FIG. 3-22 Hidden mechanical advantage inside machine.

It is not always realized that the simple lever is just one special case of a general rule that applies to all kinds of machine parts—bell-crank lever, derrick, gearing, pulley drive, block and fall, wedge, screw, etc.

In fact, the rule is so general that it works even where the actual construction of the machine or device is completely hidden and secret, as in Fig. 3-22. Here you don't know what's in the box except that if you push down steadily on handle *A*, platform *B* moves steadily upward a much shorter distance.

Evidently this is a device for *increasing force*. How much? Measurement shows that moving the handle down 7 in. raises the weight platform 1 in. Since the output movement is one-seventh of the input movement, this output force must be 7 times the input force. This means that a 100-lb down push on *A* will lift a 700-lb weight at *B* if the friction in the machine can be neglected.

Principle of Work

This rule naturally follows from the principle of work: *If nothing is wasted in friction, the work output of any mechanical device equals the work input.*

Work equals force multiplied by the distance the point of application of the force moves in the direction of the force. If a 3-lb weight is lifted 2 ft against gravity, the work is $3 \times 2 = 6$ ft-lb.

Here's another way to put the rule: *A machine can increase force at the expense of distance or can increase distance at the expense of force.*

Figure 3-23 shows a beam used as a lever to raise a 3-ton load with a 1-ton hoist. Since the hoist chain at the left is 3 times as far as

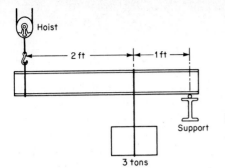

FIG. 3-23 Beam used as a lever raising 3 tons.

the load from the right-hand pivot, the load on the hoist will be one-third of 3 tons, or 1 ton.

What about the load on the right-hand support? The answer is easy to get by either of two methods. Simplest is to remember that the hoist and the right support together must carry the total load of 3 tons. Since the hoist carries 1 ton, the remaining load on the right support is 2 tons.

The other way is to use the rule of levers again, this time calling the left support the fulcrum. Then the lever arm of the 3-ton load is 2 ft and of the right support 3 ft, so the force on the right support will be two-thirds of 3 tons = 2 tons.

Bell-Cranks

The principle of levers is as easy to apply to a bell-crank lever as to a straight lever, particularly if the push or pull on each arm is at right angles to the arm. In Fig. 3-24 the arm-length ratio is 2 to 1,

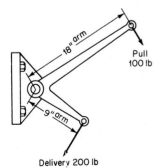

FIG. 3-24 Bell crank for delivering double force.

so any push on the 18-in. arm delivers double force at the 9-in. arm.

More Force, Less Distance

So far, we have discussed two main points. Any lever or other device to multiply force does so at the expense of distance. Even a lever doesn't give you something for nothing; it doesn't deliver any more work than is fed into it. But a lever does convert work into more convenient form. For example, a man isn't strong enough to lift a certain heavy rock, so he uses a long easy stroke on a crowbar to lift the heavy rock a much shorter distance.

In general, neglecting friction, a lever or other force-multiplying device divides the distance as much as it multiplies the force. For example, if the lever arms are 4 to 1, the force is multiplied by 4 and the input movement is divided by 4, so the work output equals the work input.

We now come to an important subject. You might call it *true lever arms* or *invisible lever arms,* since often the true lever arm is not the same as the metal rod that appears to be the lever arm.

The curved handle works exactly as easy and as hard as a straight handle with the same center-to-center distance from axis to handle. In Fig. 3-25 the fancy curves A, B, and C, work out exactly the same as D, except for the eye appeal and the extra cost for metal and patterns.

Note, however, that the radius of the crank is the true lever arm only when the push is in the direction of motion, that is, along the tangent of the circle of rotation or at right angles to the radius from the center of rotation to the point where the force is applied to the lever.

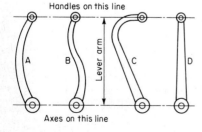

FIG. 3-25 Curved handles act like straight handles.

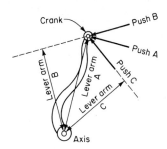

FIG. 3-26 True crank arm for directions of push.

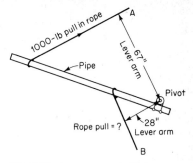

FIG. 3-27 Arrangement of pipes and ropes to multiply force.

Angular Pulls on Levers

If the force is applied in any other direction, the length of the lever arm is reduced and becomes the perpendicular dropped from the center of rotation to the line of action of the force extended.

Figure 3-26 shows the true crank arm for various directions of push and makes it clear why the greatest leverage is obtained when the push is in the direction of motion.

Figure 3-27 shows an arrangement of pipe and two ropes to multiply force in some special situation where right-angle pulls were not possible. Dropping perpendiculars from the pivot to the lines of pull, we find that the 1000-lb pull of A acts at a lever arm of 67 in., and the resulting pull on B at a lever arm of 28 in. Dividing 67 by 28, we see that the pull-in must be 2.4 times that in A, or 2400 lb.

GIN POLE AND GUY ROPE

Figure 3-28 shows a very practical application of this rule, because the guy rope must be strong enough to carry the load. Every rigger knows that the guy should be well back from the pole to avoid excessive tension. The reason for this is made clear in the second sketch. We have here a lever pivoting about the point where the pole rests on the ground. Measuring the right angles, we see that the guy rope operates at a lever arm of 8 ft and the load at a lever arm of 10 ft, so the tension in the rope will be 10/8 × 10 tons = 12.5 tons.

It is clear from this figure that the tension in the guy rope will ex-

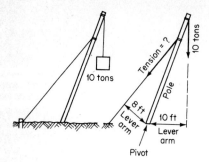

FIG. 3-28 Gin pole and guy rope do many jobs.

ceed the weight lifted if the perpendicular distance from the pivot to the guy is less than the horizontal distance from the pivot to the line of the load.

CENTRIFUGAL FORCE

Figuring centrifugal force is a *must* for engineers. Figure 3-29 shows three cases of a 2000-lb car rounding a curve. In Fig. 3-29*a* the car goes 20 mph around a 50-ft curve. The side thrust on the tires (another name for centrifugal force) is 1070 lb. In Fig. 3-29*b* the same car takes the same curve at 40 mph, or twice as fast. But the side thrust isn't just doubled, it's 4 times as great, or 4280 lb.

What happens when this same car travels at the same speed around a curve of twice the radius (Fig. 3-29*c*)? Force drops to half, or 2140 lb. This means that in Fig. 3-29*b* the *centrifugal force goes up as the square of the speed.* It's 4 times for double speed, 9 for triple. *The force is inversely proportional to the radius of curvature.* If we double the radius, we cut the force in half. This last rule compares two objects running at the same linear speed (not rpm).

The formula is stated as Rule 1, below. See if you can figure the side thrust on the cars in Fig. 3-29. Be sure to use the right value for K. Our answers are rounded off.

   Rule 1:

where S = *speed of moving object*
       R = *radius of curve it follows*
       F = *centrifugal force per pound of object weight, lb*

$$F = K \times S \times \frac{S}{R}$$

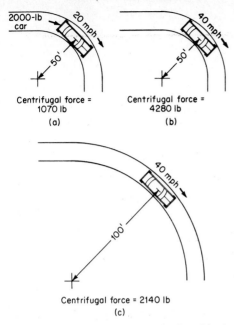

Centrifugal force = 1070 lb
(a)

Centrifugal force = 4280 lb
(b)

Centrifugal force = 2140 lb
(c)

FIG. 3-29 Rounding a curve, a moving object's centrifugal force goes up in proportion to the square of the speed and inversely as the radius of the curve.

When S is in miles per hour and R is in feet, $K = 0.0671$. When S is in feet per second and R is in inches, $K = 0.375$. Total force is F times the pounds the object weighs.

In Terms of RPM

For most rotating machinery it's easier to figure centrifugal force from rpm than linear speed. Consider the 2-lb ball swinging around a shaft in Fig. 3-30. Compare these three cases with those in Fig. 3-29. Going from Fig. 30(a) to (b), we double the rpm and the force goes up 4 times, just like doubling the car speed in Fig. 3-29. Now compare Fig. 3-29c with Fig. 3-30c. In the first case doubling the radius halved the force. But in Fig. 3-30 doubling the radius doubles the force. Why? At constant rpm, increasing the radius directly increases linear rim speed.

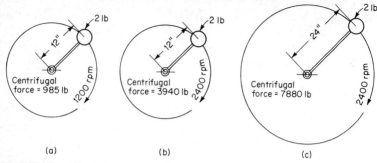

FIG. 3-30 Centrifugal force goes up in proportion both to the radius and the rpm squared.

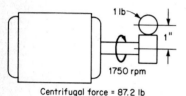

FIG. 3-31 Unbalance acts like a weight set off-center.

Try the formula in Rule 2 for the case in Fig. 3-31. Unbalance in rotating machine acts like a weight set off center. Use Table 3-1 to get F for other speeds. For other weights, multiply by the number of pounds and by inches of radius. For even rpm, Table 3-1 is very handy. Use it to check answers in Fig. 3-30.

TABLE 3-1

rpm	F, lb per lb per in. radius
600	10.2
900	23.0
1200	41.0
1800	92.1
2400	164
3000	256
3600	368

Rule 2: *If F is centrifugal force in pounds per pound of weight rotating at radius R, then*

$$F = \text{rpm} \times \text{rpm} \times \frac{R}{K}$$

When R is in feet, $K = 2920$. When R is in inches, $K = 35{,}100$.

Again multiply F by the number of pounds the rotating object weighs to get the total centrifugal force.

RULES FOR CALCULATING ROTATION _____

Look at a spinning disk (Fig. 3-32). Each point moves in a circle. For example, point B moves in a circle of radius OB. The arc described by any point in a given time will be in direct proportion to its radius. Thus if C is twice as far as A from center O, it will move twice as far and twice as fast.

Figure 3-33 shows how to work this out graphically. Let arrow Dd represent the known velocity of point D in both direction and amount. Draw Od. Then Aa is the velocity of A, Bb of B, and Cc of C because construction makes each arrow proportional to its radius.

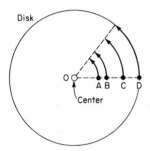

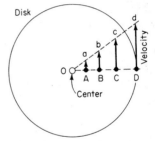

FIG. 3-32 Points A, B, C, and D move in arcs.

FIG. 3-33 Each point moves perpendicular to the radius.

In the bell crank (Fig. 3-34) point A moves at right angles to its radius and with a speed proportional to its radius or arm, and the same for B. So if the speed of A is 3 units, that of B must be 2 units.

The shape of the body makes no difference. In Fig. 3-35 the body spins around point O. Given Bb as speed of point B, find the speed of point C. Draw Ob. Transfer angle A to OC and draw Cc.

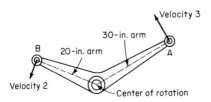

FIG. 3-34 Points A and B move at right angles to the radii.

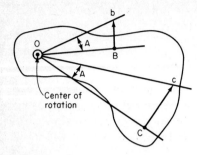

FIG. 3-35 If *Bb* is the rotational velocity of *B*, repeat the same angle for *C*.

The velocity of *C* will be *Cc* because constructions make the ratio of *Cc* to *Bb* the same as that of *OC* to *OB*.

If the center of rotation is unknown, it can be found from the known motion of any two points, say, *A* and *B* (Fig. 3-36). The perpendiculars to velocities of *A* and *B* must intersect at the center of rotation.

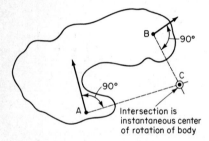

FIG. 3-36 If the motion of *A* and *B* is known, lines through them perpendicular to the velocities intersect at center *C*.

Figure 3-37 shows a practical application of this principle. At any given instant the whole connecting rod is rotating about a single point, the instantaneous center. Motions of the two ends of the rod are known. The crank end is moving in the crank circle and the

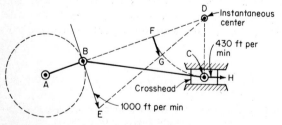

FIG. 3-37 The text explains how to find the crosshead speed of *CH*.

crosshead end in a straight line. Perpendiculars to these motions at these points are BD and CD, so their intersection D is the instantaneous center for the whole connecting rod. This means that every point in the connecting rod is rotating about D at this particular instant. For each point in the rod the momentary velocity is proportional to the radius drawn from D to the given point and is at right angles to that radius. It follows that the velocity of crosshead C will be to that of crank B as DC is to DB.

Lay off crank velocity BE (here taken as 1000 ft per min). Draw DE. With O as center swing arc CF. Then FG is the speed of the crosshead. Transfer it to CH. It scales 430 ft per min.

TORQUE, MOMENT, OR TWIST

Now we come to what is variously known as *torque, moment,* or *twisting effect.* This business of leverage is something every practical person understands to some degree. The lever arm is exactly the same as with a straight crank measuring the same in a straight line from axle to handle.

Let's pin down a few fundamentals. You apply a force to a wheel, lever, or other body operating on a shaft, pivot, or fulcrum. To figure the torque, moment, or twisting effect (they are all the same thing), multiply the amount of the force by the lever arm. *Be sure to measure the lever arm from the center of rotation along a line perpendicular to the direction of action of the force.*

Say a worker is pushing 50 lb at the end of a 20-lb pump handle. If she is pushing square with a line drawn from her hand to the center of rotation, the effect or moment or torque is $50 \times 20 = 1000$ lb-in. But let's say she is careless and pushes at a less effective angle so that the perpendicular from the center to the line of action of her push is only 18 in. Then her torque is $50 \times 18 = 900$ lb-in.

In many cases a single clockwise torque balances a single counterclockwise torque. In the usual problem, both lever arms and one force are known. What is the unknown force? The logical procedure is to write

One torque = other torque

Unknown force times its arm = known force times its arm

Then solve this equation for the unknown.

PROBLEM: What force at 10-in. arm balances 25 lb at 15-in. arm?

SOLUTION:

$$\text{One torque} = \text{other torque}$$
$$10 \times \text{unknown} = 25 \times 15 = 375 \text{ lb-in.}$$
$$\text{Unknown} = \frac{375}{10} = 37.5 \text{ lb} \quad Ans.$$

Leverage

To find the true lever arm (Fig. 3-38) pay no attention to the shape of the actual arm. Just measure the *perpendicular* distance from the pivot or center to the *direction line* of the applied force. To get torque, moment, or twisting effect multiply the lever arm by the applied force. Note that the crooked wrench will serve as well as the straight one if your push (as in *A*) is at right angles to the line from the center to the point of application of the force.

Balancing

Everybody knows that the smaller child must sit farther out on the seesaw. In any lever involving a fulcrum and two balanced forces one force creates a clockwise torque and the other a counterclockwise torque. For balance the two torques must be equal. Thus, in the first lever (Fig. 3-39)

$$6 \times 12 = 12 \times 6 = 72 \text{ lb-in. torque}$$

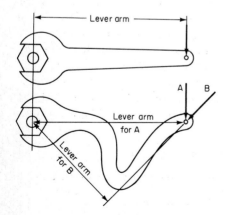

FIG. 3-38 Shape has nothing to do with true lever arm.

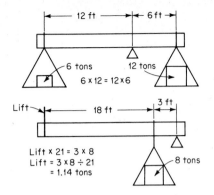

FIG. 3-39 For balancing, the two torques must be equal.

Bell Cranks

The same law applies to bell-crank levers and all sorts of irregular shapes. Just forget the shape of the arms. Note where the forces are applied and the exact directions of the forces. Then drop perpendiculars from the pivot to these direction lines. The lengths of these perpendiculars are the true lever arms.

In Fig. 3-40a the forces are applied square with the lines connecting the centers of the holes. Then the center distances, 15 and 8 in., are the true lever arms and

$$8 \times \text{unknown} = 15 \times 40 = 600 \text{ lb-in.}$$
$$\text{Unknown} = \frac{600}{8} = 75 \text{ lb}$$

In Fig. 3-40b the lever arms measure 14.5 and 5.5 in., so

$$5.5 \times \text{unknown} = 14.5 \times 40 = 580 \text{ lb-in.}$$
$$\text{Unknown} = \frac{580}{5.5} = 105 \text{ lb}$$

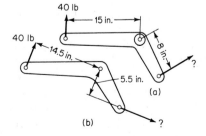

FIG. 3-40 Bell cranks; note where forces are applied and their exact direction.

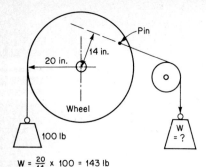

FIG. 3-41 Special torque problems are easy to solve.

$$W = \frac{20}{14} \times 100 = 143 \text{ lb}$$

Special cases

The disk problem (Fig. 3-41) shows how easy it is to solve all sorts of special problems if you have a clear understanding of torque. Note that the 100-lb weight, acting on a tangent to the wheel, exerts a counterclockwise torque of $20 \times 100 = 2000$ lb-in. Torque of the unknown weight is $14 \times W$. Then

$$14 \times W = 2000 \qquad \text{and} \qquad W = \frac{2000}{14} = 143 \text{ lb}$$

MOMENTS ON BEAMS _____

So far we have considered two general cases of balancing forces. *First,* where all the forces intersect at a single point, there is no turning tendency. *Forces intersecting at a single point are in balance when the force polygon or triangle is a closed figure.* With this rule you can find the unknown force in a balanced setup.

Next come levers, where all rotation is around a fixed known pivot or axis. Here we find that the moment (turning effect) of any force is the product of the force by its lever arm. The lever arm is the distance from the pivot to the force *measured perpendicular to the line of action of the force.*

Now we come to a beam problem, finding the load on each support. Here moments are again involved. Note also that the forces are generally parallel (usually up and down). In these beam problems it isn't necessary to specify any particular point as a *pivot.* You can choose any point you wish as an imaginary pivot. And no matter what point you select, the right-hand moments measured from that point will equal the left-hand moments.

Also note that in any beam the total load on the two supports must equal the total load on the beam. The only problem is to find out how this total is divided between the two supports. Various methods are shown.

In all the problems pictured, the weight of the beam itself has been neglected. If it is important enough to consider, just add half the weight of the beam to the figured load on each support.

Center Load

For this center loading (Fig. 3-42) or any other symmetrical loading, common sense tells us that each support must carry half of the load. If you turn the picture upside down (lower sketch) you get a balance or seesaw, but the answer is still the same.

Load off Center

In Fig. 3-43 common sense tells us that $A + B = 800$ lb. Also it's obvious that B is much greater than A. How much greater? Try bal-

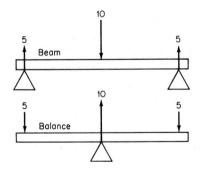

FIG. 3-42 In center loading, each support carries half the load.

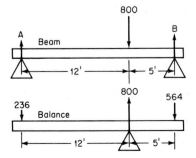

FIG. 3-43 B must be greater than A to balance.

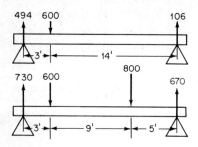

FIG. 3-44 Several loads; figure each load separately, then add.

ancing moments around the point where the 800-lb load is applied. Then $5B = 12A$, so

$$B = {}^{12}/_5A = 2.4A$$

Then $$800 = A + B = A + 2.4A = 3.4A$$

and $$A = \frac{800}{3.4} = 236 \text{ lb}$$

so that $$B = 800 - 236 = 564 \text{ lb}$$

Several Loads

METHOD 1: Figure the supports for each load in (Fig. 3-44) separately; then add up. For the 600-lb beam load the support loads are 494 and 106 lb. For the 800-lb beam load the support loads have already been figured (Fig. 3-43) as 236 and 564 lb. Then we see (lower sketch) that the combined loads must give $236 + 494 = 730$ lb at the left support and $564 + 106 = 670$ lb at the right support

METHOD 2: Figure 3-45 shows this method, which is just as easy as method 1. First balance the moments around the left support as a center. This gives

$$18B = 2.5 \times 4 + 2 \times 8 + 3 \times 12 + 3.5 \times 16 = 118 \text{ ton-ft}$$

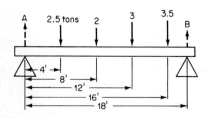

FIG. 3-45 Many loads; first balance moments around the left support as a center.

The total of A and B must be

$$2.5 + 2 + 3 + 3.5 = 11 \text{ tons}$$

so $$A = 11 - 6.56 = 4.44 \text{ tons}$$

SUGGESTED READING

Higgins, Alex, and Stephen M. Elonka: "Boiler Room Questions and Answers," 2d ed., McGraw-Hill Book Company, New York, 1976. (Over 100 calculations.)

Hicks, Tyler G.; "Standard Handbook of Engineering Calculations," McGraw-Hill Book Company, New York, 1972.

4

HOW TO READ STEAM TABLES

Steam tables are used to calculate problems involving heating water, making steam, and superheating. They are tabulated values of various properties of saturated steam such as boiling point, specific volume, sensible heat, latent heat, and total heat of saturated vapor or of superheated vapor calculated for a wide range of pressures.

The tables show that each pressure has a corresponding boiling point and that as the pressure rises, the following changes take place: (1) boiling-point temperature *rises,* (2) sensible heat *increases,* (3) latent heat *decreases,* and (4) total heat *increases* slowly until pressure approaches the so-called *critical point* of 3206.2 psia.

SATURATION: PRESSURES AND TEMPERATURES _____

Here we look at excerpts from one of the three principal tables from "Thermodynamic Properties of Steam," by J. H. Keenan and F. G. Keyes, originally published by John Wiley & Sons, Inc.; the ASME and others have prepared similar tables since. Table 4-1 (their table 2) gives the properties of saturated water liquid and vapor for various pressures. Meanings of the columns are ex-

TABLE 4-1 Saturation Pressures*

Abs. Press., Sq. psi p (1)	Temp., °F t (2)	Specific Volume		Enthalpy			Entropy			Internal Energy			Abs. Press., psi p (14)
		Sat. Liquid v_f (3)	Sat. Vapor v_g (4)	Sat. Liquid h_f (5)	Evap. h_{fg} (6)	Sat. Vapor h_g (7)	Sat. Liquid s_f (8)	Evap. s_{fg} (9)	Sat. Vapor s_g (10)	Sat. Liquid u_f (11)	Evap. u_{fg} (12)	Sat. Vapor u_g (13)	
170	368.41	0.01822	2.675	341.09	854.9	1196.0	0.5266	1.0324	1.5590	340.52	771.4	1111.9	170
172	369.35	0.01823	2.645	342.10	854.1	1196.2	0.5278	1.0302	1.5580	341.52	770.5	1112.0	172
174	370.29	0.01824	2.616	343.10	853.3	1196.4	0.5290	1.0280	1.5570	342.51	769.7	1112.2	174
176	371.22	0.01825	2.587	344.09	852.4	1196.5	0.5302	1.0259	1.5561	343.50	768.8	1112.3	176
178	372.14	0.01826	2.559	345.06	851.6	1196.7	0.5313	1.0238	1.5551	344.46	767.9	1112.4	178

*This sample section of the table is entered with the saturation pressure. It gives the properties of saturated liquid and saturated vapor (see text for explanation). The following brief description refers to the columns as numbered at the bottom. 1: Saturation pressure, psia. 2: Saturation temperature, °F. 3: Specific volume of the saturated liquid, cu ft per lb. 4: Specific volume of saturated vapor, cu ft per lb. 5: Enthalpy of saturated liquid (this is the heat in Btu that must be added to convert 1 lb of liquid at 32°F into liquid at the indicated temperature if pressure throughout heating is maintained constant at the value given in column 1). 6: Enthalpy of evaporation (this is the heat in Btu that must be added to 1 lb of saturated liquid to convert it into 1 lb of saturated vapor; the entire operation takes place at saturation pressure). 7: Enthalpy of saturated vapor (this is the sum of columns 5 and 6).

SOURCE: Abstracted by permission from "Thermodynamic Properties of Steam," by J. H. Keenan and F. G. Keyes, published by John Wiley & Sons, Inc.

plained in the footnote to the table. *Vapor* means steam, and *liquid* means *water.* Most engineers have a fair understanding of *saturation,* but a little explanation will make it clearer.

When water is exactly at the boiling temperature for the given pressure, it is said to be at the *saturation point* or to be *saturated.* The same is true of steam. For example, at atmospheric pressure (14.7 psia) the boiling temperature of pure water is 212°F. Either water or steam at 212°F is saturated if the pressure is 14.7 psia.

At saturation the vapor and the liquid are in perfect balance; they can be in contact without either gaining at the expense of the other. If steam is in contact with water in a closed container, both *must* be saturated.

For the benefit of engineers who are familiar with the older steam tables only, we will explain that *enthalpy* is the name for what used to be called *heat* in such expressions as heat of the liquid, heat of vaporization, and total heat of steam.

To get a better understanding of the steam tables, let's carry 1 lb of water through the various operations implied in the first line of Table 4-1.

We start with 1 lb of water at 32°F. For theoretical exactness (in view of the definition of enthalpy given in the footnote to Table

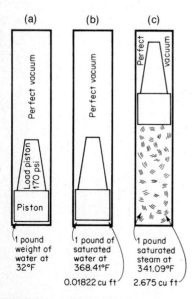

FIG. 4-1 Illustrating data on the 170-lb line of Table 4-1.

4-1) this water will be subjected to an absolute pressure of 170 psia as shown in (Fig. 4-1a), and this pressure will be kept constant throughout subsequent operations. A vacuum above the piston eliminates the effect of atmospheric pressure, so that the indicated pressure is absolute.

Heated up to 368.41°F (Fig. 4-1b) water absorbs 341.09 Btu (column 5) and expands slightly to 0.01822 cu ft (column 3 in Table 4-1).

Any further heating must produce steam, because water at 170 lb pressure cannot get any hotter than 368.41°F and remain a liquid. Figure 4-1c shows the cylinder at the exact moment of complete evaporation. Going from Fig. 4-1b to c, we see that the heat put in (column 6) is 854.9 Btu and the increase in volume is 2.657 cu ft (not shown in Table 4-1). The final volume of the vapor is 2.675 cu ft (column 4). The total heat supplied (above 32°F) is 341.09 + 854.9 = 1196.0 Btu.

Any further heating of the vapor, with the liquid all gone, will cause a rise in temperature above 368.41°F, the saturation temperature. This is called *superheating* and will be discussed later.

In defining *enthalpy,* we indicated that the enthalpy of saturated liquid water at 170 psia is exactly equal to the heat that must be supplied to warm 1 lb of water from 32°F to the saturation temperature (368.41°F) if the water is subjected to a pressure of 170 psia throughout the heating. Actually the enthalpy is all this *plus* the heat equivalent of the pumping work required to force the 32°F water under the loaded piston at the start of the process.

This correction doesn't amount to much, only about $\frac{1}{2}$ Btu in this case. Some engineers never had much trouble figuring the amount of heat required to warm 1 lb of water from one temperature to another. They never paid attention to the pressure and often figured the heat added by merely subtracting the low temperature from the high. So they figured it took 300 Btu to heat 1 lb of water from 100 to 400°F.

But to be precise, we pick the two enthalpies out of the steam tables and take the difference. Using modern tables, this gives 374.97 − 67.97 = 307 Btu, or 7 Btu *more* than the straight difference of the temperatures in this example.

The answer figured this last way will be good enough for most practical calculations, but again it is open to question by the experts, who point out that the difference of the enthalpies is *not* exactly the net heat required unless the heating is performed under certain special pressure conditions (not often existing).

The more we try to explain this, the more confused the reader will get. So just remember the following when doing ordinary figuring: *Forget all the refined definitions of the enthalpy of the liquid. Take it to be merely the heat required to warm the liquid from 32°F to the given temperature, regardless of the pressure. This rule will be close enough for most practical purposes if the pressure does not exceed 500 psia.*

For the enthalpy of vaporizations, the precise definition is the same as the practical one: heat added to convert 1 lb of saturated liquid water into saturated vapor at the same pressure and temperature.

Enthalpy of saturated vapor will be the sum of the enthalpy of the liquid and that of vaporization. It is what used to be called total heat of saturated steam.

Enthalpy of superheated vapor is the enthalpy of saturated vapor at the same pressure plus the additional heat required to superheat the saturated vapor.

Disregarding the fine points already mentioned, the following rule is good enough for ordinary engineering work at pressures under 500 psia: *To convert water at any temperature into water at higher temperature or into steam at any condition, the heat required is equal to the final enthalpy minus the initial enthalpy.*

PROBLEM 1:   *How much heat is required to heat 1 lb of water from 94 to 202°F?*

SOLUTION: From Table 4-2

$$
\begin{aligned}
\text{Enthalpy of liquid at 202°F} &= 170.00 \text{ Btu} \\
\text{Enthalpy of liquid at 94°F} &= \underline{\ \ 61.98} \text{ Btu} \\
\text{Difference} &= 108.02 \text{ Btu}
\end{aligned}
$$

PROBLEM 2:   How much heat is required to convert 1 lb of feedwater at 208°F into saturated steam at 174 psia?

SOLUTION:

From Table 4-1, enthalpy of saturated steam at 174 psi
$$
\begin{aligned}
&= 1196.40 \text{ Btu} \\
\text{From Table 4-2 enthalpy of feedwater at 208°F} &= \underline{\ \ 176.04} \text{ Btu} \\
\text{Heat applied (difference)} &= 1020.36 \text{ Btu}
\end{aligned}
$$

TABLE 4-2 Saturation: Temperatures

Temp., °F t	Abs. Pressure		Specific Volume			Enthalpy			Entropy			Temp., °F t
	Lb. Sq. psi p	in. Hg p	Sat. Liquid v_f	Evap. v_{fg}	Sat. Vapor v_g	Sat. Liquid h_f	Evap. h_{fg}	Sat. Vapor h_g	Sat. Liquid s_f	Evap. s_{fg}	Sat. Vapor s_g	
90	0.6982	1.4215	0.01610	468.0	468.0	57.99	1042.9	1100.9	0.1115	1.8972	2.0087	90
91	0.7204	1.4667	0.01611	454.4	454.4	58.99	1042.4	1101.4	0.1133	1.8927	2.0060	91
92	0.7432	1.5131	0.01611	441.2	441.3	59.99	1041.8	1101.8	0.1151	1.8883	2.0034	92
93	0.7666	1.5608	0.01611	428.5	428.5	60.98	1041.2	1102.2	0.1169	1.8838	2.0007	93
94	0.7906	1.6097	0.01612	416.2	416.2	61.98	1040.7	1102.6	0.1187	1.8794	1.9981	94
200	11.526	23.467	0.01663	33.62	33.64	167.99	977.9	1145.9	0.2938	1.4824	1.7762	200
202	12.011	24.455	0.01665	32.35	32.37	170.00	976.6	1146.6	0.2969	1.4760	1.7729	202
204	12.512	25.475	0.01666	31.14	31.15	172.02	975.4	1147.4	0.2999	1.4697	1.7696	204
206	13.031	26.531	0.01667	29.97	29.99	174.03	974.2	1148.2	0.3029	1.4634	1.7663	206
208	13.568	27.625	0.01669	28.86	28.88	176.04	972.9	1148.9	0.3059	1.4571	1.7630	208

SOURCE: Abstracted by permission from "Thermodynamic Properties of Steam," by J. H. Keenan and F. G. Keyes, published by John Wiley & Sons, Inc.

ADDING HEAT TO WATER AND STEAM _____

So far, we have learned how *easy* it is to solve problems with
steam-table enthalpies *if* we don't have to split hairs too fine. Any
practical engineer who is satisfied with an answer correct to a fraction of 1% can use the following rule for all cases of simple heating
and cooling where the pressure is *not* over 500 psia. *The heat required
to convert liquid water at any initial temperature or steam at any initial
pressure, temperature, and condition to liquid water at any final temperature or steam at any final pressure, temperature, and condition is the difference in enthalpy between the two states.*

SUPERHEATED VAPOR _____

For liquid water, take the enthalpy as that of saturated liquid water
at the given temperature. For superheated steam, read the *enthalpy*
directly from Table 4-3; for dry saturated steam, read *enthalpy*
directly from Table 4-1 or 4-3; for wet steam, multiply the enthalpy
of evaporation, and *add* the enthalpy of saturated liquid water.

In all these cases except wet steam, the enthalpy is read directly
from the steam tables. Here are some typical applications of this
rule.

PROBLEM 1:   Starting with 1 lb of feedwater at 206°F, how much
heat must be added to convert it into steam at 184 psia and 500°F?

SOLUTION:

From Table 4-3, enthalpy of steam at 184 psia = 1270.60 Btu
From Table 4-1, enthalpy of water at 206°F =   174.03 Btu
Heat required (difference) = 1096.57 Btu

PROBLEM 2:   If the boiler of Problem 1 generates 10.2 lb of steam
per pound of 13,200-Btu coal, what is the overall efficiency?

SOLUTION:

$$\text{Efficiency} = \frac{\text{output}}{\text{input}}$$
$$= \frac{1096.6 \times 10.2}{13,200} = 0.847 = 84.7\%$$

TABLE 4-3 Superheated Vapor

Abs. Press., psi (Sat. Temp.)		Sat. Liquid	Sat. Vapor	Temperature, °F													
				380	390	400	420	440	460	480	500	520	540	560	580	600	620
180 (373.06)	v	0.018	2.532	2.563	2.606	2.649	2.732	2.813	2.891	2.969	3.044	3.119	3.193	3.266	3.339	3.411	3.482
	h	346.0	1196.9	1201.4	1207.8	1214.0	1226.1	1237.8	1249.1	1260.2	1271.0	1281.7	1292.3	1302.8	1313.2	1323.5	1333.8
	s	0.5325	1.5542	1.5596	1.5672	1.5745	1.5884	1.6015	1.6139	1.6258	1.6373	1.6483	1.6590	1.6694	1.6795	1.6894	1.6990
182 (373.96)	v	0.018	2.505	2.532	2.575	2.617	2.700	2.780	2.858	2.934	3.009	3.084	3.157	3.229	3.301	3.372	3.443
	h	347.0	1197.0	1201.0	1207.4	1213.7	1225.8	1237.5	1248.8	1259.9	1270.8	1281.5	1292.1	1302.6	1313.0	1323.4	1333.7
	s	0.5336	1.5532	1.5580	1.5656	1.5729	1.5869	1.6000	1.6125	1.6244	1.6359	1.6470	1.6577	1.6681	1.6782	1.6880	1.6977
184 (374.86)	v	0.018	2.479	2.501	2.544	2.586	2.668	2.748	2.825	2.901	2.975	3.049	3.121	3.193	3.264	3.334	3.404
	h	348.0	1197.2	1200.6	1207.0	1213.3	1225.5	1237.2	1248.6	1259.7	1270.6	1281.4	1292.0	1302.5	1312.9	1323.3	1333.6
	s	0.5348	1.5523	1.5564	1.5640	1.5714	1.5854	1.5986	1.6111	1.6230	1.6345	1.6456	1.6563	1.6667	1.6769	1.6867	1.6964
186 (375.75)	v	0.018	2.454	2.472	2.514	2.556	2.637	2.716	2.793	2.868	2.942	3.015	3.086	3.157	3.228	3.297	3.367
	h	348.9	1197.3	1200.2	1206.6	1212.9	1225.2	1236.9	1248.3	1259.5	1270.4	1281.2	1291.8	1302.3	1312.7	1323.1	1383.4
	s	0.5359	1.5514	1.5548	1.5625	1.5699	1.5839	1.5971	1.6097	1.6217	1.6332	1.6443	1.6550	1.6654	1.6756	1.6854	1.6951
188 (376.64)	v	0.018	2.429	2.443	2.485	2.527	2.607	2.685	2.761	2.836	2.909	2.981	3.052	3.123	3.192	3.261	3.330
	h	349.9	1197.5	1199.7	1206.2	1212.6	1224.8	1236.6	1248.1	1259.2	1270.2	1281.0	1291.6	1302.1	1312.6	1323.0	1333.3
	s	0.5370	1.5506	1.5532	1.5609	1.5683	1.5824	1.5957	1.6083	1.6203	1.6318	1.6429	1.6537	1.6641	1.6743	1.6842	1.6938

SOURCE: Abstracted by permission from "Thermodynamic Properties of Steam," by J. H. Keenan and F. G. Keyes, published by John Wiley & Sons, Inc.

PROBLEM 3:   How much heat must be added to 1 lb of 95% dry steam at 180 psia to superheat the steam to a total temperature of 560°F? (Work this entirely from Table 4-3.)

SOLUTION:

Enthalpy of vaporization = 1196.9 − 346.0 = 850.9 Btu
Enthalpy of wet steam
    = 346.0 + (0.95 × 850.9) = 808.4 + 346.0 = 1154.4 Btu
Enthalpy of superheated steam = 1302.8 Btu
        Enthalpy of wet steam = 1154.4 Btu
                Heat added =   148.4 Btu

EXPANDING STEAM

If we keep a given weight of wet steam at constant pressure and gradually apply heat, the steam will get drier and drier until it becomes dry saturated. It will then start superheating, with a steady rise in temperature. Any movement in this direction (from wet steam to drier steam, or from a lower superheat to a higher) may be called an *improvement* in steam quality. Conversely any movement in the opposite direction may be called a *lowering* of steam quality.

When steam is throttled, its quality is always improved. If it was dry saturated, it becomes superheated. If it was superheated, it becomes more highly superheated. If it was wet, it becomes drier and perhaps superheated as well. These statements refer to true throttling, which is the *reduction of pressure without performance of useful work.*

Turbine vs. Reducing Valve

It is often said that an engine or turbine exhausting to process acts as a reducing valve. This is not strictly correct; the turbine extracts useful power from the steam, so that the enthalpy of its exhaust steam is less than the enthalpy of steam lowered to the same pressure by a reducing valve.

Figure 4-2 shows this clearly for the expansion of steam from a dry saturated condition at 174 psia pressure to a back pressure of 16 psia. Initial enthalpy equals 1196.4 Btu.

For straight throttling the rule is that enthalpy after expansion is

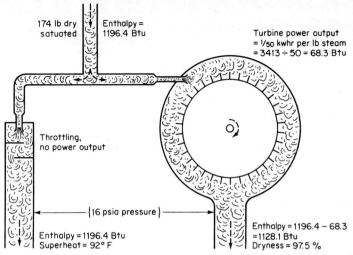

174 lb dry saturated ↓ Enthalpy = 1196.4 Btu

Turbine power output
= 1/50 kwhr per lb steam
= 3413 ÷ 50 = 68.3 Btu

Throttling, no power output

{16 psia pressure}

Enthalpy = 1196.4 Btu
Superheat = 92° F

Enthalpy = 1196.4 − 68.3
= 1128.1 Btu
Dryness = 97.5 %

FIG. 4-2 Throttling usually raises steam quality, while expansion through a turbine usually reduces quality.

the same as before. Thus the steam's final enthalpy must be 1196.4 Btu. The enthalpy of *dry saturated steam* at 16 psia is 1152.0 Btu, so the steam must be superheated the equivalent of the difference, or 44.4 Btu. Roughly, 1 Btu will superheat steam about 2°F, so the superheat after throttling will be about 89°F.

TABLE 4-4   Enthalpy at 16 psia from Table 4-3

	Btu
Saturated water	184.4
Evaporation	967.6
Dry saturated steam	1152.0
Steam superheated to 300°F	1192.5
D, Superheated to 320°F	1202.0

Table 4-4 gives data for 16 psia pressure. From this, exact superheat of throttled steam can be figured as follows:

	Enthalpy	Steam temp., °F
	1202.0	320
	−1192.5	−300
Difference	9.5	20

This is the first step in what is called *interpolation,* the process used to find at what temperature between 300 and 320°F the enthalpy is 1196.4 Btu. Next perform the following subtraction:

$$1196.4$$
$$-1192.5$$

Difference   3.9

It is clear that the temperature will exceed 300°F by 3.9/9.5 × 20°F. This is 8°F, so the final steam temperature will be 308°F. Since saturation temperature at 16 psia is 216°F, the superheat is 308 − 216 = 92°F.

Condition of Turbine Exhaust

Next consider expansion of the same steam through the turbine. Since 1 kWhr = 3413 Btu, and since the turbine produces $1/50$ kWhr per pound of steam, the reduction in enthalpy per pound will be 3413 ÷ 50 = 68.3 Btu. This assumption neglects generator losses and heat radiated from the turbine shell but is not far wrong.

The enthalpy of the exhaust steam will be about 1196.4 − 68.3 = 1128.1 Btu. Dry saturated steam at 16 psia contains 1152.0 Btu, so the turbine exhaust steam must be wet. Enthalpy of evaporation at 16 psia is 967.6 Btu, or 9.68 Btu for each 1% of moisture. Since 1152.0 − 1128.1 = 23.9 Btu, the moisture in the exhaust steam will be 23.9 ÷ 9.68 = 2.5%. Therefore the turbine exhaust steam will be 97.5% dry, whereas steam discharged from the reducing valve was superheated 92°F.

USING ENTROPY

Entropy is not much used in figuring everyday operations, but you should remember *two* facts: (1) entropy is a mathematical device convenient to designers of engines, turbines, and compressors, (2) the entropy of steam does not change when steam is expanded through a theoretically perfect turbine but always increases when steam is expanded through an actual (imperfect) turbine.

Let's use the second fact to solve a simple problem involving entropy and a *perfect turbine.* This perfect turbine is an imaginary machine completely free from friction between the steam on the one hand, and the nozzles, blades, disks, etc., on the other, free from any swirls and eddies that might cause internal friction in the steam and free from bearing friction or heat loss from the turbine casing. Obviously no such machine has been built or ever will be, but it gives an ideal with which designers and operators can compare actual machine performance.

Let us assume that this turbine receives throttle steam at 400 psia and 600°F and expands it down to an absolute pressure of 20 psia. The problem is to find the theoretical steam rate of this turbine and the final condition of the steam. The data in Table 4-5 are taken from the steam tables.

Since the turbine is "perfect," the entropy of the steam won't change during the expansion. We must therefore find a condition at which the exhaust steam at 20 psia will have an entropy of 1.5894. At the exhaust pressure the entropy of liquid is 0.3356 (see Table 4-5) and of dry saturated steam is 1.7319. It is clear, then, that the exhaust is something more than liquid water and something less than dry steam—therefore wet steam. But how wet?

Call the dryness factor of the exhaust steam X. Then the entropy of the exhaust steam must be that of the saturated liquid plus the fraction X of the entropy of evaporation, or $0.3356 + 1.3962X$. Since this must equal the original entropy of the throttle steam, we have

$$0.3356 + 1.3962X = 1.5894$$
$$1.3962X = 1.5894 - 0.3356 = 1.2538$$
$$X = \frac{1.2538}{1.3962} = 0.898$$

This means that the exhaust from the perfect turbine will be 89.8% dry or 10.2% wet.

The next step is to figure the corresponding enthalpy of the exhaust steam. This will be the enthalpy of the saturated liquid plus 89.8% of the enthalpy of evaporation, or

TABLE 4-5

	Enthalpy	Entropy
Steam at 400 psi 600°F	1306.9	1.5894
Saturated liquid at 20 psia	196.2	0.3356
Evaporation at 20 psia	960.1	1.3962
Saturated vapor at 20 psia	1156.3	1.7319

$$196.2 + (960.1 \times 0.898) = 196.2 + 862.2 = 1058.4 \text{ Btu}$$

When steam is expanded through a perfect turbine, the difference between the throttle enthalpy and the exhaust enthalpy is converted into useful work. Thus, for each pound of steam the useful work in heat units is

$$\begin{array}{r} 1306.9 \\ -1058.4 \\ \hline 248.5 \text{ Btu} \end{array}$$

Since 1 hp = 2544 Btu per hr, the steam rate of this perfect turbine will be 2544 ÷ 248.5 = 10.2 lb steam per hp-hr.

Since 1 kWhr = 3413 Btu per hr, if the perfect turbine drives a perfect generator, its overall steam rate will be

$$\frac{3413}{248.5} = 13.7 \text{ lb steam per kWhr}$$

To see what might be possible with an actual steam turbine, we need to know or assume a *turbine efficiency,* a number expressing the performance of an actual machine in terms of the *perfect turbine.* Suppose this efficiency is 70%; then the steam rate of the actual turbine per hp-hr will be

$$\frac{10.2}{0.7} = 14.6 \text{ lb}$$

Steam rate per kilowatthour will be

$$\frac{13.7}{0.7} = 19.6 \text{ lb}$$

HOW TO USE THE MOLLIER CHART

In a pocket in the back of the Keenan and Keyes steam tables is a chart nearly 3 × 4 ft. This most modern form of the well-known Mollier chart is a graphic steam table covering pressures all the way from 0.2 to 5400 psia and steam qualities from deep in the wet-steam region up to superheated steam of 1200°F total temperature.

The gridwork lines of the chart represent enthalpy and entropy. Vertical lines are constant entropy, and horizontal lines are constant enthalpy. Therefore, for any point on this chart you can read at once the enthalpy, the entropy, the steam pressure, and either the moisture in the steam on one hand or superheat and total temperature on the other.

If any two of these properties are known, they give an intersection and thereby determine a point from which the other properties can be read directly. This operation is perfectly simple although the confusion of lines on the chart makes it look hard.

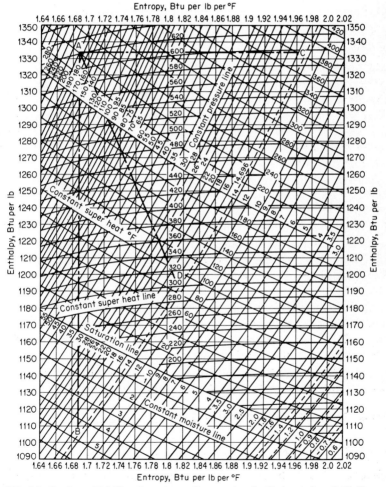

FIG. 4-3 Section of Mollier chart (some lines omitted). (*Redrawn from J. H. Keenan and F. G. Keyes, "Thermodynamic Properties of Steam," by John Wiley & Sons, Inc., New York.*)

The chart in Fig. 4-3 is not intended for practical use but merely to show how to use the original.

Point *A* at the intersection of the lines for 200 psia and 620°F total temperature represents steam at that condition. Note that the line for 240°F superheat goes through this point, so that is the superheat corresponding to 620°F at 200 psia. This figure can be more exactly determined from the steam tables as 238°F.

Reading horizontally, we see that the enthalpy is 1333 Btu per lb. Reading vertically, we find the entropy, 1.686 Btu per lb per °F.

Expansion of Steam

The Mollier chart can be used to show the results of various types of expansion of steam. For example, expansion in a "perfect" engine or turbine is without change of entropy and must therefore be represented by a vertical line. Thus line *AB* represents expansion without change of entropy to 16 psia. Note that the exhaust steam contains 4.3% moisture and has an enthalpy of 1110 Btu per lb.

Enthalpy drop during expansion is 1333 − 1110 = 223 Btu, so the "perfect" turbine would have a steam rate of 3413 ÷ 223 = 15.3 lb per kWhr.

When steam is throttled through a reducing valve, the enthalpy remains constant, so the line *AC* represents throttling to 16 psia. Note here that the final temperature of the steam is 596°F and the corresponding superheat is 380°F. Throttling increases superheat or quality.

The expansion of steam in an actual turbine always falls between that in a perfect turbine on the one hand and in a reducing valve on the other. Its expansion can be represented by a line like *AD*. Thus the common statement that a turbine exhausting to process acts as a reducing valve is not strictly true because the turbine exhaust is at lower quality than that of a reducing valve.

SOME TYPICAL STEAM PROBLEMS _____

1. HEAT IN WATER _____

PROBLEM: Does 1 lb of water in a boiler contain as many heat units as that quantity converted into steam at 100 lb or any other pressure?

SOLUTION: First, we must establish that water in a boiler is at the *same* temperature as the steam. Thus, before the water can be converted into steam, it must receive additional heat, which is called the *latent heat of evaporation*.

Therefore, for 100 psig we learn from the steam tables that the water and steam are at a temperature of 338°F and that each pound of the water contains 309 Btu above 32°F. But for conversion into steam, each pound of water must, in addition, receive 879.8 Btu, which is the latent heat of evaporation at the stated pressure. So the total heat contained by 1 lb of the steam in this case is 309 + 879.8 = 1188.8 Btu. *Ans.*

2. TRANSFER OF HEAT REQUIRES DIFFERENCE OF TEMPERATURES

PROBLEM: If at sea level 15 lb of steam at atmospheric pressure is blown into water in an open drum containing 150 lb of water at the boiling point, what temperature would the water attain?

SOLUTION: The temperature of dry saturated steam at atmospheric pressure is 212°F, and the boiling point of water under atmospheric pressure is also at the same temperature. Thus there could be *no* transfer of heat because the temperature would be the *same* and the temperature of the water would remain unchanged. *Ans.*

3. DISCHARGE OF STEAM JETS

PROBLEM: Calculate the quantity of steam at 100 lb boiler pressure that would be used by a steam jet having four nozzles, each $\frac{1}{16}$-in. diameter discharging into a boiler ash pit.

SOLUTION: Discharge is given approximately by Napier's rule for flow of steam through orifices when the final absolute pressure is less than 58% of the initial absolute pressure:

Flow, lb per sec

$$= \text{absolute initial pressure} \times \frac{\text{area of orifice, sq in.}}{70}$$

In this problem, for an initial pressure of 115 psia (100 + 15) and four orifices, each of $\frac{1}{16}$ in. diameter, the total area would be

$$\frac{1}{16} \times \frac{1}{16} \times 0.7854 \times 4 = 0.01228 \text{ sq in.}$$

Thus, by the formula the discharge would amount to

$$115 \times \frac{0.01228}{70} = 0.02017 \text{ lb of steam per sec}$$

or $0.02017 \times 60 \times 60 = 72.6$ lb per hr   *Ans.*

4. WHAT PRICE EXHAUST STEAM? _____

PROBLEM: Does any system of exhaust-steam *accounting* get away from the fact that at times exhaust used by the factory departments would otherwise be wasted? Should they be charged live-steam rates for a dump product?

SOLUTION: The value of the exhaust steam should be based on its heat content, just as with *live* steam. In either case, the department is buying just so much *heat.*

Exhaust wasted to atmosphere should be wasted at the power plant and charged against electrical generation. In this way it sets up a bogie for the power engineer—utilization of the many possible ways of improving heat balance to cut down exhaust waste.

If a department were given dump rates on exhaust steam, it would simply mean that power-generating costs would *rise,* which is taking money out of one pocket to put it in another.

5. HEAT REQUIRED FOR GENERATING WET STEAM _____

PROBLEM: What is the formula for determining how much heat is required to generate 1 lb of steam at 150 psig of 98% quality from feedwater at 120°F?

SOLUTION: The number of Btu contained per pound of steam is given by

$$H_w = h + qL \tag{1}$$

where H_w = number of Btu above 32°F in 1 lb of wet steam
       h = heat of liquid = number of Btu required to heat 1 lb of water from 32°F to temperature of evaporation corresponding with pressure
       L = latent heat of evaporation = number of Btu contained by 1 lb of dry saturated steam at stated pressure in addition to h

q = quality or fraction of whole pound of steam that has received latent heat of evaporation

If t is the temperature of the feedwater, then $t - 32$ is the number of Btu contained by the water above 32°F *before* any heat is added to it in the boiler. And if x is the quantity of heat required for generating 1 lb of the steam, then

$$x = H_w - (t - 32) = H_w + 32 - t \qquad (2)$$

Substituting the value of H_w in (1) gives

$$x = + qL + 32 - t \qquad (3)$$

For steam at 150 psig (165 psia) in this problem, the steam tables of properties of dry saturated steam give

$h = 338.2$ and $L = 856.8$ $q = 98\%$ $t = 120$

We substitute in (3) to find heat required:

$x = 338.2 + (0.98 \times 856.8) + 32 - 120 = 1089.8$ Btu   *Ans.*

6. STEAM FORMULA FOR TOTAL HEAT _____

PROBLEM: Is there a formula for obtaining the total heat of dry saturated steam, knowing the temperature?

SOLUTION: Yes, but it is an approximate formula. The total heat of steam or number of Btu required to raise 1 lb of water at 32°F to a given temperature and convert it *all* into dry saturated steam at that temperature is *approximately* calculated for a temperature t in the Fahrenheit scale by the formula

Total heat = $1086 + 0.305t$ *Ans.*

NOTE: A simple and precise equation that will cover *all* temperatures cannot be formulated because of the variation of the *specific* heat and heat transformed into work in raising the water to different temperatures and then converting it into steam of corresponding pressures.

For application to ordinary temperatures of steam in *rough* calculations, the above formula may be considered sufficiently accurate, but for *close* computations, the total heat values used should be obtained by consulting standard tables of the properties of steam.

7. HORSEPOWER OUTPUT OF BOILER _____

PROBLEM: Calculate the horsepower output of a steam boiler working at 160 psia steam pressure and evaporating 3400 lb of water per hr from feedwater at 140°F.

SOLUTION: The heat put into 1 lb of steam at 160 psia, with feedwater at 140°F, is 1195.1 − (140 − 32) = 1087.1 Btu. Then

$$\text{Equivalent evaporation} = \frac{3400 \times 1087.1}{970.3}$$

$$= 3809 \text{ lb of water per hr}$$

$$\text{Boiler hp} = \frac{3809}{34.5} = 110 \text{ hp} \quad Ans.$$

8. FACTOR OF EVAPORATION FOR GENERATING SUPERHEATED STEAM _____

PROBLEM: State the factor of evaporation when under actual conditions a boiler generates steam at 200 psig with 100°F superheat from feedwater at 212°F. How many pounds of water has to be evaporated per boiler horsepower?

SOLUTION: An absolute pressure of 200 psig would be equal to 215 psia, and according to the steam tables, 1 lb of steam at that pressure superheated 100°F contains 1259 Btu above 32°F. Thus if the feedwater temperature is 212°F, each pound of feedwater for conversion into steam of the stated pressure and quality must receive (1259 + 32) − 212 = 1079 Btu.

NOTE: Unless otherwise provided, a combined boiler and superheater should be treated as *one* unit, and the equivalent of the work done by the superheater should be included in the evaporative work of the boiler. Evaporation of 1 lb of water from and at 212°F requires 970.4 Btu. Therefore, under the actual conditions, the factors of evaporation would be

$$\frac{1079}{970.4} = 1.111$$

Because a boiler horsepower is equivalent to the evaporation of 34.5 lb of water from and at 212°F per hr (according to *one* method of rating), under the conditions stated a boiler horsepower would require evaporation of

$$\frac{34.50}{1.111} = 31.05 \text{ lb of water per hr} \quad Ans.$$

9. SUPERHEATED CONDITION FOR REDUCED PRESSURE _____

PROBLEM: Assume that a reducing valve is placed on a 100-psig steam line carrying dry saturated steam. If the valve is set to reduce pressure to 20 psig, will the steam delivered to the low-pressure side be superheated?

SOLUTION: During bull sessions in power plants one often hears the argument that a reducing valve is also a superheater. But is it? Neglecting the heat lost by radiation, a given weight of steam discharged through the reducing valve will contain as much heat as it had before passing through the reducing valve.

We know that 1 lb of dry saturated steam at 100 psig (115 psia) contains 1188.8 Btu and 1 lb of dry saturated steam at 20 psig (35 psia) contains 1166.8 Btu. Thus, without loss of heat in passing through the reducing valve, each pound would contain 1188.8 − 1166.8 = 22 Btu *more* than necessary for a saturated condition at the reduced pressure. So the steam *would* be in a superheated condition for the reduced pressure.

Checking the steam tables for the properties of superheated steam, we learn that for a pressure of 20 psig and a heat content of 1188.8 Btu, the temperature would be 303.7°F. And since the temperature of dry saturated steam at 20 psig is 259.3°F, the steam would be superheated:

$$303.7 - 259.3 = 44.4°F \quad Ans.$$

10. WATER BLOWN OUT OF GAGE GLASS _____

PROBLEM: Calculate quantity of water discharged from blowing down a 72-in.-diameter 18-ft-long fire-tube boiler. The boiler has flat ends, and water is blown down $1\frac{1}{2}$ in. from a water level 17 in. below the underside of the shell.

SOLUTION: The cross-sectional area of the steam space can be found by the approximate formula for the area of a segment of a circle:

$$\text{Area of segment} = \frac{4H^2}{3}\sqrt{\frac{2R}{H} - 0.608}$$

where H = height of segment
      R = radius of arc

When the height of the steam space is 17 in. and $2R$ is equal to 72 in., by substitution in the formula, the cross-sectional area of the steam space will be

$$\frac{4 \times 17 \times 17}{3}\sqrt{\frac{72}{17} - 0.608} = 733.9 \text{ sq in.}$$

And when the height is $1\frac{1}{2}$ in. lower, or $18\frac{1}{2}$ in. *below* the top of the shell, the sectional area of the steam space will be

$$\frac{4 \times 18.5 \times 18.5}{3}\sqrt{\frac{72}{18.5} - 0.608} = 826.9 \text{ sq in.}$$

Thus the cross-sectional area of the water discharged will be

$$826.9 - 733.9 = 93 \text{ sq in.}$$

For an 18-ft length of shell, the volume of water discharged will be

$$\frac{93}{144} \times 18 = 11.62 \text{ cu ft}$$

Obviously, the weight of water discharged depends on its temperature. Thus if the boiler pressure was 100 psi, the water temperature would be 338.1°F (from steam tables). At that temperature, water has a density of 54 lb per cu ft, so the weight of water discharged would be about

$$11.62 \times 54 = 627.48 \text{ lb} \quad Ans.$$

SUGGESTED READING

Higgins, Alex, and Stephen M. Elonka: "Boiler Room Questions and Answers," 2d ed., McGraw-Hill Book Company, New York, 1976.
Hicks, Tyler G.: "Standard Handbook of Engineering Calculations," McGraw-Hill Book Company, New York, 1972.

5

HEAT TRANSFER

Heat is energy, and putting it to useful work efficiently is the primary job of the power engineer. The trick is to get heat to flow where needed while keeping it from escaping until *all* possible heat has been extracted.

We learn that heat moves in three ways only: (1) by conduction, (2) by convection, and (3) by radiation. Before getting into applied heat calculations in this chapter, let's first quickly review these three methods of heat flow and transfer.

CONDUCTION

According to the kinetic theory, heat is conducted through matter by a series of kicks or pushes. High-temperature molecules move fast; low-temperature molecules move slowly. When we heat one end of the iron rod (Fig. 5-1), the molecules there move faster and bump those next in line into faster motion, and so on down the rod.

Conduction, then, is heat transmission by the mechanical bumping of one particle on the next. This applies to liquids and gases also, but there's a difference in the way the molecules act. In a solid the molecule swings around its home base, like a grazing

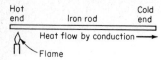

FIG. 5-1 Heat flows gradually from the hot end of iron to the cold end.

horse wandering around on the end of a tether. In a liquid the molecules have more freedom; they wander around from one place to another but are never completely free from their fellow molecules, rather like a man dodging through a circus crowd. In a gas the molecules shoot around freely, like bullets flying in open space. Each keeps going in one direction until it strikes another or the wall of the container and then caroms off like a billiard ball.

In all three cases, despite these differences, heat conduction is by bumps alone. However, in liquids and gases some of the heat transfer will always be by convection and radiation. That's why it is often so hard to tell what fraction of the observed heat transfer is by each method. For example, when you stand some distance from a room radiator, you are heated to a substantial degree by both radiation and convection and to a very slight degree by conduction through the air.

CONVECTION

We might call convection "slow freight or express." Convection, (Fig. 5-2) applies only to fluids (liquids and gases). Heat carried by convection is that carried by the actual movement of the substance. It is simple mechanical transportation, nothing else. The fluid movement may be *natural* (caused by so-called thermal currents) or it may be *forced circulation* (as by a fan). In either case the gas or liquid moves up to a hot surface, is heated, and moves away to a cooler spot, where it dumps its load of heat.

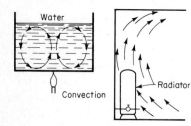

FIG. 5-2 Convection carries heat by movement of water, air, or other fluid. At the radiator, heat sets up fluid currents.

RADIATION

Radiation can be likened to radio broadcasting with good reason. Radiant heat travels out in a straight line with a speed of 186,282 miles per sec, exactly the same as light, X-rays, and radio waves. Naturally you can't measure this 670-million-mph speed without special instruments, but any engineer can satisfy himself that radiant heat moves very fast by the simple test illustrated in Fig. 5-3. The ordinary electric heater sends out most of its heat by radiation, with the speed of light. Have a helper slip a large card across the face of the heater. The instant he does so you will feel coolness—no waiting.

All bodies radiate heat. Even a cake of ice placed near a steam radiator radiates heat to the radiator. Meanwhile, the radiator sends far more heat to the ice, so there is a net transfer of heat from the radiator to the ice, causing the ice to melt.

Figuring radiation is a bit complicated. The basic law is that each body radiates in proportion to the fourth power of its absolute temperature. Thus if the absolute temperature is doubled, its radiation will be 16 times as great ($2 \times 2 \times 2 \times 2 = 16$).

Because of this fourth-power effect, radiation piles up faster and faster as the temperature rises. When you are standing near a warm body, you receive heat partly by convection and partly by radiation. If the temperature is moderate with good air currents, most of the heat may come by convection. If temperature is very high, as with a white-hot billet, most of the heat will come by radiation.

Convected heat requires air, water, or some other fluid for its transmission. Radiant heat will go perfectly through a vacuum. For example, the radiant heat of the sun travels 98 million miles through vacuum to the earth in 8 min.

Flow of heat by conduction is like the flow of electricity from a

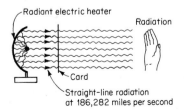

FIG. 5-3 Radiant heat travels as fast as light. A card will cut off heat in less than a millionth of a second.

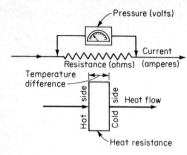

FIG. 5-4 Heat conduction follows the same law as steady electrical flow.

higher potential to a lower. After conditions get steady, heat conduction follows a law exactly like Ohm's law in electricity, as the following discussion will show (Fig. 5-4).

Ohm's law says that electrical flow (amperes) equals pressure (volts) divided by resistance (ohms). The heat-conduction law says that heat flow through a body by conduction equals the temperature difference between the hot and cold sides divided by the heat resistance. If you double the temperature difference, heat will flow twice as fast. If you double the resistance, heatflow will be cut in half.

PRACTICAL PROBLEMS

Now let us see how the laws of conduction are applied to practical problems and add a word about figuring the surface of heat-transfer equipment.

First remember that the conduction of heat follows the same law as the conduction of electricity: *The heat conduction, in Btu per hour, is equal to the temperature difference between entering and leaving faces multiplied by the conductance.*

The example in Fig. 5-5 will make this clearer. Silver is the best conductor of heat, with copper a close second. The *specific conductance* of copper is about 220. That means that if one face of a *1-ft cube* of copper is 1°F hotter than the opposite face, heat will flow from the hot face to the cold at the rate of 220 Btu per hr.

Let's apply this fact to the case shown, where a copper bar 1 in. square and 2 ft long is kept 300°F at one end and 200°F at the other. Find the heat flow. Both its smaller cross section and its greater length will give this bar a smaller conductance than the 1-ft

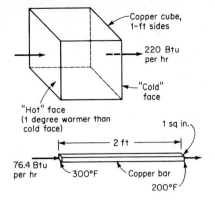

FIG. 5-5 The conductivity of the copper bar is 76.4 Btu per hr.

cube. Since the area is divided by 144 and the length is multiplied by 2, the conductance of the bar will be $220 \div 144 \div 2 = 0.764$ Btu per hr per °F difference. The temperature difference is $300°F - 200°F = 100°F$, so the heat flow will be $100 \times 0.764 = 76.4$ Btu per hr.

Here is another example. At the other extreme from copper is an insulating material like 85% magnesia with a specific conductivity of about 0.04.

Consider a slab of this insulation 2 in. thick and 1 ft square with one side at 300°F and the other at 100°F. Since the piece is $\frac{1}{6}$ ft thick, its conductivity will be 6 times that of the 1-ft cube, or $6 \times 0.04 = 0.24$ Btu per hr per °F. The temperature difference is 200 °F, so the heat flow will be $200 \times 0.24 = 48$ Btu per hr.

HEATING BOILER WATER

Standard pressure of the atmosphere at sea level is taken as 14.7 psia. At this pressure the barometer reads 30 in. of mercury (in height). The temperature at which water boils rises with the pressure. At the standard atmosphere of 14.7 psia, water boils at 212°F (Fig. 5-6a).

In airplanes, and on high mountains, the pressure is less, so water boils at a lower temperature. For example (Fig. 5-6b), at 11.5 psia (23.5 in. barometer) water boils at 200°F.

If vacuum equipment brings the pressure down to 0.5 psia (that

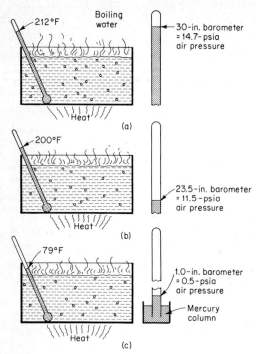

FIG. 5-6 Effect of atmospheric pressure on boiling temperature.

is, 1 in. barometer, or 29 in. vacuum) water boils at 79°F. You can hold your hand in it comfortably (Fig. 5-6c).

Expansion.

When heated from 32 to 212°F, liquid water expands about 4%. Table 5-1 gives weights at various temperatures.

At 212°F 1 lb of water occupies only 0.0167 cu ft. When evaporated, this expands 1600 times to form 26.7 cu ft of steam at 212°F and 14.7 psia.

Steam is compressible, about like air, so 1 lb by weight of steam occupies less and less space as the pressure rises. At 100 psig (114.7 psia) 1 lb of steam occupies 3.9 cu ft. At 445 psig saturated steam weighs 1 lb per cu ft.

TABLE 5-1 Weight of 1 cu ft of Water at Various Temperatures

Temp.	Weight, lb
32	62.4
70	62.3
100	62.0
150	61.2
200	60.1
212	59.8

For practical purposes, at temperatures under 400°F, 1 Btu is the heat required to warm 1 lb of liquid water 1°F. So, to heat 2000 lb of water from 80 to 180°F (100° rise) takes 100 × 2000 = 200,000 Btu. If this same water cools from 180 to 80°F, it will give off 200,000 Btu.

In Fig. 5-7, to heat 1 lb of water from 80 to 212°F takes 212 − 80 = 132 Btu. If further heat is supplied, with the fluid under atmospheric pressure through the floating piston, the water will start to turn into steam, raising the piston.

Latent Heat

When 970 Btu has been supplied, all the liquid will have been converted into saturated steam. In this case the total heat required to convert 1 lb of water at 80°F into saturated steam at 212°F and 14.7 psia is 132 + 970 = 1102 Btu. The 970 Btu is the latent heat of vaporization for this pressure and temperature.

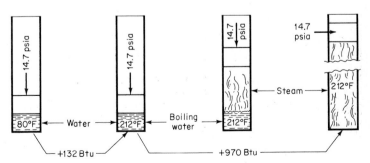

FIG. 5-7 Work on piston by water or vapor at various temperatures.

STEAM FOR HEATING WATER

It is easy to figure the amount of steam required for water heating. For many purposes the round-figure allowance of 1000 Btu per lb of steam is close enough.

Suppose, then, we want to heat 5780 lb of water from 60 to 180°F. The rise is 120°, so the water absorbs 120 Btu per lb, or a total of 5780 × 120 = 693,600 Btu. If each pound of steam supplies 1000 Btu, the steam required will be 694 lb. This, of course, takes no account of the heat required to warm up the metal of the tank or the heat lost from the tank and the water surface during the heating-up period.

Now let's refigure this problem using actual steam-table data instead of the round 1000 Btu per lb. Total heat (enthalpy) of saturated steam at 5 psig (20 psia) is 1156 Btu per lb. The amount of heat transferred to water is this minus heat in condensate at its final temperature, which in turn depends on the method of heating.

Consider the case where the water is heated by direct contact with the steam (Fig. 5-8). Here the final temperature of the condensate must be 180°F, and its final heat (enthalpy) 180 − 32 = 148 Btu per lb. Then the heat given up per pound of steam will be 1156 − 148 = 1008 Btu per lb. Steam required to heat the 693,000 lb of water will then be 693,600 ÷ 1008 = 688 lb.

If we want to correct this for the heat required to warm up the tank, it's not difficult, assuming that the metal starts at 60°F and

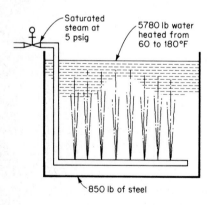

Saturated
steam at
5 psig

5780 lb water
heated from
60 to 180°F

850 lb of steel

FIG. 5-8 The heat per pound of steam is the difference between the total heat of the steam and that of the condensate at 180°F.

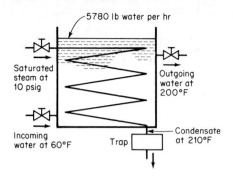

FIG. 5-9 Heat supplied for heating water by a steam coil in a tank.

rises to 180°F just like the water. If the metal is iron, steel, brass, or copper, its heat-absorbing capacity (specific heat) is about one-tenth that of water, so all you have to do is to add one-tenth the weight of the tank to the weight of the water contained. The equivalent weight of water would then be (for a 850-lb steel tank) 5780 + 85 = 5865 lb, the heat absorbed 5865 × 120 = 703,800 Btu, and the steam required 703,800 ÷ 1008 = 698 lb, practically the same as figured before.

As another example, consider Fig. 5-9, showing 5780 lb of water per hr heated by 10-psig steam supplied to a submerged coil. Here the tank is maintained continuously at 200°F, new water being fed in at 60°F to replace the 5780 lb per hr drawn off at 200°F. In this case the heat capacity of the tank makes no difference, since its temperature does not change.

The amount of heat given up per pound of steam will depend upon the cooling of the condensate. If condensate leaves at 10°F above water temperature, its temperature will be 210°F and its heat (enthalpy) 210 − 32 = 178 Btu. Then heat given up per pound of steam will be 1160 − 178 = 982 Btu; steam required per hour = 5780 × (200 − 60) ÷ 982 = 824 lb.

If the tube is well insulated against heat loss, the arrangement shown in Fig. 5-10, or some equivalent, gives the greatest efficiency because it cools the condensate down almost to the temperature of the entering cold water—let's say within 10°F. Then condensate

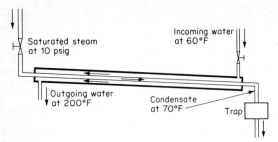

FIG. 5-10 Heating with steam in counterflow exchanger is efficient.

leaves at 70°F, with 70 − 32 = 38 Btu, and heat given off per pound of steam is 1160 − 38 = 1122 Btu. The steam required to heat 5780 lb per hour will be 5780 × (200 − 60) ÷ 1122 = 721 lb.

HEAT MIXTURES

We can add cold water to hot water to temper it, or hot water to cold to produce a larger quantity of water warm enough for some particular use. We can cool water by adding ice. All we have to do is remember these two commonsense rules:

   Rule 1: *Heat in the mixture equals heat in its components.*

   Rule 2: *Heat lost by the hot body equals heat gained by the cold body.*

   Pick either rule (whichever happens to be more convenient for the problem in hand). Set up the problem and solve it by simple algebra. Here's a demonstration:

PROBLEM 1:   What will happen if we mix 4200 lb of water at 190°F with 1250 lb of water at 60°F?

SOLUTION: It is clear that we will have 5450 lb of water at some temperature lower than 190°F and higher than 60°F. To find the actual temperature use either rule 1 or rule 2. Let's try rule 1 first.

   Since heats are normally measured above water at 32°F, the heat in 1 lb of water at 190°F is 190 − 32 = 158 Btu. Similarly, the heat in 1 lb of water at 60°F is 60 − 32 = 28 Btu. Then, by rule 1,

$$\text{Heat in mixture} = \text{heat in components}$$
$$\text{Heat in 5450 lb} = \text{heat in 4200 lb} + \text{heat in 1250 lb}$$

$$\text{Heat in 5450 lb} = (4200 \times 158) + (1250 \times 28)$$
$$= 663{,}600 + 35{,}000 = 698{,}600 \text{ Btu}$$

$$\text{Heat in 1 lb of mixture} = \frac{698{,}600}{5450} = 128 \text{ Btu}$$

To get the final temperature of the mixture add 32°, which gives 160°F.

PROBLEM 2: How much water at 70°F must be added to each thousand pounds of water at 205°F to temper it to 160°F?

SOLUTION: Here rule 2 will be convenient. Use the letter C to represent the unknown quantity of cold water required. First, 1000 lb of water is cooled from 205 to 160°F, a heat loss of $1000 \times (205 - 160) = 45{,}000$ Btu. Second, C lb of water is heated from 70 to 160°F, a heat gain of $90C$ Btu. Then, by rule 2,

$$\text{Heat gained by cold water} = \text{heat lost by hot water}$$
$$90C = 45{,}000$$
$$C = \frac{45{,}000}{90} = 500 \text{ lb}$$

Therefore add 500 lb of 70°F water to each 1000 lb of water at 205°F to get 1500 lb of 160°F water.

PROBLEM 3: How much ice will be required to cool 800 lb of water from 80 to 40°F, assuming that all the ice is completely melted in the mixture?

SOLUTION: To melt 1 lb of ice at 32°F into water at 32°F requires 144 Btu. If the ice melts and then rises to 40°F, the heat it takes up will be $144 + 8 = 152$ Btu per lb. The water is cooled 40° and therefore loses a total of $40 \times 800 = 32{,}000$ Btu. Then, by rule 2, letting I represent the number of pounds of ice required

$$\text{Heat gained by ice} = \text{heat lost by water}$$
$$152I = 32{,}000$$
$$I = \frac{32{,}000}{152} = 210 \text{ lb of ice required}$$

PROBLEM 4: What will the final temperature of 200 lb of water at 60°F be if it is used to quench 100 lb of iron at 900°F?

SOLUTION: The specific heat of iron and steel is very close to 0.1, meaning that they require only 0.1 Btu to raise the temperature of 1 lb 1°F. When the quenching is over and a steady state is attained, both iron and water will be at same unknown temperature T.

The heat lost by iron will be

$$100 \times (900 - T) \times 0.1 = 9000 - 10T$$
$$\text{Heat gained by water} = 200 \times (T - 60) = 200T - 12,000$$

By rule 2

$$\text{Heat gained by water} = \text{heat lost by iron}$$
$$200T - 12,000 = 9000 - 10T$$
$$210T = 21,000$$

or

$$T = \frac{21,000}{210} = 100°F$$

SOME TYPICAL HEAT-TRANSFER PROBLEMS —————

1. CONDENSED STEAM ————————————————

PROBLEM: Steam at 100 psig is discharged into an open tank containing 400 gal of water. Calculate the quantity of steam that will be condensed (steam used) in raising the temperature of the water from 40°F to its boiling point of 212°F.

SOLUTION: The initial 400 gal of water weighs $400 \times 8^{1}/_{3} = 3333$ lb. Neglecting losses of heat from radiation, to raise the temperature from 40°F to the temperature of boiling at atmospheric pressure will require $3333 \times (212 - 40) = 573,276$ Btu.

Assuming that dry saturated steam is supplied at the pressure of 100 psig (115 psia), each pound (weight) of the steam will contain 1189.7 Btu above 32°F. Thus in becoming condensed to 212°F, the steam parts with $1189.7 + (32 - 212) = 1009.7$ Btu. Because heating the water will absorb 573,276 Btu, the amount of steam condensed will be

$$\frac{573,276}{1009.7} = 567.7 \text{ lb} \quad Ans.$$

2. WIND VELOCITY _____

PROBLEM: How important is wind velocity in heating calculations?

SOLUTION: If the building is normally exposed to wind, it is best to allow 10 to 20% for wind. For example, a 4-in. brick wall must be doubled in thickness to give the *same* coefficient in a 15-mph wind as in still air.

Air leakage through a plain $8^{1/2}$-in. brick wall is zero in still air but 7.8 cu ft per sq ft per hr with a wind of 15 mph. Usually, on exposed buildings, computations are based on a wind velocity of 15 mph. **NOTE:** Data can be obtained from the American Society of Heating and Ventilation Engineers.

3. RELATIVE EFFECT OF LOW- AND HIGH-PRESSURE RADIATORS _____

PROBLEM: Calculate the relative effectiveness of dry room radiators supplied with exhaust steam at a pressure of 2 psig compared with one supplied with live steam at 100 psig.

SOLUTION: Assuming that there is complete removal of air from the radiators and perfect circulation of steam, the heat radiated for 1 sq ft of surface may be considered as directly in proportion to the difference of temperature of the steam within the radiator and the room temperature in the immediate vicinity of the radiator.

EXAMPLE: If the room temperature maintained near the radiator is 90°F, the temperature of steam at 2 psig is 218.5°F and the temperature of steam at 100 psig is 338°F. Then the relative effectiveness per square foot of radiation would be as 218.5 − 90 for the exhaust steam is to 338 − 90 for the steam at 100 psig, or as 100 is to 193. *Ans.*

4. LEAKY TRAPS IN GRAVITY HEATING SYSTEM _____

PROBLEM: Assume that faulty radiator traps return condensate at about 190°F and that before going to the sewer, the condensate flows through a heat exchanger, which lowers temperature to about 100°F in the process of preheating domestic hot water. In this case, as long as the heat in the condensate is used, would there be any saving in finding and repairing the faulty traps?

SOLUTION: Radiator traps for gravity steam systems are usually designed to operate at a temperature slightly below that of atmospheric steam, so the condensate temperature does *not* necessarily indicate leaking traps. If the temperature rises to 200 or 210°F, it will be time enough to search.

In this case, a greater saving (about 4½%) can be made by running the condensate to the boiler as feedwater instead of wasting the 100°F water to sewer. All this requires is a gravity condensate-return trap. Traps should be checked and repaired during the summer, because *one* defective trap may hold steam back from other radiators.

5. SAVING STEAM FOR HEATING WATER _____

PROBLEM: Assume that 90-psig steam is used through a pipe heating coil to heat water in a 2000-gal uninsulated steel tank. The tank is filled 3 times a day with 60°F water, which is heated by the coils to 190°F in about 1 hr. Will any steam saving result if a reducing valve is installed to reduce steam pressure from 90 to 25 psig entering the heating coils?

SOLUTION: Not only would saving *not* be made, but heating time would be increased to 1½ hr. Here's why. With an uninsulated tank, the longer heating time would result in about 50% *greater* heat loss through radiation. That would require about 7 lb per hr *more* steam for the new low-pressure heating. About 15 lb per hr of steam could be saved by insulating such a tank.

But a *much* greater saving could result by using the 90-psig steam *first* to drive a steam engine (pump, any small piston-valve engine), which from its exhaust steam would provide about 230 hp-hr of power a day. This is about 28 hp of *free* energy through an 8-hr working day. *Ans.*

6. TEMPERATURE FOR MIXTURE OF STEAM AND WATER _____

PROBLEM: If 5 lb (weight) of dry steam at 5 psig is mixed at atmospheric pressure with 10 lb of water at 60°F, what will the temperature and condition of the resulting mixture be?

SOLUTION: Since 1 lb (weight) of dry saturated steam at 5 psig (20 psia) contains 1156.2 Btu above 32°F, 5 lb of dry saturated steam will contain 1156.2 × 5 = 5781 Btu above 32°F.

Since 1 lb of water at 60°F contains 60 − 32 = 28 Btu above 32°F, 10 lb will contain 28 × 10 = 280 Btu above 32°F. Mixing the steam and water together makes a total of 5781 + 280 = 6061 Btu above 32°F. Combining 5 lb of steam with 10 lb of water, we have 15 lb. Each pound of the mixture contains 6061 ÷ 15 = 404 Btu above 32°F. Then the temperature of the mixture will be

$$404 + 32 = 436°F \quad Ans.$$

7. FUEL SAVED BY HEATING FEEDWATER _____

PROBLEM: To save fuel, a feedwater heater is installed which raises (with waste heat) the water temperature from 50 to 210°F. If the boiler generates steam at 90 psig, what is the percentage saving in fuel?

SOLUTION: At 90 psig, or 105 psia, 1 lb of dry saturated steam contains 1187.2 Btu above 32°F. When the feedwater is at the temperature of 50°F, or 50 − 32 = 18°F above 32°F, for conversion into steam at the stated pressure, each pound must receive 1187.2 − 18 = 1169.2 Btu. When the feedwater is at 210°F, each pound of feedwater evaporated requires 210 − 50 = 160 Btu *less,* or only

$$\frac{1169.2 - 160}{1169.2} \times 100 = 86.3\%$$

as much heat for conversion into steam. Thus the gain is 13.7%. *Ans.*

PROBLEM: Assume a boiler pressure of 120 psig where condensate is returned to a tank at 180°F. What is the percentage of saving if the condensate is returned to heating coils and then through steam traps at 240°F, instead of directly at 180°F?

SOLUTION: In both cases, remember that each pound of feedwater converted into steam at 120 psig (135 psia) will contain 1191.6 Btu above 32°F. When the feedwater temperature is 180°F, each pound of feedwater for conversion into steam will receive (1191.6 + 32) − 180 = 1043.6 Btu.

When the feedwater temperature is 240°F, each pound of feed-water will have to receive (1191.6 + 32) − 240 = 983.6 Btu, or (1043.6 − 983.6) × 100 ÷ 1043.6 = 5.75% more heat. *Ans.*

NOTE: In this case, whether the actual saving in fuel is from the use of traps instead of a receiving tank and feed pump depends on the relative steam economies of the trap or feed pump that may be in use. *Ans.*

8. EQUIVALENT EVAPORATION

PROBLEM: How many pounds of feedwater at 212°F evaporated into steam at 70 psig would be equivalent to the evaporation of 30 lb of water from a temperature of 100°F into steam at 70 psig?

SOLUTION: Since 1 lb of steam at 70 psig (85 psia) contains 1183.4 Btu above 32°F, the evaporation of 30 lb of feedwater from a temperature of 100°F into steam at 70 psig will require

$$[1183.4 - (100 - 32)] \times 30 = 33,162 \text{ Btu}$$

For evaporation from a temperature of 212°F into steam at 70 psig, each pound of feedwater will require

$$1183.4 - (212 - 32) = 1003.4 \text{ Btu}$$

Thus to obtain an evaporation into steam at 70 psig is equivalent to the conversion of 30 lb of feedwater from 100°F into steam at 70 psig. This will require the evaporation of

$$\frac{33,162}{1003.4} = 33.05 \text{ lb of feedwater at 212°F} \quad Ans.$$

PROBLEM: What is the percentage saving with an exhaust-steam feedwater heater where the boiler pressure is 90 psig and the feed-water is heated from 50 to 170°F?

SOLUTION: Steam tables show that 1 lb of dry saturated steam at 90 psig, or 90 + 15 = 105 psia, contains 1188.1 Btu above 32°F. When the feedwater is at 50°F, or 50 − 32 = 18°F, for conversion into steam we find that each pound of feedwater requires 1188.1 − 18 = 1170 Btu.

If the feedwater has a temperature of 170°F, for its conversion into steam each pound will require 170 − 50 = 120 Btu *less* than

TABLE 5-2 Percentage of Fuel Saved by Heating Feedwater with 100-psi Exhaust Steam

Initial temperature of feedwater, °F	Final temperature of feedwater, °F											
	120	130	140	150	160	170	180	190	200	210	220	230
40	6.80	7.65	8.72	9.35	10.45	11.05	12.20	13.07	13.95	14.80	15.70	16.55
50	5.95	6.85	7.92	8.57	9.70	11.28	11.45	12.32	13.20	14.10	15.00	15.85
60	5.10	6.04	7.12	7.57	8.90	9.50	10.70	11.60	12.45	13.35	14.25	15.15
70	4.25	5.23	6.27	6.97	8.07	8.72	9.87	10.75	11.65	12.55	13.45	14.35
80	3.40	4.39	5.43	6.15	7.24	7.91	9.05	9.95	10.85	11.75	12.70	13.60
90	2.55	3.54	4.57	5.32	6.40	7.09	8.22	9.13	10.05	10.95	11.90	12.80
100	1.70	2.68	3.68	4.47	5.53	6.26	7.38	8.30	9.22	10.15	11.05	12.00
110	0.85	1.80	2.78	3.61	4.65	5.41	6.52	7.43	8.38	9.30	10.35	11.15
120	0	0.91	1.88	2.73	3.75	4.55	5.63	6.58	7.50	8.45	9.40	10.30
130	0	0	0.95	1.84	2.84	3.68	4.74	5.68	6.63	7.60	8.55	9.45
140	0	0	0	0.92	1.90	2.98	3.83	4.80	5.75	6.70	7.65	8.60
150	0	0	0	0	0.97	1.97	2.90	3.85	4.83	5.80	6.75	7.72

when the temperature is 50°F. Thus, if the feedwater heater is operated without increasing back pressure on steam machinery (pumps, engines, etc.), the saving will be

$$\frac{120}{1170.1} = 0.1026 = \text{about } 10^{1}/_{4}\% \quad Ans.$$

Feedwater heaters heat the feedwater before it enters the boiler, thus increasing the efficiency of the entire plant. Table 5-2 shows the percentage of fuel saved by using 100-psi exhaust steam for heating feedwater. There are various types of heaters: straight tube, bent tube, etc. Steam for heating is usually extracted from the main turbine or engine in large plants but in smaller plants from exhaust steam, where it has already done work.

In a well-designed heater, the temperature of the water leaving it is 10 to 15°F under the temperature of the steam used for heating. Feedwater heaters have from 2.5 to 4 sq ft of heating surface per 1000 lb of feedwater per hr.

SUGGESTED READING

Elonka, Stephen M., and Joseph F. Robinson: "Standard Plant Operators' Questions and Answers," vols. I and II, McGraw-Hill Book Company, New York, 1959.

6

COMBUSTION

Understanding the chemistry of combustion and the calculations and formulas necessary to achieve top efficiency with today's costly fuels has *never* been more important. The burning of coal, oil, or gas is a chemical reaction. These fuels contain many *different* atoms in many different combinations, but the only important heat-producing atoms in commercial fuels are carbon (C) and hydrogen (H). Here we'll explain the *minimum* chemistry and math necessary to save fuel dollars.

UNDERSTANDING COMBUSTION

The oxygen for combustion comes from the air supplied by the furnace. Air is 23% oxygen by weight and 21% by volume. The remainder of the air is mostly nitrogen, which plays *no* part in combustion.

The table in Fig. 6-1 shows the atoms of hydrogen, carbon, and oxygen. In the table "Weight" means the atomic weight (weight of one atom), using hydrogen as the standard. Thus carbon weighs 12 and oxygen 16.

To understand the word "valence" in the table try picturing the

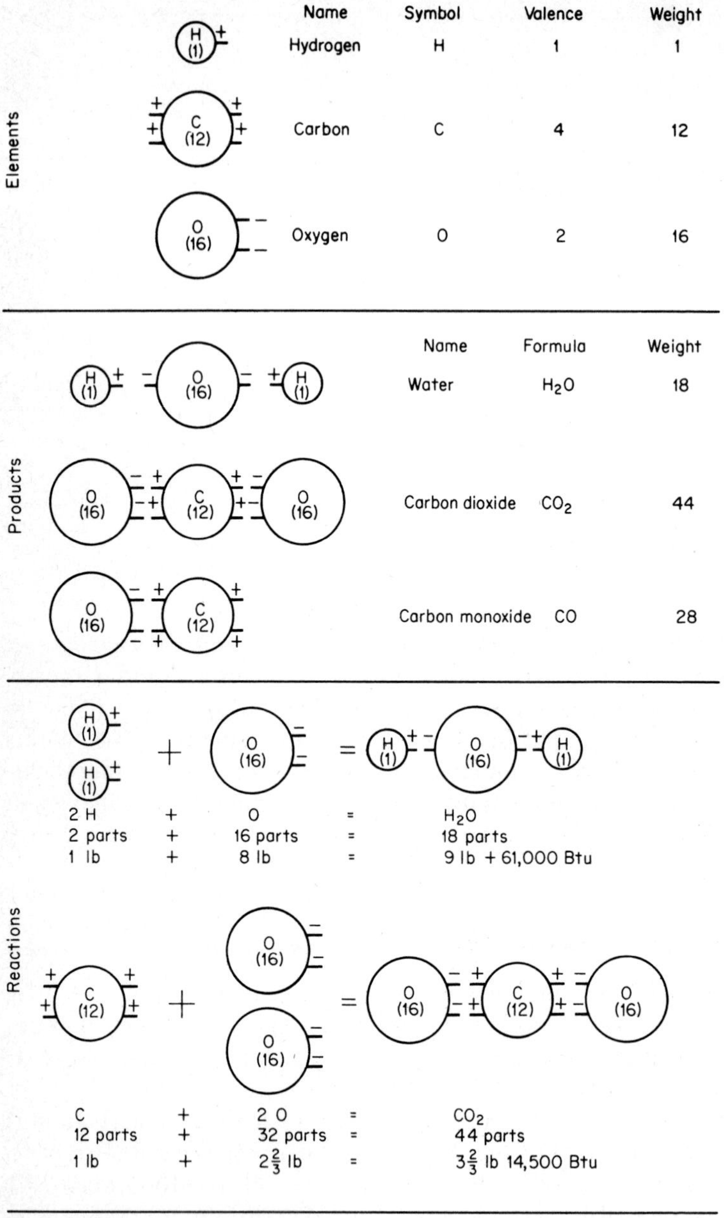

	Name	Symbol	Valence	Weight
	Hydrogen	H	1	1
	Carbon	C	4	12
	Oxygen	O	2	16

Elements

	Name	Formula	Weight
	Water	H_2O	18
	Carbon dioxide	CO_2	44
	Carbon monoxide	CO	28

Products

Reactions

2 H	+	O	=	H_2O
2 parts	+	16 parts	=	18 parts
1 lb	+	8 lb	=	9 lb + 61,000 Btu

C	+	2 O	=	CO_2
12 parts	+	32 parts	=	44 parts
1 lb	+	$2\frac{2}{3}$ lb	=	$3\frac{2}{3}$ lb 14,500 Btu

FIG. 6-1 Table of combustion chemistry to help clarify elements, products, and reactions for better fuel economy.

valence number as the number of *hooks* or bonds available to tie this atom to other atoms. The plus bonds pictured will pair with the minus bonds on other atoms.

Under Products, the water molecule contains two atoms of hydrogen and one of oxygen, so its formula is H_2O. Note that all the bonds are paired up (plus to minus) and that the weight of the molecule is 18, the sum of the weights of its atoms.

In the formula for carbon monoxide, two of the carbon hooks are unused, indicating that carbon monoxide is the product of imperfect combustion.

BURNING HYDROGEN AND CARBON

Under Reactions (Fig. 6-1) we see how hydrogen and carbon burn. The first line shows how two atoms of hydrogen combine with one of oxygen to make one of water (H_2O). The formula balances, meaning that the weight of products equals the weight of combining elements. Also every atom on the left shows up on the right, and every valence bond is paired. The same is true when carbon and oxygen combine to form CO_2.

MATHEMATICS OF COMBUSTION

Did you know that it takes more than 10 tons of air to burn 1 ton of 13,500-Btu coal? All this air eventually goes up the stack, although in a different chemical form. To estimate the theoretical amount of air required to burn 1 lb of coal, divide the heating value of the coal by 1350. Thus, for the 13,500-Btu coal, the theoretical air needed is

$$\frac{13,500}{1350} = 10 \text{ lb}$$

Since furnaces and firing can never be perfect, no actual furnace could burn this coal with only 10 lb of air. There *must* be some excess air.

An excess of 20 or 30% is reasonable in a small boiler furnace. With 30% excess air the furnace would use up 13 lb of air for every pound of coal fired. Since no matter is ever destroyed, and since very little material goes through the grate, nearly 14 lb of hot gas would go up the stack for every pound of coal fired. To heat 1 lb of flue gas 1°F it takes about $\frac{1}{4}$ Btu.

PROBLEM: The boiler-room temperature is 80°F, and the stack temperature is 530°F. What is the stack loss in hot dry gas?

SOLUTION: The temperature rise is

$$530 - 80 = 450°F$$

and the stack loss in the hot dry gas is

$$450 \times \frac{1}{4} \times 14 = 1575 \text{ Btu per lb of coal fired}\quad Ans.$$

Assume that poor equipment and operation raise stack temperature to 580°F and excess air to 80%. Air supplied per pound of coal would be 18 lb, and stack gases would weigh 19 lb per pound of coal fired. Then, temperature rise would be

$$580 - 80 = 500°F$$

Also, loss in hot, dry flue gas would be

$$19 \times \frac{1}{4} \times 500 = 2375 \text{ Btu per lb coal}$$

The way to determine the excess air is to analyze the flue gas for CO_2, using an Orsat or a CO_2 recorder. Take a sample at the point where the gas leaves the boiler setting. Flue temperature should be measured at the same point. Knowing the CO_2 percentage allows a close estimate of excess air from one of the three charts in Fig. 6-2.

Then use a short cut to approximate the percentage of coal heat lost up stack in the hot dry gas. *For the theoretical amount of air allow 1.8% loss for 100°F rise above boiler-room temperature.*

PROBLEM: If flue temperature is 520°F when the boiler room is 90°F, calculate the stack loss.

SOLUTION: The rise will be $520 - 90 = 430°F$. With the theoretical air supply the stack loss will be $4.3 \times 1.8 = 7.7\%$ *Ans.*

Increase this figure proportionately to allow for the excess air.

EXAMPLE: If the fuel is anthracite coal and the CO_2 is 12%, the excess air is 60% (from chart). Then the actual flue loss is

$$1.6 \times 7.7 = 12.3\%\quad Ans.$$

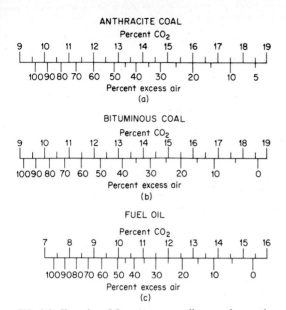

FIG. 6-2 Knowing CO_2 percentage allows a close estimate of the excess air needed for various fuels.

CORRECT CO_2 SAVES MONEY _____

Every engineer knows that high carbon dioxide (CO_2) in the boiler flue gas is a good thing, within certain practical limits. The reason isn't always as clear. It's *not* a matter of complete combustion.

Carbon, completely burned, turns into CO_2, so it's a natural mistake to assume that high CO_2 means that the fuel has been completely consumed. Yet there's no connection between CO_2 percentage and the completeness of combustion; you can have it complete with 6% CO_2 and incomplete with 15%.

Well, then, what's wrong with low CO_2? Here's the real answer. *Low CO_2 is proof that flue gas is heavily diluted with a lot of excess air.* This excess air goes to waste up the stack at a fairly high temperature ("heating up the sky"), which is a big money loss.

Now let's get down to some simple combustion arithmetic but in a somewhat unusual form. Start with 100 cu ft of air. That happens to be just the amount theoretically needed to burn up $2/3$ lb carbon, which will be our fuel supply for this example.

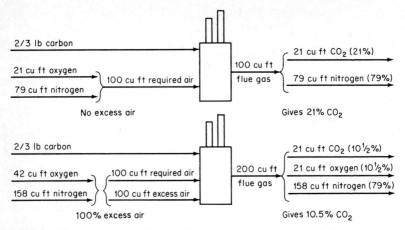

FIG. 6-3 What comes out as flue gas depends on what goes in as fuel and air.

Air is 21% oxygen by volume (Fig. 6-3). Only the oxygen really burns with the coal. The remaining 79% is nitrogen, which goes along for a free ride but doesn't have any chemical action.

One more point, when oxygen burns with carbon, the volume of the CO_2 produced (figured back to room temperature) equals the volume of oxygen actually consumed. So now we can write

$^2/_3$ lb carbon + 21 cu ft oxygen + 79 cu ft nitrogen
                        = 21 cu ft CO_2 + 79 cu ft nitrogen

We start with 100 cu ft of air and end with 100 cu ft of flue gas. All the oxygen disappears, and we find 21% CO_2 in the flue gas.

Now if you supply 200 cu ft of air instead of 100 cu ft to burn this $^2/_3$ lb of coal, it will include 100% excess air. How will this show up in the flue-gas analysis? Remember that only 21 cu ft of oxygen can really burn here. Then

$^2/_3$ lb carbon + 42 cu ft oxygen + 158 cu ft nitrogen
        = 21 cu ft CO_2 + 21 cu ft oxygen + 158 cu ft nitrogen

The flue gas composition is

	Cu ft	%
CO_2	21	10.5
Oxygen	21	10.5
Nitrogen	158	79.0
	200	100.0

What happened? We doubled the total air supplied (100% excess air). As a result we cut the flue-gas CO_2 in half, from 21% to 10.5%. The illustrations follow the same arithmetic.

This general idea holds true for actual fuels that aren't pure carbon. But don't try to use the foregoing figures for commercial fuels. Hydrogen in bituminous coal and fuel oil changes the figures some.

HOW CARBON BURNS

In an average bituminous coal more than 80% of the total heating value is in the carbon contained. Even boiler oil averages about 85% carbon by weight, although the hydrogen contained does represent about 40% of the oil's heat value. That's why learning how carbon burns is the first and most important step in understanding combustion.

When carbon burns, it merely combines chemically with oxygen in the air. Air is 23% oxygen by weight and 21% by volume.

Normally (complete combustion) one atom of carbon combines with two atoms of oxygen to make one molecule of carbon dioxide. The reaction is

$$C + 2O = CO_2$$

where CO_2 stands for a molecule that contains 1 atom of carbon (C) and 2 atoms of oxygen (O).

Using the formula and the atomic weights, it's easy to figure how much oxygen will burn 1 lb of carbon to CO_2. The atomic weight of carbon, that is, the weight of its atom compared with an atom of hydrogen, the lightest atom, is 12. The atomic weight of oxygen is 16. So we have, in terms of parts by weight,

$$12 \text{ parts C} + 32 \text{ parts O} = 44 \text{ parts CO}_2$$

If we divide everything by 12, we get,

$$1 \text{ lb C} + 2.66 \text{ lb O} = 3.66 \text{ lb CO}_2 \text{ (Fig. 6-4)}$$

Sometimes (with air short) some of the carbon burns incompletely to carbon monoxide (CO). Then chemists write the reaction as

$$C + O = CO$$

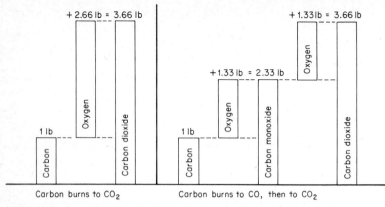

FIG. 6-4 Some combustion chemistry all power engineers should memorize.

Thus

$$12 \text{ parts C} + 16 \text{ parts O} = 28 \text{ parts CO}$$

Dividing by 12, we get

$$1 \text{ lb C} + 1.33 \text{ lb O} = 2.33 \text{ lb CO}$$

To burn this 2.33 lb of CO to CO_2 takes another 1.33 lb of oxygen and gives 3.66 lb of CO_2.

Note that burning 1 lb of carbon to CO_2 requires exactly 2.66 lb of oxygen and gives 3.66 lb of CO_2. This relationship holds true whether conversion occurs in one step or in two.

HOW HYDROGEN BURNS

Carbon and hydrogen are the only important sources of heat in commercial fuels. Although carbon comes first in importance, hydrogen is a big factor, particularly with gas and oil fuels.

Uncombined hydrogen is the simplest and lightest element, a gas so light that 1 lb fills 188 cu ft. Heating value per pound is 61,000 Btu. Per cubic foot, it's only 325 Btu, much less than manufactured city gas.

Here are some interesting facts. As soon as you connect the battery in Fig. 6-5a, the water starts decomposing into its elements. Oxygen collects in the tube over the left electrode (anode, or *plus*)

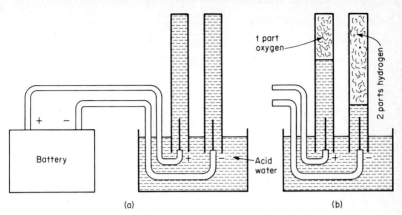

FIG. 6-5 Electric current (*a*) splits water into its constituents, 1 part oxygen (by volume) and 2 parts hydrogen. By weight (*b*) water is 8 parts oxygen and 1 part hydrogen.

and hydrogen over the right (cathode, or *minus*). At every moment the volume of hydrogen is exactly double the volume of oxygen.

If you then take oxygen and hydrogen in these proportions and burn them slowly or fast (explosion) (Fig. 6-6*a*), they merely recombine to form water. After the gases have been recombined by explosion or burning, nothing is left in the bomb but a little water vapor. That's why water from the tank will then be sucked up to fill the bomb completely.

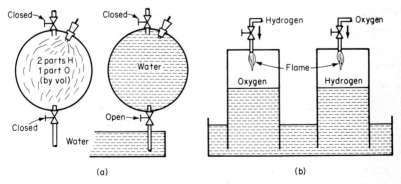

FIG. 6-6 Proportions of hydrogen and oxygen produced by electrolysis from a perfect explosive mixture (*a*), and (*b*) either gas will burn in the other.

TABLE 6-1   Chemical Facts

	Symbol	Relative weight				
Hydrogen atom	H	1		$2H_2$	$+ O_2$	$= 2H_2O$
Hydrogen molecule	H_2	2	Weights	$\begin{cases} 4 \\ 1\ lb \end{cases}$	$\begin{matrix} + 32 \\ + 8\ lb \end{matrix}$	$\begin{matrix} = 36 \\ = 9\ lb \end{matrix}$
Oxygen atom	O	16				
Oxygen molecule	O_2	32	Volume	2	$+ 1$	$= ?$

In Fig. 6-6b note that a jet of either gas will burn in the other. Also, that the water will keep rising until it extinguishes the flame, since there are no gaseous combustion products.

In Table 6-1 note the weight relation: 1 lb of hydrogen combines with 8 lb of oxygen to make 9 lb of water. By volume it is an entirely different story. When gases react chemically, the volumes are proportional to the number of molecules. Thus, two molecules (two volumes) of hydrogen combine with one molecule (one volume) of oxygen (Fig. 6-5b).

This volume rule applies only to gases, not to the liquid water produced. In fact, burning 2 cu ft of hydrogen with 1 cu ft of oxygen produces only about $\frac{1}{600}$ cu ft of water.

FIGURING HEAT LOST UP STACK _____

Actual stack loss in the hot gases depends on both the excess air and the stack temperature.

PROBLEM: What is the percentage stack loss in hot gases for a bituminous coal if the stack-gas temperature is 580°F, the room temperature 80°F, and the CO_2 in flue gas 14.2%?

SOLUTION: The scale for bituminous coal (Fig. 6-7) shows that excess air is 30%. The temperature rise is stack temperature minus room temperature, or 580°F − 80°F = 500°F. The loss is easy to figure from this handy chart. As shown by the dotted line, run a straightedge from 500 on the left scale through 30 on the center scale. It cuts the right scale at 12.2%. Thus 12.2% of the coal's heat is wasted, "heating up the sky."   *Ans.*

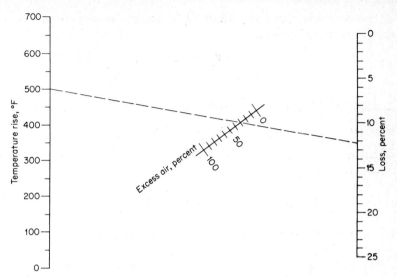

FIG. 6-7 Chart gives percentages of fuel heat wasted in the hot flue gas for hard and soft coal and fuel oil.

SOME TYPICAL COMBUSTION CALCULATIONS _____

1. HEAT ENERGY REALIZED PER POUND OF COAL _____

PROBLEM: What percent of the heat energy in fuel is realized by a steam turbine in a plant where the coal used contains 12,000 Btu per lb, the evaporative economy of the boilers is 7 lb of water per pound of dry coal, the economy of the turbine is 32 lb of water per indicated horsepower (ihp), and the mechanical efficiency of the turbine is 88%?

SOLUTION: From the evaporation of 7 lb of water per pound of coal, the fuel consumption would be $32 \div 7 = 4.57$ lb of coal per ihp-hr. Thus for 88% mechanical efficiency, the energy realized would be

$$\frac{33,000 \times 60}{4.57} \times 0.80 = 346,608 \text{ ft-lb}$$

or

$$\frac{346,608}{778} = 445.5 \text{ Btu per lb of coal}$$

Thus for coal containing 12,000 Btu per lb, the percent of heat energy realized would be

$$\frac{445.5 \times 100}{12,000} = 3.7\% \quad Ans.$$

2. AIR REQUIRED FOR BURNING COAL

PROBLEM: Calculate the air required for burning 1 lb of coal.

SOLUTION: Air required for the combustion of 1 lb of coal is given approximately by

$$\text{Weight of air, lb} = 12C + 35\left(H - \frac{O}{8}\right)$$

in which C, H, and O represent the parts of a pound of carbon, hydrogen, and oxygen respectively in 1 lb of coal.

For perfect combustion most fuels combine with about 12 lb of air per pound of the fuel. But in burning the fuel, to ensure that each atom of carbon will meet with an abundance of oxygen for complete combustion, more air must be admitted to the furnace than is necessary for the combination.

The weaker the draft the more excess air will be required for this purpose. With natural draft it is usual to provide for a supply of about 100% excess air and with forced draft about 50%. As 1 lb of air at 62°F has a volume of 13.14 cu ft, with natural draft the provision for air supply should be about $12 \times 2 \times 13.14 = 315$ cu ft. With forced draft about $12 \times 1.5 \times 13.14 = 236$ cu ft per lb of coal to be burned. *Ans.*

NOTE: For best economy, the quantity of air actually supplied should be no more than required under the conditions for obtaining the highest percentage of CO_2 in the flue gas.

3. HEAT LOSS FROM MOIST COAL

PROBLEM: Calculate heat loss of coal due to its moisture content. Assume a coal of 13,000 Btu (dry basis), 8% moisture, 60°F temperature of coal as fired, and 550°F stack temperature.

SOLUTION: Burning wet coal is costly because its moisture must first be evaporated and superheated before it can escape at flue temperature at atmospheric pressure. Because heat is thus rejected to the chimney, any moisture in coal, in addition to being a dead weight to transport, results in wasted heat. The heat loss can be determined by the formula

Loss, Btu per lb dry coal
$$= M[212 - t + 970.4 + 0.47(T - 212)]$$

where M = moisture per lb of dry coal, lb
   t = room (ambient) temperature, °F
   T = temperature of flue gases, °F
   970.4 = latent heat of evaporation at 212°F (see steam tables)
   0.47 = mean specific heat of superheated steam

Substituting in the formula, we find the heat loss to be

$$0.08[(212 - 60) + 970.4 + 0.47(550 - 212)] =$$
$$0.08[(152 + 970.4) + (0.47 \times 338)] =$$
$$0.08[1122.4 + 158.86] =$$
$$0.08 \times 1281.25 = 102.5 \text{ Btu per}$$
lb of coal

or $\dfrac{102.5 \times 100}{13,000}$ = about 0.8% of heat in dry coal   *Ans.*

NOTE: This shows that with small percentages of moisture, the heat loss amounts to about 1% for each 10% moisture in this coal.

4. LOSS FROM COMBUSTIBLE REMAINING IN ASHES _____

PROBLEM: Calculate the loss from combustible remaining in ashes when the coal as fired contains 12,890 Btu per lb and 12.6% ash, the refuse contains 40% combustible, and the coal costs $40 per ton.

SOLUTION: Each 100 lb of coal containing 12.6% ash would consist of $(1 - 0.126) \times 100 = 87.4$ lb of combustible and 12.6 ash. If refuse from firing consisted of 40% combustible and $100 - 40 = 60\%$ ash, the refuse from firing 100 lb of coal would contain $(12.6 \div 60) \times 40 = 8.4$ lb of combustible. Also the loss of combustible contained in the coal would be $(8.4 \times 100) \div 87.4 = 9.6\%$.

Thus if the coal contained 12,890 Btu per pound of combustible, there would be a loss of 9.6% of 12,890 = 1237 Btu per lb of coal. And with coal costing $40 per ton, there would be a loss of 9.6% × $40 = $3.84 per ton of coal used.   *Ans.*

Expressed algebraically, if

a = percentage of ash in coal

c = percentage of combustible in refuse

$100 - c$ = percentage of ash

then
$$\frac{a}{100 - c} \times c \times \frac{100}{100 - a} = \text{loss, \%}$$

If, as in the example, a = 12.6 and c = 40, by substitution the formula becomes

$$\left(\frac{12.6}{100 - 40} \times 40\right) \frac{100}{100 - 12.6} = 9.6\% \text{ loss} \quad \textit{Ans.}$$

5. COAL REQUIRED FOR HEATING AIR

PROBLEM: A fan delivers 36,000 cu ft of air per min through steam-heating coils. What amount of coal of 10,000 Btu per lb will be required to raise the temperature of the air from − 10 to 70°F?

SOLUTION: The specific heat of dry air at constant pressure is about 0.2376. At − 10°F the weight per cubic foot would be about 0.0882 lb. As the elevation of temperature would be 80°F, the heat required would be 36,000 × 60 × 0.0882 × 0.2376 × 80 = 3,621,252 Btu per hr.

Allowing a boiler efficiency of 60% to be obtained with coal of 10,000 Btu per lb gives

$$\frac{3,621,252}{10,000 \times 0.6} = 604 \text{ lb of coal per hr} \quad \textit{Ans.}$$

6. SPECIFIC GRAVITY CORRESPONDING TO BAUMÉ DEGREES

PROBLEM: Give specific-gravity values corresponding to Baumé degrees and show how the specific gravity of a liquid is estimated from the degrees Baumé.

SOLUTION: Corresponding values of the Baumé scale and specific gravity within the limits most used in connection with petroleum are as follows:

Density, °Bé	Specific gravity	Density, °Bé	Specific gravity
20	0.9333	34	0.8536
22	0.9210	36	0.8433
24	0.9090	38	0.8333
26	0.8974	40	0.8235
28	0.8860	42	0.8139
30	0.8750	44	0.8045
32	0.8641	46	0.7954

Specific gravity of a liquid is estimated from the degrees Baumé by the following formulas:

For liquids lighter than water:

$$\text{Sp. gr.} = \frac{140}{130 + °\text{Bé}} \qquad (1)$$

For liquids heavier than water:

$$\text{Sp. gr.} = \frac{145}{145 - °\text{Bé}} \quad Ans. \quad (2)$$

NOTE: The specific gravity of an oil is determined by the use of two types of hydrometers, conventional form and the Baumé, used for fluids *lighter* than water.

7. REDUCTION OF BAUMÉ READING TO POUNDS OF OIL PER GALLON

PROBLEM: If the Baumé reading of a fuel oil or distillate is known, how are the pounds per gallon estimated?

SOLUTION: The weight per gallon will be equal to the weight of a gallon of pure water multiplied by the specific gravity or weight of the oil, compared with the weight of an equal volume of pure water.

At 62°F 1 U.S. gal of pure water weighs 8.3356 lb, and 1 Imperial gal of pure water at the same temperature weighs 10 lb. To convert degrees Baumé to specific gravity, from Problem 6, formula (1) is used. Thus for an oil lighter than water, if the reading according to the Baumé hydrometer is 21°Bé,

$$\text{Sp. gr.} = \frac{140}{130 + 21°\text{Bé}} = 0.927$$

and the weight is

$$8.3356 \times 0.927 = 7.727 \text{ lb per U.S. gal} \quad Ans.$$

8. WEIGHT OF DISCHARGED STACK GASES _____

PROBLEM: If 1 ton of carbon is burned in a furnace using 20 lb of air per pound of fuel, how many pounds of carbon dioxide, free oxygen, and nitrogen would be discarded up the smoke stack, assuming that the rare gases are classed with the nitrogen?

SOLUTION: We know that 1 ton of carbon weighs 2000 lb and that to burn 1 lb of carbon of CO_2 requires 2.66 lb of oxygen. Thus in burning 1 lb of carbon to CO_2, we send up the stack 1 lb of carbon + 2.66 lb of oxygen = 3.66 lb of CO_2, and for 2000 lb of carbon there will be $2000 \times 3.66 = 7320$ lb of CO_2 discharged up the chimney.

Air contains 0.23 parts by weight of oxygen; thus 20 lb of air contains $20 \times 0.23 = 4.6$ lb of oxygen. Therefore the total oxygen supplied to burn 2000 lb of carbon is $2000 \times 4.6 = 9200$ lb of oxygen. But since combustion of the carbon required only $2000 \times 2.66 = 5320$ lb of oxygen, $9200 - 5320 = 3880$ lb of free oxygen will be discharged.

Because air contains 0.77 parts nitrogen by weight,

$$2000 \times 20 \times 0.77 = 30{,}800 \text{ lb of nitrogen}$$

will be received and discharged up the chimney. *Ans.*

9. EFFICIENCY OF BOILER, FURNACE, AND GRATE _____

PROBLEM: Calculate the percentage of efficiency of boiler, furnace, and grate obtaining an evaporation equivalent to 10.95 lb of water from and at 212°F per pound of dry coal containing 14,645 Btu per lb.

SOLUTION: Expressed as a formula,

Efficiency of boiler, furnace, and grate

$$= \frac{\text{heat absorbed by boiler per lb of fuel fired}}{\text{heat of perfect combustion per lb of fuel}}$$

As evaporation of 1 lb of water from and at 212°F requires 970.4

Btu, the heat absorbed by evaporation of 10.95 lb will be

$$970.4 \times 10.95 = 10,625.9 \text{ Btu}$$

For coal containing 14,645 Btu per lb, the efficiency of boiler, furnace, and grate will be

$$\frac{10,625.9}{14,645} = 0.7255 = \text{about } 72\frac{1}{2}\% \quad Ans.$$

10. SMOKESTACK CAPACITY

PROBLEM: A smokestack has a flue diameter of 36 in. and a height of 78 ft. Calculate the capacity increase if the height is raised to 100 ft and the size of the flue at the top is reduced to 34 in. diameter.

SOLUTION: Assuming the same temperature of chimney gases, the force or pressure of the draft at the base of chimney will be directly as the height, or $(100 - 78) \times 100 \div 78 = $ about 28% greater. *Ans.*

NOTE: This increased draft will permit use of lower-grade fuel. Since discharge capacity is directly as the square root of the stack height and about proportion to the area, the boiler capacity with the proposed dimensions would be to the present capacity as $34 \times 34\sqrt{100}$ is to $36 \times 36\sqrt{78} = 11560/11446$ or about 1% greater. *Ans.*

11. HOW TO FIGURE THE WEIGHT OF ANY GAS

PROBLEM: Give the formula for finding the weight per cubic foot of a gas.

SOLUTION: Power engineers should know the constant by which the weight of a cubic foot of any gas can be approximately determined from its molecular weight. At atmospheric pressure (14.7 psia) and 60°F the relation is

$$\text{Weight per cu ft} = \frac{\text{molecular weight}}{376}$$

$$\text{Cubic ft per lb} = \frac{376}{\text{molecular weight}}$$

The molecular weights of a few common gases are as follows:

Name	Formula	Mol. wt.	Name	Formula	Mol. wt.
Nitrogen	N_2	28	Hydrogen	H_2	2
Oxygen	O_2	32	Ammonia	NH_3	17
Carbon dioxide	CO_2	44	Air	. . .	28.8*

* This is a weight average based on 4 parts nitrogen and 1 part oxygen.

EXAMPLE: The weight of 1 cu ft of CO_2 at 14.7 psia and 60°F would be

$$\frac{44}{376} = 0.117 \text{ lb}$$

And the number of cubic feet in 1 lb would be

$$\frac{376}{44} = 8.55 \quad Ans.$$

12. EXCESS AIR, GENERAL FORMULA _____

PROBLEM: Given the percentage of CO_2 in the flue gases, how is the percentage of excess air determined?

SOLUTION: First, we know that excess air is admitted in *excess* of the theoretically required amount to furnish enough oxygen for complete combustion of the fuel, according to its chemical composition. But *no* general formula can be constructed for determining the percent of excess air in the flue gases without reference also to the CO and O_2 present.

When assuming, as in the case of anthracite coals, that the air supply is principally required for the combustion of carbon, an approximation of percentage of excess air based on the percentage of CO_2 can be found by subtracting the observed percentage of CO_2 from 20.7, dividing the remainder by the observed percentage, and *then* multiplying by 100.

Let us take the CO_2 as 8%. Then the approximate percentage of excess air passing through the fire is

$$\frac{20.7 - 8}{8} \times 100 \quad \text{or} \quad \left(\frac{20.7}{8} - 1\right) \times 100 = 158.8\% \quad Ans.$$

NOTE: For a more accurate method, first determine the percentage of excess air from the amount of CO_2 and the oxygen in the flue gases.

SUGGESTED READING _____

Higgins, Alex, and Stephen M. Elonka: "Boiler Room Questions and Answers," 2d ed., McGraw-Hill Book Company, New York, 1976.

Elonka, Stephen M., and Anthony L. Kohan: "Standard Boiler Operators' Questions and Answers," McGraw-Hill Book Company, New York, 1969.

Elonka, Stephen M., and Joseph F. Robinson: "Standard Plant Operators' Questions and Answers," vols. I and II, McGraw-Hill Book Company, New York, 1959.

7

FORCES AT WORK

Power engineers work daily with pressures of water, steam, oil, air, city gas, and other fluids and with the forces exerted on machinery they operate. Here we cover a few basic calculations also used in the construction and repair of energy-producing equipment so extremely important for *safe* operation.

FIGURING PRESSURES ————————————————

We'll start by assuming a weightless gas (no such thing); Fig. 7-1 shows an irregular container full of this gas under pressure. If pressure is 100 psig, as shown, it will be the *same* at every other point in the system, regardless of distance, level, or direction. This is illustrated by the little pistons of 1 sq in. cross section.

If the hydraulic press (Fig. 7-2) is filled with water or oil, a downward push of 1000 lb on the small plunger will produce an upward push of 100,000 lb on the large. Here the actual fluid pressure per square inch is the *same* on both plungers, but this pressure acts on 100 times the projected area in the case of the ram (larger plunger) and hence multiplies the force 100 times. (NOTE: Areas of circles are proportional to the squares of their diameters. If the diameter

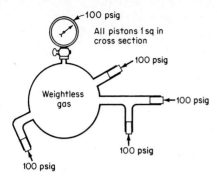

FIG. 7-1 Pressure is the same everywhere, regardless of distance.

is multiplied by 10, the area is multiplied by $10 \times 10 = 100$.) In Fig. 7-2, the bottoms of the plunger and ram are at same level, so the weight of the liquid makes no difference.

Every now and then some inventor announces that he will increase the push on an engine piston by making the piston head conical (Fig. 7-3) so the pressure will act on *more* area. Such attempts are always licked by the fact that the push on each square inch of conical head acts at an angle with the piston rod. The components in the direction of the rod add to give exactly the *same* piston push as if the piston head were flat. With any piston or plunger the total push equals the pressure per square inch times the square inches of cross-sectional (projected) area. In the case of a piston, this cross section is that of either cylinder or piston (they are the same). In the case of a plunger, be sure to figure the area from the plunger diameter, not the inside diameter of the cylinder.

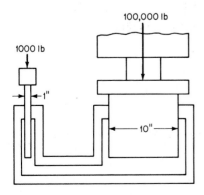

FIG. 7-2 Here 1 psi on the small piston produces 100 psi on the large one.

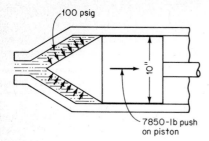

FIG. 7-3 A larger area on the piston head does not increase push.

PRESSURE IN TANKS _____

To determine the strength of a tank or pressure vessel, for example, the all-welded one of Fig. 7-4, we consider the various *ways* in which it might fail and figure each separately. Here the hemispherical heads are overstrength and give assurance that the tanks must fail in the straight part, if anywhere.

Consider first a circular failure (Fig. 7-5) and then a longitudinal one (Fig. 7-6). In Fig. 7-5 the "piston" area is that of a 10-in. circle (78.5 sq in.), so the separating force is $100 \times 78.5 = 7850$ lb. This is resisted by a steel ring of 10 in. internal diameter and $1/4$ in. thick. The inside circumference is $3.14 \times 10 = 31.4$ in., so the metal section area (approximately) is $31.4 \times 1/4 = 7.85$ sq in. Then the unit stress in the steel is $7850 \div 7.85 = 1000$ psi, which is safe by an extravagant margin.

For the break shown in Fig. 7-6 (neglecting any reinforcement by the heads), the force on the "piston" is $10 \times 10 \times 100 = 10,000$ lb. The resisting metal has an area of 5 sq in. (two strips 10 in. $\times$ $1/4$). Thus the unit stress in the metal is $10,000 \div 5 = 2000$ psi, still extra safe, but double the unit stress for a ring break.

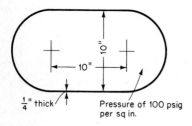

FIG. 7-4 What area of this tank is the weakest?

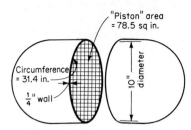

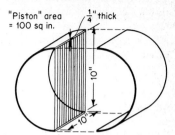

FIG. 7-5 The separating force is $100 \times 78.5 = 7850$ lb.

FIG. 7-6 The longitudinal force is $10 \times 10 \times 100 = 10,000$ lb.

Tensile Stress

When a tensile test specimen (Fig. 7-7) is stretched to the breaking point, the material tends to *neck down. Tensile strength* of the material in *pounds per square inch* is the total breaking tension divided by the *original* cross section.

At any tension short of breaking, the *unit stress* is the actual total tension divided by this same original cross section.

Up to a certain unit stress, called the *elastic limit,* the metal stretches in exact proportion to the applied load and the unit stress. Beyond that the metal starts to *give* a little and stretches more and more for a given increase in unit stress.

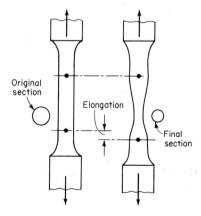

FIG. 7-7 Tensile test piece, before and after pulling.

Compression

The *compressive strength* of a material is tested by crushing a short block. The total crushing load divided by the original cross section is the compressive strength in pounds per square inch.

Shear

In the same way, if the section is sheared across (as in a power shear) the *shearing strength* is the total force required divided by the cross-sectional area sheared.

Factor of Safety

This is ultimate strength divided by actual stress.

Bolts and Pins

Figure 7-8 shows two applications. What is the unit tensile stress at the thread root of the bolt at the left? [The cross-sectional area at the thread root of a 1-in. (U.S. Standard) bolt is 0.551 sq in.] Then unit stress is $3000 \div 0.551 = 5440$ psi. For Class *B* bolt steel of 60,000 psi tensile strength, the factor of safety is $60,000 \div 5440 = 11.0$.

The 1/2-in. pin at the right (Fig. 7-8) has a cross-sectional area $0.5 \times 0.5 \times 0.785 = 0.196$ sq in. Since the pin is in *double shear,* the total sheared area is $2 \times 0.196 = 0.392$, so the shearing unit stress is $2500 \div 0.392 = 6380$ psi.

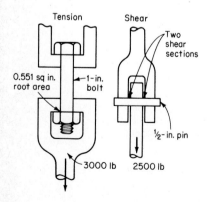

FIG. 7-8   Tension and shear at work.

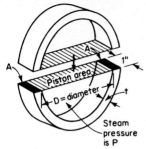

Steam force on shaded
area equals total tension
in two metal sections, so
P x D = 2 x t x s,
then P = 2 x t x s ÷ D

FIG. 7-9 How to derive formula
for shell stress in pressure vessels.

Stress in Shell

In a seamless or welded tube or drum under internal pressure, the tendency to split lengthwise is double the tendency to split around. Thus, unless the circular seams are very weak, such shells or drums *always* fail by splitting lengthwise (longitudinally).

Figure the shell strength without seams; then correct for the efficiency of the longitudinal joint. Consider a half slice of shell 1 in. long (Fig. 7-9). Fluid pressure tends to split this into two halves, both of which are shown. If the internal diameter (inches) is D and fluid pressure is P, the force on the shaded *piston area* is $P \times D$. This force is resisted and balanced by the pull of the two metal sections A. This resisting force is $2 \times t \times s$, where t is the shell thickness and s is the unit stress. From this relation we derive the shell formula $P = 2 \times t \times s \div D$.

If the diameter is 30 in., thickness 0.5 in., and safe unit stress 15,000 psi, safe pressure for a seamless shell is $2 \times 0.5 \times 15,000 \div 30 = 500$ psi. If the shell has a longitudinal riveted seam of 80% efficiency, the allowable pressure for 15,000 psi stress is $0.80 \times 500 = 400$ psi.

Heat Stresses

Almost any form of iron or steel (except cast iron) has a *modulus of elasticity* around 30,000,000. That means that a stress of 1 psi will

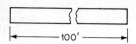

To expand 1 in. per 100 ft
requires 120°F temp.
rise or tension of
25,000 psi

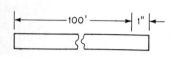

FIG. 7-10 Thermal tension in rigidly held iron or steel.

stretch it 1/30,000,000 times its own length. This relation holds right up to the elastic limit.

To put it another way, stretching iron or steel 1 in. per 100 ft (1200 in.) produces a tensile stress of $1/1200 \times 30,000,000 = 25,000$ psi. The same increase in length can be caused by a temperature rise of 120°F (say, from 80 to 200°F).

It follows that if a piece of steel rod or pipe of any length is heated to 200°F, then rigidly held at both ends, and cooled to 80°F, the resulting tensile stress will be 25,000 psi (Fig. 7-10). This figures about 200 psi for each degree of change.

SOME TYPICAL BOILER CALCULATIONS

1. MAXIMUM ALLOWABLE WORKING PRESSURE

PROBLEM: With a factor of safety of 6, calculate the highest allowable working pressure for a cylindrical boiler shell 72 in. in diameter, made of $1/2$-in. steel plate of 55,000 lb tensile strength and 85% efficiency of longitudinal joint.

SOLUTION: The formula for determining the maximum allowable working pressure for a cylindrical shell is

$$P = \frac{TS \times t \times E}{R \times FS}$$

where P = maximum allowable working pressure, psi
TS = tensile strength of shell plates, psi cross-sectional area
t = minimum thickness of shell plates, in.

E = efficiency of longitudinal joint

R = radius (one-half inside diameter of the outside course the shell) in.

FS = lowest factor of safety allowed

Substituting the given values leads to

$$P = \frac{55,000 \times 0.5 \times 0.85}{36 \times 6} = 108.2 \text{ psi} \quad Ans.$$

2. STRESSES OF GIRTH AND LONGITUDINAL SEAMS _____

PROBLEM: Show by calculation why the girth seam of a boiler is twice as strong as the longitudinal seam.

SOLUTION: The strength of a joint is no greater because it is used as a girth seam, but the stress pulling the joint apart is only one-half as much per unit length of a girth seam as per unit length of a longitudinal seam.

As an example, suppose a cylindrical shell is 72 in. in diameter. Then the whole length of a girth seam is $72 \times 3.1416 = 226.195$. The gross area of a head 72 in. in diameter is $72 \times 72 \times 0.7854 = 4071.5136$. Thus each pound pressure per square inch causes a stress of $(1 \times 4071.5136) \div 226.195 = 18$ lb per inch length of the girth seam. But for a 1-in. length of a longitudinal seam each pound pressure per square inch causes a stress of $\frac{1}{2}(1 \times 72) = 36$ lb, or twice as much as the stress per inch of length of the girth seam. *Ans.*

3. HYDROSTATIC TEST PRESSURE FOR BOILER _____

PROBLEM: If a boiler safety valve is to be set to blow at 250 psig, what should the hydrostatic test pressure be?

SOLUTION: The boiler should be subjected to a hydrostatic test of $1\frac{1}{2}$ times the maximum allowable working pressure, and the test pressure should be under proper control so that the required test pressure is not exceeded by more than 2%.

Thus the safety valve is to be set to blow at 250 psig, the boiler should be subjected to a hydrostatic test of

$$1\frac{1}{2} \times 250 = 375 \text{ psig} \quad Ans.$$

4. EXPLODING BOILER

PROBLEM: How much energy does a boiler containing 60,000 lb of water at 180 psia release if it explodes?

SOLUTION: To understand what happens, assume a slow-motion picture of the explosion. Imagine 60,000 lb of water at 180 psia and 373°F in a cylinder. The first slight drop in pressure causes a small part of the water to flash to steam, which pushes against the piston as it expands.

The process continues, with more and more water flashing to steam at lower and lower pressure as the piston moves. The energy release is the sum of the work done by the expansion of steam, down to atmospheric pressure. This amounts to about 1,000,000 Btu, or about 778,000,000 ft-lb. That is enough to lift a weight of 400,000 lb about 2000 ft *straight up.* *Ans.*

SUGGESTED READING

Elonka, Stephen M., and Anthony L. Kohan: "Standard Boiler Operators' Questions and Answers," McGraw-Hill Book Company, New York, 1969.

Higgins, Alex, and Stephen M. Elonka: "Boiler Room Questions and Answers," 2d ed., McGraw-Hill Book Company, New York, 1976.

8

FLUID PRESSURE, FLOW, AND ORIFICES

The weight of a fluid, the effect of fluid motion, measuring water flow, and figuring orifices and tank capacities (volumes) are all covered in this chapter, along with miscellaneous calculations.

WATER PRESSURE

In Chap. 7 we learned that a "weightless" fluid at rest in a connected system of pipes and tanks has the *same* pressure in all parts of the system. Also that the pressure acts *equally* in all directions. Now let us consider the effect of the *weight* of the fluid and the effect of *motion*.

EFFECT OF DEPTH

PROBLEM: The open-top tank (Fig. 8-1a) is 1 ft sq and full of water. What is the total pressure on the square piston 3 ft down?

SOLUTION: Weight of water in tank = $3 \times 62.4 = 187$ lb

The sides of the tank, being vertical, carry *no* part of this weight, so the downward force on the piston must be 187 lb. The pressure is therefore 187 lb per sq ft, or

$$\frac{187}{144} = 1.3 \text{ lb per sq in.}\quad Ans.$$

Now consider the larger open-top tank (Fig. 8-1*b*) with a 1-ft square piece of thin sheet metal set horizontally in the water 3 ft below the surface. The full 187 lb weight of 3 cu ft of water pushes *down* on the top of this sheet. Balancing this is 187 lb pushing *up* on the bottom of the sheet, because pressure at a given level acts equally in *all* directions. At any depth under the free surface of liquid exposed to atmospheric pressure, the pressure in pounds per square root equals the depth in feet multiplied by 62.4 (the weight of 1 cu ft of water).

Figure 8.2*a* shows a column of water 1 in. square and 1 ft high. Its weight will be 62.4 ÷ 144 = 0.434 lb. It follows that the gage pressure at a point 1 ft below the surface of water exposed to atmospheric pressure will be 0.434 psi. For any other submergence (for *head*) multiply the submergence in feet by 0.434 to get the pressure in pounds per square inch. If the free surface of the water is under pressure, add this to the pressure gained by submergence.

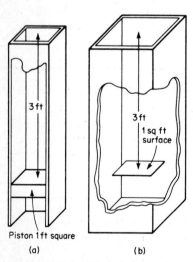

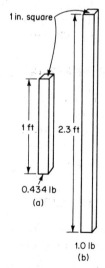

FIG. 8-1 Pressure on 1 sq ft 3 ft down is 3 times the weight of 1 cu ft of water.

FIG. 8-2 Weight of water columns.

A column of water 1 in. sq and 2.3 ft high (Fig. 8-2*b*) weighs 1 lb. Thus 2.3 ft of head will create a pressure of 1 psi.

PROBLEM: What head of water will create a pressure of 50 psi?

SOLUTION: $50 \times 2.3 = 115$ ft   *Ans.*

BUOYANCY

A body partly or wholly submerged is buoyed upward by a force equal to the weight of water displaced. Thus, if the dead weight of a ship and contents is 50,000 tons, the water displaced by its hull below the waterline must weigh 50,000 tons. Figure 8-3 shows how this *law* follows directly from the increase of water pressure with depth. Start with a 1-ft cube of wood weighing 40 lb (Fig. 8-3*a*) and push it down until its top is flush with the water surface. Since the bottom of the cube is now submerged 1 ft, the upward force on this whole bottom will be 62.4 lb. This must be the buoying effect, since there is *no* water pressure on the top of the cube and since the horizontal pressure on the sides of the cube has *no* vertical effect. Subtracting the weight of the block, we get a net buoyancy of

$$62.4 - 40 = 22.4 \text{ lb}$$

This is *not* changed if the block is submerged more deeply. If the block is submerged 1 ft, for example (Fig. 8-3*b*), there will be a downward force of 62.4 lb on the top but the upward force on the bottom (now submerged 2 ft) will be

$$2 \times 62.4 = 124.8 \text{ lb}$$

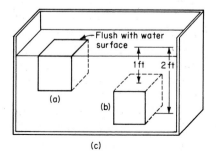

FIG. 8-3 A body partly or completely submerged loses weight equal to the weight of the water displaced.

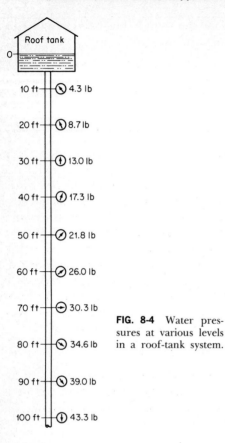

FIG. 8-4 Water pressures at various levels in a roof-tank system.

so the difference will still be 62.4 lb as before and the net buoyancy is $62.4 - 40 = 22.4$ lb.

From this we learn that, in general, any body partly or completely submerged loses weight equal to the weight of water displaced. Naturally, a floating body sinks until it displaces its own weight of water. Thus, a block of wood two-thirds as dense as water will float with two-thirds of its volume submerged.

Proving that pressure increases 0.434 lb for every foot of submergence, Fig. 8-4 shows the pressures at various levels in a piping system connected to an open roof tank. Note that pressure shows correct only when water is at rest. Flow of water in any part of the system will greatly *disturb* the pressure distribution.

MEASURING WATER FLOW

Water is spouting from the end of the level pipe in Fig. 8-5. The flow can be measured with a caliper or ruler by first finding how far the jet moves horizontally in inches while falling 1 ft. Multiply this by the square of the jet diameter and by 0.82. For the measurements shown, the flow is

$$38 \times 2.1 \times 2.1 \times 0.82 = 137 \text{ gpm} \quad \textit{Ans.}$$

Any horizontal water jet falls 1 ft in the first $^1/_4$ *sec.* This holds whether the jet is fast or slow. Also, while the jet falls faster and faster as it moves out, its horizontal velocity remains the same as when it left the pipe.

Thus measurements in Fig. 8-5 show that the water leaves the pipe with a horizontal velocity of 38 in. in $^1/_4$ sec. It follows that the discharge rate (water flow) must be proportional to this measurement. It must also be proportional to the area of the jet, which in turn is proportional to the square of the jet diameter. Thus, to get the flow in gallons per minute, multiply the horizontal measurement by the square of the diameter and by the correct constant, which happens to be 0.82.

Note that a horizontal water jet takes the same shape as the path of a weight dropped from a plane (Fig. 8-6) and that the vertical rate of fall is the same if the weight is dropped from a stationary balloon. The weight, like the water jet, will fall 1 ft in the first $^1/_4$ sec, whether it is dropped from a balloon or from a plane traveling 300 mph.

To plot the trajectory of the weight from the plane, draw vertical lines equally spaced by the distance the plane travels in 1 sec. Then locate the weight 16 ft down on the 1-sec line, 64 ft on the 2-sec line, etc., as shown. Then draw a smooth curve through the points.

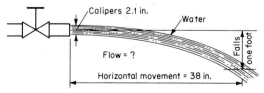

FIG. 8-5 Gallons per minute can be measured with a caliper and ruler.

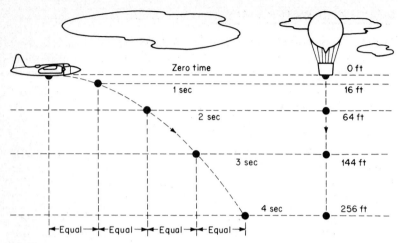

FIG. 8-6 Regardless of the amount of horizontal motion, the object falls at same rate of speed.

Air resistance throws the curve off somewhat at high speeds, but this will not apply in the case of the water jet.

ORIFICES MEASURE FLOW

You don't have to study hydraulics to be sure that for a given orifice, greater pressure will produce greater flow and the same pressure will *always* produce the *same* flow. So any kind of orifice or nozzle with a presure gage anywhere behind it can be used to measure the flow through the nozzle.

Figure 8-7a shows a bank of three spray heads. At any point between the control valve and the first spray head install a pressure gage. For each gage reading there can only be *one* rate of water flow. If the flow can be measured once at various gage readings and these points are plotted, it will be easy to find the flow for *any* gage reading.

Let's say such a job must be done in a hurry. Take a pail or container and find, by weighing, how much water it will hold. Then adjust the control valve until the gage reads 10 lb. Wait until the water is flowing out of the catch pan at a steady rate, then shove the empty pail under the discharge and time the number of seconds required to fill the pail.

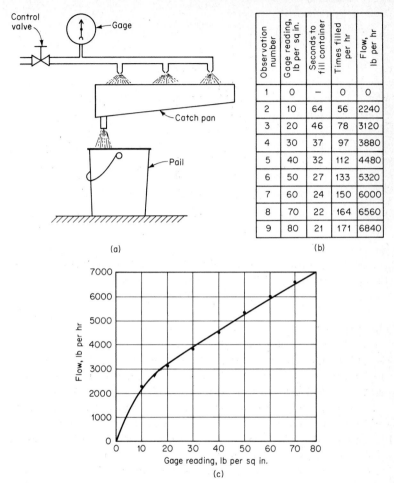

Observation number	Gage reading, lb per sq in.	Seconds to fill container	Times filled per hr	Flow, lb per hr
1	0	—	0	0
2	10	64	56	2240
3	20	46	78	3120
4	30	37	97	3880
5	40	32	112	4480
6	50	27	133	5320
7	60	24	150	6000
8	70	22	164	6560
9	80	21	171	6840

FIG. 8-7 Any combination of sprays backed by a pressure gage is a flowmeter. (*a*) Measure time required to fill pail for each of a series of gage readings; (*b*) flow for each measurement; (*c*) calibration curve for reference.

Repeat this process by 10-lb pressure steps. Then tabulate this information as shown in the first three columns of Fig. 8-7*b*. Now consider the 10-lb line in this table. At this gage reading, it took 64 sec to fill the pail. Since there are 3600 sec in 1 hr, the existing rate of flow would fill the pail

$$\frac{3600}{64} = 56 \text{ times per hr}$$

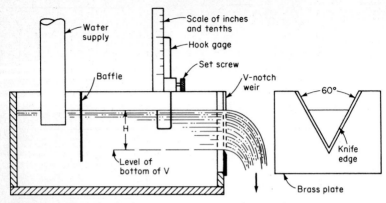

FIG. 8-8 A V-notch wier is an accurate means of measuring water flow in an open channel.

This gives column 4 of the table. If the pail holds 40 lb of water, the flow per hour at 10-lb gage reading will be

$$40 \times 56 = 2240 \text{ lb}$$

This process is repeated for each pressure.

With the table complete, plot the rates of flow against the corresponding gage readings and draw a smooth average curve through the points (Fig. 8-7c). Post this curve on a board near the gage and you have a *flowmeter* of fair accuracy.

To find the flow rate at any later time, read the pressure gage and take the corresponding flow from the chart. This method can be applied to many power and process devices—cooling towers, washers, and spray equipment.

Figure 8-8 shows a convenient and accurate means of measuring water flowing in an open channel. It is the V-notch weir. V notches of either 60 or 90° are commonly used. Each head corresponds to a definite rate of flow, but the formula is too complicated for everyday use.

FIGURING ORIFICES

Let's consider orifices widely used to measure the flow of water and other fluids. The metal-plate orifice in Figs. 8-9 and 8-10 is beveled to a sharp knife edge with the flat on the *upstream* side.

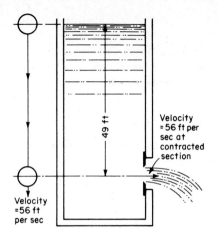

FIG. 8-9 The speed velocity of the jet at the contracted section equals that of a body falling (from rest) from water-surface level to the level of the orifice center.

With an orifice of this type the jet area will always contract about 40% after leaving the orifice. The velocity of the water at the contracted section (called the *vena contracta*) will be practically the same as that of a body falling freely from rest a vertical distance equal to the head of water on the orifice. The formula is

Velocity = 8 × square root of head

In this formula the head is measured in feet and the velocity comes out in feet per second. The head (Fig. 8-9) is 49 ft. Since the square root of 49 is 7, the velocity will be

8 × 7 = 56 ft per sec

If the contracted section in this case is 0.01 sq ft, the flow will be 56 × 0.01 = 0.56 cu ft per sec. *Ans.*

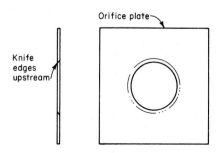

FIG. 8-10 A bevel orifice has a sharp knife edge, with the flat side upstream.

The practice is to use the *full* area of the orifice and then multiply the flow thus figured by a correction factor, or *coefficient*, to allow for the contraction and for the slight loss of water velocity.

For the sharp-edge orifice mounted in a box or pipe much larger than the orifice, the coefficient may be taken as 0.60. Then the flow formula will be

Flow = 8 × square root of head × orifice area × 0.60

The head must be in feet and the orifice area in square feet. Flow will come out in cubic feet per second.

PROBLEM: How much water will a pressure of 100 psi force through a 1-in. round sharp-edged orifice?

SOLUTION:

Area of 1-in. circle = 0.785 sq in. = 0.00545 sq ft
Head = 100 × 2.3 = 230 ft
Square root of head = 15.2
Flow = 8 × 15.2 × 0.00545 × 0.6
= 0.40 cu ft per sec   *Ans.*

SOME TYPICAL FLUID CALCULATIONS _____

1. CAPACITY OF WOODEN TANK _____

PROBLEM: Calculate the quantity of water contained in a wooden water-tower tank of the following dimensions: inside measurements, bottom diameter 18 ft, top diameter 17 ft, depth (height) 14 ft.

SOLUTION: The volume for this shape is given by the prismoidal formula:

Volume = $\dfrac{\text{depth}}{6}$ × (area of top + area of bottom

+ 4 times cross-sectional area at middepth)

Thus

Area at 17 ft diam = 17 × 17 × 0.7854 = 226.98 sq ft
Area at 18 ft diam = 18 × 18 × 0.7854 = 254.47 sq ft

Diameter at middepth is

$$\frac{18 + 17}{2} = 17.5 \text{ ft}$$

Area at middepth is 17.5 × 17.5 × 0.7854 = 240.53 sq ft. By substitution the formula becomes

Volume = $^{14}/_6$[226.98 + 254.47 + (4 × 240.53)] = 3368.33 cu ft

or   3368.33 × 7.48 = 25,195 gal   *Ans.*

2. CAPACITY PER INCH DEPTH

PROBLEM: Calculate the number of gallons contained per inch depth of an oil tank with vertical sides and a diameter of 10 ft $^1/_2$ in. What should the diameter be to contain 50 gal per inch of depth?

SOLUTION: Since 1 U.S. gal contains 231 cu in., this tank of 120.5 in. diameter would contain

$$\frac{120.5 \times 120.5 \times 0.7854}{231} = 49.37 \text{ gal per in. depth}$$

To contain 50 gal per inch of depth, the diameter must be

$$\sqrt{\frac{231 \times 50}{0.7854}} = 121.26 \text{ in.-about 10 ft } 1^1/_4 \text{ in.}   \textit{Ans.}$$

3. INCH OF WATER PRESSURE

PROBLEM: Explain the value of 1 in. of water pressure expressed in pounds or ounces per square inch.

SOLUTION: Pressure exerted per inch of depth of an incompressible liquid is the same pressure per square inch as the weight of 1 cu in. of the liquid.

At standard temperature of 62°F 1 cu ft of water weighs 62.355 lb. Assuming water to be incompressible, 1 in. of water pressure is equal to

$$\frac{62.355}{1728} = 0.03609 \text{ psi} = 0.03609 \times 16$$
$$= 0.5774 \text{ oz per sq in.}   \textit{Ans.}$$

4. CONVERSION OF INCHES OF VACUUM TO POUNDS PER SQUARE INCH _____

PROBLEM: Calculate the pressure equivalent to 26 in. of vacuum as indicated on a mercury column.

SOLUTION: Consider a column of mercury 1 in. high at ordinary temperature. Such a column would exert a pressure of 0.491 psi. The term "inches of vacuum" signifies the number of inches of mercury-column pressure *less* than the pressure of the atmosphere at the place it is observed.

When a vacuum gage indicates 26 in. of vacuum, the pressure is $26 \times 0.491 = 12.766$ psi *less* than the pressure of the atmosphere at that place. Also, the absolute pressure of the atmosphere varies with the elevation of the place. For example, at sea level it usually is assumed to be 14.7 psi. So at sea level the absolute pressure for 26 in. of vacuum would be

$$14.7 - 12.766 = 1.934 = \text{about 2 psia.} \quad Ans.$$

5. CAPACITY OF CYLINDRICAL TANKS _____

PROBLEM: Give a short rule for computing the number of gallons contained by a cylindrical tank of 72 in. diameter and 18 ft long having flat heads. Also give the allowance made when the heads of the tank are bumped to a slight radius.

SOLUTION: The formula for the capacity of a cylindrical tank with flat heads is

$$\text{Gallons capacity} = d^2 \times L \times 0.0408$$

where d = diameter of tank, in.
L = length of tank, ft

Thus cubical content in U.S. gallons of the flat-headed tank in this problem is

$$\frac{(72 \times 72 \times 0.7854) \times (18 \times 12)}{231} = (72)^2 \times 18 \times 0.0408$$
$$= 3.807.13 \text{ gal} \quad Ans.$$

where h = height of a bumped head, in.
d = diameter of bumped head, in.

The volume of one bumped head is

$$\frac{\left(\dfrac{h}{2} \times 0.7854 \times d^2\right) + (h^3 \times 0.5236)}{231} = \frac{h^3 \times 0.7854 \times d^2}{2 \times 231}$$
$$+ (h^3 \times 0.00226)$$

Thus two bumped heads contain the same number of gallons as a cylinder of diameter d and length h,

$$2(h^3 \times 0.00226) \text{ gal}$$

For complete capacity the formula including both bumped heads is

$$\text{Gallons capacity} = \left(d^2 \times \text{length of sides, ft} + \frac{h}{12}\right)$$
$$\times 0.0408 + 2(h^3 \times 0.00226)$$

NOTE: Tanks for holding liquids under atmospheric pressure usually are provided with heads that are bumped so little that the value obtained for $2(h^3 \times 0.00226)$ is only a small percentage of the total tank capacity. When there are two equal bumped heads, the capacity is given close enough for most practical purposes by the formula

$$\text{Number of gal} = (\text{diam. in.})^2 \times \text{length of side}$$
$$+ \text{height of head, ft} \times 0.0408 \quad Ans.$$

6. CUBIC YARDS IN FOUNDATION CONCRETE _____

PROBLEM: Calculate the number of cubic yards of concrete contained in an engine foundation 4 ft × 12 ft at the top, 6 ft × 14 ft at the base, and 5 ft 6 in. deep, with sides and ends battered.

NOTE: To *batter* means to give a receding upward slope of the outer face of a wall or other structure.

SOLUTION: When all dimensions are in feet, the contents in cubic feet is given by the prismodial formula

$$\text{Number of cu ft} = \frac{\left(\begin{array}{c}\text{area of top + area of base} \\ + \text{ 4 times sectional area at middepth}\end{array}\right)}{6 \times \text{total depth}}$$

The area of the top would be 4 × 12 = 48 sq ft, and that of the base would be 6 × 14 = 84 sq ft. The section at middepth would be

$$\left(\frac{4 + 6}{2}\right) \times \left(\frac{12 + 14}{2}\right) = 5 \text{ ft} \times 13 \text{ ft}$$

Thus the area of the middepth section would be 65 sq ft. Substituting these values and 5.5 ft for total depth gives

$$\text{Number of cu ft} = \frac{48 + 84 + (4 \times 65)}{6} \times 5.5 = 359.33 \text{ cu ft}$$

or

$$\frac{359.33}{27} = 13.31 \text{ cu yd} \quad \textit{Ans.}$$

SUGGESTED READING

Elonka, Stephen M., and Orville H. Johnson: "Standard Industrial Hydraulics Questions and Answers," McGraw-Hill Book Company, New York, 1967. (Has 25 calculations and formulas.)

Elonka, Stephen M., and Anthony L. Kohan: "Standard Boiler Operators' Questions and Answers," McGraw-Hill Book Company, New York, 1969.

Elonka, Stephen M., and Alonzo R. Parsons: "Standard Instrumentation Questions and Answers," vols. I and II, McGraw-Hill Book Company, New York, 1962. (Has 40 calculations and formulas.)

9

PUMPS AND PIPING SYSTEMS

Pumps and piping provide the arteries for fluids in energy systems. Here we cover 16 typical calculations, including velocities in pump lines, horsepower required to raise water, sizes of suction and discharge lines, pump characteristic curves, power required for pumping, water delivered by a given pipe line, and the diameter required for a steam line.

SOME TYPICAL PUMPING CALCULATIONS ————————

1. HEIGHT OF PUMPING WATER ———————————————

PROBLEM: Consider a direct-acting steam pump with steam piston 12 in. diameter and water piston of 8 in. diameter. If it is operated with steam at 110 psig, to what height in feet can the pump raise water at 70% efficiency?

SOLUTION: If the total pressure exerted on the steam piston is transmitted to the water piston, the 110 psig acting on the steam piston (opposed by back pressure of the atmosphere) will exert a pressure of

$$\frac{12^2}{10^2} \times 110 = 158.4 \text{ psig}$$

on the water piston.

A 1-ft head of water exerts a pressure of 0.433 psig, and without friction of water in the pump or pipes, the pump could raise the water to a height of $158.4 \div 0.433 = 365.8$ ft above the level assumed by the suction water under atmospheric pressure.

With 70% efficiency, the height would be

$$0.70 \times 365.8 = 256 \text{ ft} \quad \textit{Ans.}$$

2. VELOCITIES IN PUMP LINES _____

PROBLEM: What velocities are practical for waterpump suction and discharge lines, and why?

SOLUTION: The maximum velocities should *not* be exceeded, otherwise the loss of pressure from pipe friction may be too great for usual lengths of pipe lines. In the suction lines of pumps, the velocity of water should not exceed 240 ft per min. In the discharge lines the velocity of water should not be over 300 ft per min for best pump operation.

Pipe sizes approximately corresponding to these velocities are given by the formulas

$$\text{Suction diameter, in.} = \sqrt{0.1 \times G}$$
$$\text{Discharge diameter, in.} = \sqrt{0.08 \times G}$$

where G is the number of gallons pumped per minute.   *Ans.*

3. HORSEPOWER REQUIRED TO RAISE WATER _____

PROBLEM: Calculate the horsepower required to raise 2500 gal of water to a height of 60 ft.

SOLUTION: Horsepower is a rate of doing work; thus the number of horsepower required to be developed while raising 2500 gal of water to an elevation of 60 ft at a uniform rate depends on the *time* it takes. Since 1 gal of water weighs 8.33 lb, 2500 gal weighs $2500 \times 8.33 = 20{,}825$ lb.

If pumping the 2500 gal is performed in 1 hr, 20.825 ÷ 60 = 347.1 lb of water will be pumped per minute. And if elevated 60 ft, the net work performed would be

$$347.1 \times 60 = 20{,}825 \text{ ft-lb per min}$$

As 1 hp is developed by work at the rate of 33,000 ft-lb per min, the net power developed will be at the rate of

$$\frac{20{,}825}{33{,}000} = 0.6 \text{ hp}$$

Neglecting pipe friction, the power required to be developed on the steam end of a pump to develop an actual, or net, horsepower depends on its mechanical efficiency. For pumps of the size required, the mechanical efficiency would be probably only about 60%. Thus the indicated horsepower required on the steam end for developing 0.6 hp in the water end would be about

$$\frac{0.6}{0.6} = 1 \text{ ihp} \quad \textit{Ans.}$$

4. FORMULA FOR APPROXIMATE CAPACITY OF PUMP _____

PROBLEM: Explain the formula

$$g = \frac{D \times L \times N}{942}$$

for finding the number of gallons delivered by a reciprocating pump.

SOLUTION: In the formula

g = volume pumped, gpm
D = diameter of plunger or piston, in.
L = length of stroke, in.
N = number of single strokes per minute

Plunger or piston displacement in cubic inches per minute would be area of piston × length of stroke × number of single strokes per minute, or

$$D \times D \times 0.7854 \times L \times N$$

and as 1 gal equals 231 cu in.

$$g = \frac{D^2 \times 0.7854 \times L \times N}{231}$$

dividing both numerator and denominator of the second term by 0.7854 gives

$$g = \frac{D^2 \times L \times N}{294.117}$$

usually written

$$\frac{D^2 L N}{294}$$

If N is taken to represent the number of strokes of a single double-acting pump, multiply the result by 2, and if N represents the number of strokes of a duplex pump, which would be the same as two single pumps, multiply the result by 4.

Also, remember that the formula gives results larger than the actual capacity of a pump because it makes no allowances for reduction of capacity by slippage. In double-acting piston pumps displacement on one side of the piston is reduced by the area of the rod. *Ans.*

5. HORSEPOWER OF A RECIPROCATING PUMP _____

PROBLEM: Give the formula for finding the horsepower of a reciprocating pump.

SOLUTION: Five different values of horsepower of a reciprocating pump must be distinguished:

1. The indicated horsepower of the steam end, obtained from indicator diagrams of the steam end in the same way as the indicated power of a reciprocating engine

2. The brake horsepower, or power actually transmitted to the pump, which in a direct-acting steam pump consists of the indicated power of the steam end *less* the friction of parts essential to operation of the steam end

3. The indicated horsepower of the water end, obtained from indicator diagrams taken from the water cylinder to determine the power transmitted by the water piston or plunger

4. The water, or developed, horsepower to express the useful

work done by the pump, based on the actual *weight* of water discharged and total height through which the water is elevated

5. The nominal horsepower, based on the weight of water that would be displaced per minute by the plunger, or piston, if there were no slippage combined with the discharge pressure plus the lift, measured from the water level in the suction well to the height of the discharge gage

Thus, if the plunger or piston displacement is 1000 gpm, one would assume that the pump actually handles 1000 × weight of 1 gal of water, or

$$1000 \times 8^{1}/_{3} = 8333 \text{ lb of water per min}$$

If the discharge pressure indicated 40 psi and the height of the gage was 16 ft above the water level of the suction gage, the total lift would be considered as equivalent to

$$(40 \text{ psi} \times 2.3 \text{ ft per lb}) + 16 \text{ ft} = 108 \text{ ft}$$

or $\quad \dfrac{8333 \times 108}{33,000} = 27.27 \text{ nominal pump hp} \quad Ans.$

6. SIZES OF PUMP-SUCTION AND DISCHARGE LINES _____

PROBLEM: Give the formulas for determining the size of pump-suction and discharge diameters.

SOLUTION: The sizes of pump-suction and discharge piping lines are determined by the loss of pressure from pipe friction that is permissible when the pump is operated at its fullest required capacity. For a given length of pipe, the pressure required to overcome pipe friction is nearly inversely as the diameter and directly as the square of the velocity, or quantity of water flowing per minute.

Under ordinary conditions, suction pressure is constant and is sufficient to supply the pump and overcome the pipe friction and friction of the pump passages when the suction pipe diameter is of such a size that it requires no greater suction water velocity than 240 ft per min; that is, when

$$\text{Diameter of suction pipe, in.} = \sqrt{0.1 \times \text{gpm}} \quad Ans.$$

The loss of pressure permissible in a discharge line is limited only by the strength of the pump and the power available for its operation. As the loss of pressure in the discharge line for a given rate of pumpage is a matter of choice, the size of the discharge pipe may be much less than necessary for the suction line. Under average conditions, however, it is advisable to make the discharge pipe of such size that the velocity is not in excess of 300 ft per min; that is, to have

Diameter of discharge pipe, in. $= \sqrt{0.08 \times \text{gpm}}$ *Ans.*

7. FORMULA FOR COMPUTING PUMP CAPACITY _____

PROBLEM: Give the formula for estimating the capacity of a reciprocating pump.

SOLUTION: The capacity of a single double-acting pump can be calculated by the formula

$$Q = \frac{a \times F \times 12}{231}$$

where Q = displacement of one double-acting plunger, U.S. gal.
a = area of plunger, sq in.
F = piston speed, ft per min
  If d is the diameter of the plunger in inches, the formula becomes

$$Q = \frac{d^2 \times 0.7854 \times F \times 12}{231} = 0.0408 \times d^2 \times F \quad Ans.$$

NOTE: For actual capacity, the displacement by the piston rod and percentage of slip of the pump must be deducted.

8. POWER DEVELOPED BY A RECIPROCATING PUMP _____

PROBLEM: Calculate the horsepower developed by the operation of a single double-acting steam pump having a water cylinder of 14 in. bore and an 18-in. piston stroke. It makes 24 rpm (double strokes) while pumping against a head pressure if 85 psi.

SOLUTION: If we neglect the reduction of piston displacement due to the presence of the piston rod, the water horsepower (useful work) developed is

$$\frac{(85 \times \text{}^{18}/_{12})(14 \times 14 \times 0.7854)(24 \times 2)}{33,000} = 28.55 \text{ hp} \quad Ans.$$

NOTE: The power developed by the steam end would depend on the mechanical efficiency of the pump. A mechanical efficiency of 75% would require development of 28.55 ÷ 0.75 = 38.07 ihp in the steam cylinder of the pump. *Ans.*

9. STEAM PRESSURE REQUIRED FOR PUMPING _____

PROBLEM: Calculate the steam pressure required to operate a direct-acting steam pump having an 8-in.-diameter steam cylinder and 6-in.-diameter water cylinder if water is to be pumped to a height of 100 ft and suction water is supplied to the pump at 10 psi.

SOLUTION: First, the mechanical efficiency of a pump of the stated size (in good working order) would be only about 65%. As a 1-sq-in. column of water 1 ft high weighs 0.433 lb, the pressure pumped against would be

$$100 \times 0.433 = 43.3 \text{ psi}$$

But due to the head plus the pressure required to overcome friction of the water in the discharge pipe, the friction depends on the rate of pumping and the diameter, length, and fittings of the discharge pipe. Under normal conditions the loss of pressure from pipe friction would be no greater than 10 psi. If it is assumed to be equal to the suction pressure, the net resistance to movement of the water piston would be

$$6 \times 6 \times 0.7854 \times 43.3 = 1224 \text{ psi}$$

With 65% mechanical efficiency of the pump, the resistance to be overcome by the steam piston would be 1224 ÷ 0.65 = 1883 psi. For overcoming that resistance, the effective pressure required to be exerted on a direct-acting 8-in.-diameter steam piston would be

$$\frac{1883}{8 \times 8 \times 0.7854} = 37.46 \text{ psi}$$

Evidently the required boiler pressure must be equal to the effective pressure plus the back pressure and the reduction of the boiler pressure by throttling in the steam pipe and steam passages of the pump. Thus if we allow a back pressure of 4 psi and reduction by throttling of 10 psi, the required boiler pressure would be

$$37.46 + 4 + 10 = 51.46 = \text{about 52 psi}\quad Ans.$$

10. CHANGING THE HEAD OF A CENTRIFUGAL PUMP _____

PROBLEM: Assume a centrifugal pump rated at 300 gpm pumping against a head of 100 ft and driven by a 10-hp induction motor at 1750 rpm. If the head is reduced to 60 ft, will the motor be overloaded? If so, what changes must be made in the pump?

SOLUTION: Some pumps have a flat characteristic, or substantially *constant,* horsepower with change in head. Others have a rising head-delivery characteristic, which increases the horsepower as the head increases.

If characteristic curves cannot be obtained from the pump maker, it is not difficult to identify the type of pump. For example, if the pump runner is of the radial or forward-curved type, the pump is likely to *overload* the motor on decreased head. If the runner is the backward-curved type, it will probably operate satisfactorily on reduced head without change.

For a temporary job, the pump described can be used for a 60-ft head by closing the discharge valve just until discharge at this head is 300 gpm, but this uses excessive power and is not a per-

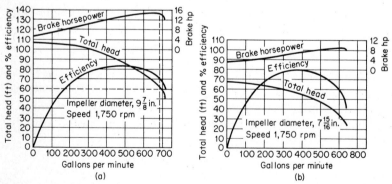

FIG. 9-1 Characteristic curve (*a*) shows (vertical dashed line) power increase; (*b*) shows power after reducing impeller diameter.

manent solution. If the discharge valve is *not* closed, the pump motor will certainly be overloaded. Figure 9-1*a* shows this by the vertical dashed line, which indicates power increase from 9.9 to 14.6 hp. This increase is due to the large increase in capacity in spite of lowered head.

Figure 9-1 show the result of a permanent change of reducing the impeller diameter. An actual test is indicated, in which the diameter was reduced from $9^7/_8$ to $7^{15}/_{16}$ in. Figure 9-1*b* also shows that the power required after reducing the impeller diameter is 5.9 hp. Obviously, some pumps have a power line that stays even with the reduced head, but even then, it is advisable to reduce the impeller diameter to save power consumption. *Ans.*

11. WEIGHT OF COMPRESSED AIR ─────────────

PROBLEM: Calculate the weight of 24 cu ft of dry air at a temperature of 125°F under a pressure of 26 psig.

SOLUTION: At atmospheric pressure, or 14.696 psia, 1 lb of dry air at 32°F, or an absolute temperature of 460 + 32 = 492°F, has a volume of 12.387 cu ft; and since the density is inversely as the absolute temperature and directly as the absolute pressure, the weight of 12 cu ft of air at the temperature of 125°F, or 460 + 125 = 585°F and pressure of 26 psig, or 26 + 14.696 = 40.696 psia, would be

$$\frac{492 \times 40.696 \times 24}{585 \times 14.696 \times 12.387} = 4.5 \text{ lb} \quad Ans.$$

12. HEIGHT OF WATER RAISED BY A STEAM TRAP ─────────

PROBLEM: Show how to calculate the height that a return steam trap will raise water.

SOLUTION: The height obviously depends on (1) the density of the water, (2) the pressure of steam acting on the water for expelling it from the trap, (3) the back pressure or pressure *ahead* of the water, and (4) the pressure required for overcoming friction of pipes, valves, and fittings.

Let us assume a density of water at 62°F, which is 62.36 lb per cu ft. A 1-ft column of water at that temperature exerts a pressure of 62.36 ÷ 144 = 0.433 psi for each pound pressure of steam in excess of back pressure and pressure required for overcoming friction. The water can be raised to a height of 1 ÷ 0.433 = 2.309 ft.

At 200°F, water weights 60.07 ÷ 144 = 0.417 psi. Thus without allowance for back pressure and pipe friction, for each pound pressure of steam acting on the surface of the water, it can be raised to a height of

$$\frac{1}{0.417} = 2.398 \text{ ft} \quad Ans.$$

13. SIZE OF PIPELINE AND POWER NEEDED FOR PUMPING

PROBLEM: (1) Calculate the diameter of iron pipe needed for a line 1200 ft long to deliver 15 gpm of water at 30 psi when pumped from a lake to an elevation of 85 ft. (2) If the pump is 5 ft above the lake, what is the pressure (static) on the pump from the line when the pump is *not* running? (3) What horsepower motor is needed for operating the pump?

SOLUTION: (1) For discharging 15 gpm through 1200 ft of smooth, clean 1¹/₄-in. iron or steel pipe, we learn from piping handbooks that the pressure needed for overcoming friction is about 42 psi; for 1¹/₂-in. pipe it is about 15 psi; and for 2-in. pipe about 6 psi. Remember that pressure increases with use because of friction in a pipeline caused by scale and corrosion. Thus, in this case, it would be best to provide a pipe of not less than 1¹/₂-in. diameter. *Ans.*

(2) With the discharge end of the line open to atmospheric pressure and the line filled with water, the static, or *standing,* pressure in the pipe at the pump is

$$(85 - 5) \times 0.433 = 34.6 \text{ psi} \quad Ans.$$

(3) Pumpage at the rate of 15 gpm with a total lift of 85 ft and discharge pressure of 30 psi (without allowance for power needed to overcome pipe friction) requires

$$\frac{30 + (85 \times 0.433)15 \times 231}{12 \times 33,000} \text{ about 0.6 net hp}$$

or water hp. If we assume a pump efficiency of 50%, the required power (neglecting pipe friction) would be

$$\frac{0.6}{0.50} = 1.2 \text{ hp}$$

At this pump efficiency, each pound pressure with discharge at the rate of 15 gpm requires

$$\frac{1 \times 15 \times 231}{12 \times 33,000 \times 0.50} = 0.0175 \text{ hp}$$

Thus the total power required using $1^1/_4$-in. pipe is

$$(0.0175 \times 42) + 1.2 = 1.9 \text{ hp}$$

For $1^1/_2$-in. pipe the power needed would be

$$(0.0175 \times 15) + 1.2 = 1.5 \text{ hp}$$

and for 2-in. pipe it would be

$$(0.0175 \times 6) + 1.2 = 1.3 \text{ hp}$$

Since pump friction increases with use of the pipeline because of an increase of roughness caused by scale and corrosion, an electric motor of not less than 2 hp should be used.   *Ans.*

14. WATER DELIVERED BY A 6-in. PIPELINE _____

PROBLEM: With a 25-ft head, what quantity of water can be delivered through a 6-in. cast-iron pipe 1000 ft long?

SOLUTION: Obviously, the highest rate of flow will be obtained when the whole head is absorbed in overcoming friction at the entrance and pipe friction through the pipe and in producing the velocity with delivery from the discharge end at atmospheric pressure.

Taking all this into consideration, figures obtained from piping handbooks for a 25-ft head available, for a *clean* 6-in. cast-iron pipe line 1000 ft long, with delivery at atmospheric pressure indicate a discharge of about 500 gpm. For delivery of 400 gpm, the loss of head is about 15 ft, leaving a discharge head of 10 ft; for 300 gal a loss of head of about 8.5 ft, leaving a discharge head of 16.5 ft; for 200 gal a loss of head of about 4 ft, leaving a discharge head of 21 ft; and for 100 gpm a loss of head of about 1 ft leaving a discharge head of 24 ft. *Ans.*

15. PRESSURE EXERTED BY WATER AND MERCURY _____

PROBLEM: Calculate the indication of a pressure gage placed at the foot of a 6-in. standpipe 100 ft high when the pipe is filled with water and when filled with mercury.

SOLUTION: Assuming that both liquids are at 62°F, the pressure of a column of water 1 ft high is 0.433 psi, and that of a column of mercury 1 ft high is 5.892 psi.

A pressure gage placed so that the center of the gage is level with the foot of the water column 100 ft high would indicate,

$$0.433 \times 100 = 43.3 \text{ psi} \quad \textit{Ans.}$$

The gage connected so that its center is level with the foot of the mercury column 100 ft high would indicate

$$5.892 \times 100 = 589.2 \text{ psi} \quad \textit{Ans.}$$

NOTE: In each case, the pressure shown by the gage depends on the height of the liquid (mercury is a metallic element that is liquid at ordinary temperatures) and is independent of the *diameter* of the standpipe. Don't be fooled by the 6-in.-diameter standpipe given here.

16. LOWER PRESSURE, LARGER SAFETY VALVE _____

PROBLEM: Consider two boilers of the *same* dimensions throughout, each provided with the same size of grate, kind of fuel, and draft. The temperature of the feedwater in *each* case is 200°F. One boiler is allowed to carry a working pressure of 50 psig, the other 150 psig. Show by calculation which should have the *larger* safety valve.

SOLUTION: The boiler with the lower pressure should have the *larger* safety valve; here's why. Napier's approximate formula for the discharge of steam from a safety valve states

$$\text{Flow, lb per sec} = \text{absolute pressure} \times \frac{\text{area, sq in}}{70}$$

This means that the escape area required is directly as the weight and inversely as the absolute pressure. Thus, the safety valve for discharging steam at 165 psia would need to have only 65/165, or about 40%, as much area of opening as for discharging as much steam as would be generated at 65 psia for the same amount of heat transmitted by the boiler. *Ans.*

NOTE: Keep in mind that gage pressure is pressure *above* atmospheric pressure. Atmospheric pressure is 14.7 psi (use 15) at sea level and decreases as height above sea level increases. The gage on steam boilers indicates *gage* pressure.

17. DIAMETER OF STEAM PIPE

PROBLEM: Calculate the diameter of a steam pipe for a continuous flow of 6000 lb per hr at pressure of 90 psig and velocity assumed to be (about) 7000 ft per min.

SOLUTION: First, the specific volume of dry saturated steam at 90 psig (105 psia) is 4.23 cu ft per lb, and the volume discharged per minute would be

$$\frac{6000 \times 4.23}{60} = 423 \text{ cu ft}$$

Handling this flow at 7000 ft per min would require a pipe with a cross-sectional area of

$$\frac{423}{7000} = 0.0604 \text{ sq ft} = 8.7 \text{ sq in.}$$

which is a diameter of 3.33 in. The nearest commercial pipe is $3\frac{1}{2}$ in. *Ans.*

SUGGESTED READING

Higgins, Alex, and Stephen M. Elonka: "Boiler Room Questions and Answers," 2d ed., McGraw-Hill Book Company, New York, 1976.
Elonka, Stephen M., and Joseph F. Robinson: "Standard Plant Operators' Questions and Answers," vols. I and II, McGraw-Hill Book Company, New York, 1959.

10

CALCULATING EFFICIENCY

Evaluating the efficiency of equipment in energy systems is a never-ending job for the plant operator. It tells him when to overhaul a unit and when to replace it. Here we cover a few basics and go right into some typical calculations needed to reduce fuel bills.

FIGURING EFFICIENCY

Almost any kind of machine efficiency is easy to figure. If a machine could give out as much as went into it, the efficiency would be 100%. That never happens, although big generators and hydro turbines get close to this perfect mark.

A machine that delivers half its input has an efficiency of 50%. One that delivers three-quarters has an efficiency of 75%, and so on. The input and output being considered may be work, heat, mechanical power, or electrical power. The important thing is to figure both the input and output in the *same* kinds of units—horsepower, kilowatthours, Btu, or foot-pounds.

EXAMPLE: Input and output are in like units in Figs. 10-1 and 10-2. In Fig. 10-1 both input and output are measured in foot-

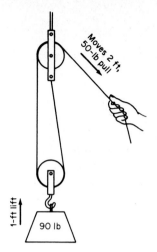

FIG. 10-1 A pull of 2 ft lifts a 90-lb load 1 ft; the efficiency is 90%.

pounds. The pull has to be 50 lb to lift 90 lb and for each 2-ft pull the load rises 1 ft. Then

$$\text{Input} = 50 \times 2 = 100 \text{ ft-lb}$$
$$\text{Output} = 90 \times 1 = 90 \text{ ft-lb}$$
$$\text{Efficiency} = \frac{90}{100} = 0.90 = 90\%$$

In the motor-generator set (Fig. 10-2) both input and output are in kilowatts. By feeding 103 kW to the motor we get 79 kW out of the generator. Then

$$\text{Efficiency} = \frac{79}{103} = 0.767 = 76.7\%$$

In Fig. 10-3 the input is indicated horsepower and output is brake horsepower, yet both are mechanical horsepower. The indi-

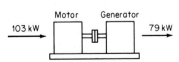

FIG. 10-2 The efficiency of this motor-generator set is 76.7%.

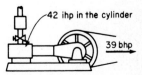

FIG. 10-3 The mechanical efficiency of this engine is 92.9%.

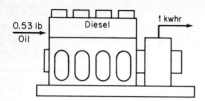

FIG. 10-4 The overall efficiency of this diesel generating set is 33.4%.

cated horsepower is the mechanical power delivered by the steam to the piston, and the brake horsepower is the mechanical power delivered by the engine to the load. Thus the efficiency of the engine in converting cylinder power into useful power (mechanical efficiency) is

$$\frac{39}{42} = 0.929 = 92.9\%$$

The diesel generating set (Fig. 10-4) is different. Here input is heat, and output is electricity. For every kilowatthour delivered this engine burns 0.53 lb of 19,300-Btu oil. The input per kilowatthour is

$$0.53 \times 19,300 = 10,230 \text{ Btu}$$

Table 10-1 shows that 1 kWhr = 3413 Btu; so

$$\text{Input} = 10,230 \text{ Btu}$$
$$\text{Output} = 3413 \text{ Btu}$$

$$\text{Efficiency} = \frac{3413}{10,230} = 0.334 = 33.4\%$$

TABLE 10-1   Conversion Factors

1 kW = 1.3415 hp	1 hp = 424 Btu per min
= 738 ft-lb per sec	= 2544 Btu per hr
= 44,268 ft-lb per min	
= 2,656,100 ft-lb per hr	1 Btu = 778.3 ft-lb
= 56.9 Btu per min	
= 3413 Btu per hr	1 kWhr = 3413 Btu
	= 1.342 hp-hr
1 hp = 0.7455 kW	
= 550 ft-lb per sec	
= 33,000 ft-lb per min	1 hp-hr = 2544 Btu
= 1,980,000 ft-lb per hr	= 0.7455 kWhr

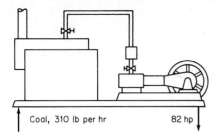

FIG. 10-5 Only 4.98% efficiency is produced by this small steam plant exhausting to waste.

Coal, 310 lb per hr   82 hp

Now assume that the simple steam plant in Fig. 10-5 blows all exhaust to waste and that when it delivers 82 hp, the fuel burned is 310 lb per hr of 13,500-Btu coal. Then 310 ÷ 82 = 3.78 lb coal per boiler horsepower, so

$$\text{Input} = 3.78 \times 13,500 = 51,030 \text{ Btu}$$
$$\text{Output} = 2544 \text{ Btu} \quad \text{(see Table 10-1)}$$
$$\text{Efficiency} = \frac{2544}{51,030} = 0.498 = 4.98\%$$

The motor in Fig. 10-6 delivers 9.2 hp at its pulley when drawing 8.4 kW from the line. What is the motor efficiency at this load? Input and output must be in the same units, so we convert the 8.4 kW input into horsepower, using the constant 1.341 from Table 10-1. Then

$$\text{Input} = 8.4 \times 1.341 = 11.26 \text{ hp}$$
$$\text{Useful output} = 9.2 \text{ hp}$$
$$\text{Efficiency} = \frac{9.2}{11.26} = 0.817 = 81.7\%$$

In Fig. 10-7 we have the reverse case, a generator is driven by a steam turbine. Generator output is 15,200 kW, and input (from the shaft of the turbine) is 23,000 hp. Then

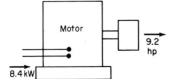

Motor

9.2 hp

FIG. 10-6 The motor efficiency here figures 81.7%.

8.4 kW

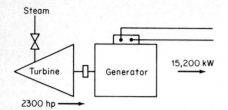

FIG. 10-7 The electric generator efficiency is 88.7%.

$$\text{Input} = 23,000 \times 0.745 = 17,135 \text{ kW}$$
$$\text{Efficiency} = \frac{15,200}{17,135} = 0.887 = 88.7\%$$

It is just as easy to figure the overall efficiency of a complete power plant. No understanding of the interior arrangements or equipment is required. For example, it is enough to know that the steam plant shown in Fig. 10-8 delivered 34,400,000 kWhr of electrical energy in a certain month during which it burned 20,400 tons of coal having a heat value of 13,300 Btu per lb.

In a case of this sort we may take input and useful output on a monthly basis, or work in terms of the input per kilowatthour output. Coal fired per month was $20,400 \times 2000 = 40,800,000$ lb. This is $40,800,000 \div 34,400,000 = 1.186$ lb per kWhr.

$$\text{Heat input per kWhr} = 1.186 \times 13,300 = 15,775 \text{ Btu}$$
$$\text{Useful output per kWhr} = 3413 \text{ Btu (see Table 10-1)}$$
$$\text{Efficiency} = \frac{3413}{15,775} = 0.216 = 21.6\%$$

The hydro plant (Fig. 10-9) is equally simple, assuming that we want overall efficiency, including the losses in penstocks and tail pipes. Since 1 cu ft of water weighs 62.5 lb, 3400 cu ft per sec is

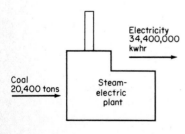

FIG. 10-8 The overall efficiency of this plant is only 21.6%.

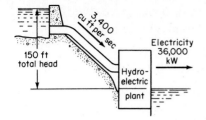

FIG. 10-9 With losses in penstock and tail pipes, the efficiency of this hydro installation is 83.4%.

212,500 lb per sec. Falling through the total head of 150 ft, this represents an energy supply of 212,500 × 150 = 31,875,000 ft-lb per sec. Since 1 kW = 738 ft-lb per sec,

$$\text{Input} = \frac{31,875,000}{738} = 43,190 \text{ kW}$$

$$\text{Efficiency} = \frac{36,000}{43,190} = 0.834 = 83.4\%$$

For the motor-driven pump in Fig. 10-10 find the overall efficiency of the system, including all losses in motor, pumps, and

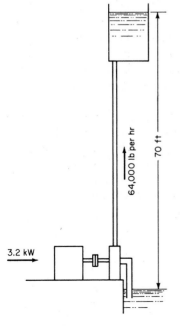

FIG. 10-10 Piping and motor losses reduce the pumping efficiency to 52.7%.

piping. In this case the input is electrical energy, and the output is the energy in 64,000 lb of water raised 70 ft. Then

$$\text{Useful output} = 64,000 \times 70 = 4,480,000 \text{ ft-lb per hr}$$
$$\text{Input} = 3.2 \times 2,656,000 = 8,499,200 \text{ ft-lb per hr}$$
$$\text{Efficiency} = \frac{4,480,000}{8,499,200} - 0.527 = 52.7\%$$

BOILER EFFICIENCY

The formula for boiler efficiency is the same as that for the efficiency of practically any other piece of power equipment: *Efficiency is the useful energy output divided by the energy input.*

In a boiler unit, we feed in Btu in the form of coal, oil, or gas. We get out useful Btu in the form of steam.

Boiler efficiency can be figured directly from the total fuel burned in a given period and the total water evaporated in the same period. It is more common to figure, first, the evaporation per pound of coal fired and the efficiency from this.

EXAMPLE: For one calendar month of regular operation in a certain plant, the coal consumed is 682,000 lb, and the steam generated is 6,411,000 lb. What is the actual evaporation per pound of coal? First, the actual evaporation per pound of coal fired is 6,411,000 ÷ 682,000 = 9.40 lb. Then, boiler efficiency = useful heat output ÷ heat input = heat to make 9.4 lb of steam ÷ heat content of 1 lb of coal.

For rough estimates of efficiency the heat content of the coal may be taken from the statement of the company supplying the coal. For accurate work the operator must collect a good average sample of the coal and send it to a laboratory for testing. Let's say the figure is 13,260 Btu per pound of coal as fired. Then, boiler efficiency = heat to make 9.4 lb of steam ÷ 13,260.

Note carefully *"heat to make* steam" is not the same as *"heat in* steam." You cannot credit the boiler with all the heat in the steam leaving the boiler, because part of it was in the water fed to the boiler. The boiler unit can be credited only with the heat *put into* the water and steam by the boiler.

All figures for "heat" in water or steam (as given in the steam tables published by ASME and others) are measured above water at

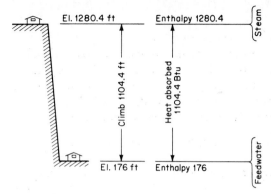

FIG. 10-11 The difference in enthalpy between feedwater and steam equals heat required to convert feedwater into steam.

32°F. That is the zero point for heat content, just as sea level is the zero point for elevations (Fig. 10-11).

To compute the vertical distance climbed in going from one locality to another, you take the difference between their elevations, both measured above sea level. To compute the amount of heat required to convert 1 lb of water at the feedwater temperature into steam at the boiler-outlet pressure and temperature, you subtract the "heat" in the water from the "heat" in the steam, both measured above water at 32°F as given in the steam tables.

Suppose the steam is delivered at 179 psig pressure and superheated to an actual temperature of 520°F. First find the *absolute* steam pressure by adding 15 lb: 179 + 15 = 194 psia. Then, turning to the steam tables, you find that the "total heat" of 1 lb of steam at 194 psia and 520°F is 1280.4 Btu.

If the feedwater temperature is 208°F, its "heat content," above water at 32°F, is merely 208 − 32 = 176 Btu. Therefore, the heat *put into* each pound by the boiler is 1280.4 − 176.0 = 1104.4 Btu. Heat put into 9.4 lb will be 10,381 Btu. Then

$$\text{Boiler efficiency} = \frac{\text{output}}{\text{input}} = \frac{\text{heat put into 9.4 lb steam}}{\text{heat in 1 lb of coal}}$$

$$= \frac{10,381 \text{ Btu}}{13,260 \text{ Btu}} = 0.783 = 78.3\%$$

Enthalpy

We have talked about the heat *in the water* and the heat *in the steam* because these expressions are old and familiar to most engineers, but, as pointed out in Chap. 4, what we have called heat in the steam is now termed the enthalpy of the vapor, and heat in the water is now enthalpy of the saturated liquid. Thus, using the modern steam tables for the given problem, we should write

Enthalpy of superheated vapor at 194 psia and 520°F
$$= 1280.4$$
Enthalpy of saturated liquid at 208°F $= \underline{\quad 176.0\quad}$
Difference $= 1104.4$ Btu

As before, the 1104.4 Btu is the heat required to make 1 lb of steam from the given feedwater.

STEAM-ENGINE EFFICIENCY _____

Here is the rule again: *Efficiency of any machine is its useful output divided by its input, both measured in the same units of power or energy.* This rule is correct for a steam engine or turbine if one clearly understands what is meant by input in this case. Since the input is heat, it is easy to assume that input is the heat in the steam supplied to the throttle of the engine or turbine. But the heat in the throttle steam, by itself, means nothing in terms of engine heat consumption because this heat is measured above 32°F, which is an arbitrary point and bears no relation to the facts of plant operation.

Another point to remember is that the engine turns some heat back to the boiler in the form of feedwater and should get credit for the hottest feedwater its exhaust could produce, that is, for the hot water at the saturation temperature corresponding to the pressure of the exhaust steam. Subtract the heat in that water from that in the throttle steam to get the net per pound charged against the engine.

This subtraction eliminates the effect of the 32°F base and leaves an absolute amount of heat, just as the difference between the two elevations, both measured above some arbitrary sea level, is the true distance you would climb in going from the bottom to the top of the chimney (Fig. 10-12).

Assume that the engine takes in superheated steam at 400°F total

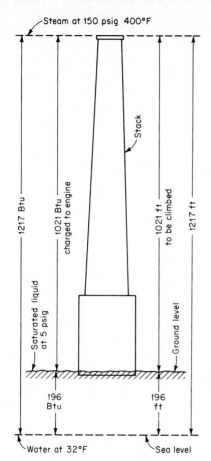

FIG. 10-12 The difference in heat content between throttle steam and feedwater at exhaust temperatures gives heat per pound chargeable as engine input.

temperature and 150 psig and exhausts at 5 psig. The steam tables show that the heat in this throttle steam is 1217 Btu per lb and that the heat of the liquid at exhaust temperature is 196 Btu. The difference (chargeable to the engine as input) is 1021 Btu per lb.

If the engine uses 30 lb of steam per hp-hr,

Input per hp-hr = 30 × 1021 = 30,630 Btu
Corresponding useful output (1 hp-hr) = 2544 Btu (Table 10-1)

$$\text{Efficiency} = \frac{2544}{30630} = 0.083 = 8.3\%$$

Exactly the same method of computation is used if the engine or turbine exhausts to condenser, provided no steam is bled from the unit. Where steam is bled for feedwater heating only, the turbine supplies the boiler, in effect, with feedwater at the exit-water temperature of the feed heater fed by the highest bleed point. Therefore, for each pound of steam delivered to the throttle, charge the turbine with the heat of throttle steam minus the heat in the water leaving the last feed heater.

Attempts have been made to standardize the figuring of efficiency where all or part of the exhaust steam and bled steam goes to heating and process, but there is no general agreement on how such cases should be computed.

It is clear, however, that any heat supplied to the process by exhaust or bled steam really becomes part of the *useful* output. Thus, where no steam is lost to condenser or atmosphere, it is sensible to look upon a steam engine or turbine as having an overall efficiency of 80 or 90%. In that case, all heat supplied is usefully employed except that small portion lost in external friction, radiation, and electrical losses. Nevertheless, it is customary to figure the efficiency of any back-pressure engine or turbine as if all its exhaust heat were completely wasted except the small portion that could be absorbed in heating feedwater.

An engine that figured very low in efficiency on this basis might in fact be part of a phenomenally efficient plant if all exhaust were utilized for process and heating.

SOME TYPICAL EFFICIENCY CALCULATIONS ――――――――

1. MECHANICAL EFFICIENCY OF AN ENGINE ――――――――

PROBLEM: Calculate (1) the mechanical efficiency and (2) brake horsepower of an engine developing 142 ihp and with *no* load on the engine 19.5 ihp.

SOLUTION: (1) The mechanical efficiency of an engine, or its efficiency considered simply as a machine, is the ratio of the brake horsepower to the indicated horsepower, or

$$\text{Mechanical efficiency} = \frac{\text{bhp}}{\text{ihp}} \quad \textit{Ans.}$$

(2) The difference between the indicated horsepower and the brake horsepower is the amount of power required to overcome friction. With most steam engines this difference, called the *friction horsepower,* is practically constant for all loads from zero to full load. Thus the brake horsepower developed for any indicated power is assumed to be the indicated horsepower *minus* the friction horsepower, or horsepower indicated when the engine runs at its regular speed with no load. Thus in this example

$$\text{bhp} = 142 - 19.5 = 122.5$$

$$\text{Mechanical efficiency} = \frac{\text{bhp}}{\text{ihp}} = \frac{122.5}{142} = 0.86 = 86\% \quad Ans.$$

2. THE DIFFERENCE BETWEEN THERMAL EFFICIENCY AND ENGINE EFFICIENCY

PROBLEM: (1) What is thermal efficiency of a steam engine, and (2) how does it differ from the engine efficiency?

SOLUTION: (1) The proportion of total heat consumption which is converted into work is called the *thermal efficiency.* It is found by dividing 2544 (Btu equivalent to 1 hp-hr) by the number of heat units actually consumed per horsepower-hour. The quotient is multiplied by 100 to express the thermal efficiency in percent. The formula is

$$\text{Thermal efficiency} = \frac{2544}{W(H_1 - q_2)}$$

where W = steam as supplied per ihp-hr, lb
  H_1 = total heat above 32°F per lb of steam at initial conditions prevailing before throttle valve
  q_2 = heat of liquid above 32°F in 1 lb of water at temperature of saturated steam at exhaust pressure

(2) *Engine efficiency* is the ratio obtained by dividing the heat equivalent of the actual work done by the heat available for an ideal engine. The accepted standard for the ideal steam engine is the Rankine cycle. Engine efficiency is obtained from

$$\text{Engine efficiency (ihp)} = \frac{2544}{W(H_1 - H_2)}$$

where W = steam per ihp-hr, lb
H_1 = total heat above 32°F per lb of steam at initial conditions prevailing before throttle valve
H_2 = total heat above 32°F per lb of steam after adiabatic expansion from initial conditions to final pressure

NOTE: H_1 and H_2 can be found from any total heat-entropy diagram, supplied with steam tables published by the ASME. $H_1 - H_2$ is the heat available for work.

SUGGESTED READING

Elonka, Stephen M., and Anthony L. Kohan: "Boiler Operators' Questions and Answers," McGraw-Hill Book Company, New York, 1969.

Elonka, Stephen M., and Joseph F. Robinson: "Standard Plant Operators' Questions and Answers," vols. I and II, McGraw-Hill Book Company, New York, 1959.

11

HORSEPOWER OF
HEAT ENGINES

Finding boiler horsepower and indicated horsepower of engines and measuring brake horsepower involve fairly simple calculations. They help the plant operator understand his equipment and get the maximum efficiency from each unit. Here we'll start with boiler horsepower, an old-fashioned measure that should be abolished but is still used by some license examiners.

BOILER HORSEPOWER

Years ago an ASME committee decided that a good noncondensing engine of that day would take 30 lb of steam per hr to generate 1 mechanical horsepower. Also that the average boiler of that day could generate about 3 lb of steam per sq ft of water-heating surface. Thus 10 sq ft would generate 30 lb, and 10 sq ft should be rated as 1 boiler horsepower; therefore 30 lb of steam per hr would develop 1 boiler horsepower. So 1 boiler horsepower was stated as $34\frac{1}{2}$ lb of steam per hr from and at 212°F, meaning the evaporation of $34\frac{1}{2}$ lb of water at 212°F into steam at the same temperature at atmospheric pressure.

Because boilers don't usually run under these conditions, a

factor of evaporation was invented to convert actual evaporation from and at 212°F. If the feedwater temperature is 184°F and the steam is at 100 psig and 500°F, this factor is 1.16. This means that it takes 1.16 times as much heat to generate 1 lb of steam under these conditions as from, and at, 212°F.

Let's assume that a boiler operating under these conditions has 2000 sq ft of heating surface and generates 65,000 lb per hr. The rated boiler horsepower will be

$$\frac{2000}{10} = 200$$

The 65,000 lb per hr will be equivalent to

65,000 × 1.16 = 75,400 lb from, and at, 212°F

Dividing 75,400 by 34.5, we get 218 developed horsepower. Then

$$100 \times \frac{218}{200} = 109\% \text{ rating}$$

But 10 sq ft of water-heating surface in a modern boiler will generate anywhere from 50 to 500 lb of steam per hour (500 lb in many large central-station boilers), and some large modern turbines use as little as 5 lb of steam per hp-hr, instead of 30. So 1 boiler horsepower can serve anywhere up to 100 mechanical horsepower.

The makers and users of large boilers discarded *boiler horsepower* long ago. Both the capacity and actual loads of such units are clearly stated as so many pounds of steam per hour, and that's that. In some smaller plants boiler horsepower still hangs on and may for years to come, but it really doesn't rate the boiler's capacity.

INDICATED HORSEPOWER OF ENGINE

Work is merely force times the distance moved. If we pull 50 lb to drag a weight 100 ft across the floor, the work is 50 × 100 = 5000 ft-lb.

The power of a steam or internal combustion engine may refer to either the *brake* horsepower delivered at the shaft or the *indicated* horsepower as determined from the diagrams drawn by an engine indicator that shows the pressure at all points of the stroke.

The *indicated horsepower* of an engine is merely the net power delivered to the piston faces by the expanding steam or gas in the cylinder. The amount of work so performed in 1 min divided by 33,000 will be the indicated horsepower.

The first and most important step is finding the net useful push on the piston. Remember that the work delivered to the piston during the working stroke is partly offset by the work the piston returns to the steam or gas during the exhaust stroke.

In Fig. 11-1*a* pressure falls as shown by the curve when the piston face moves from *A* to *B*. Find the average pressure from the average height of the curve between *A* and *B*. This average pressure, in pounds per square inch, multiplied by the area of the piston face in square inches gives the average force or push on the piston. This force multiplied by length *AB* gives the work done during the stroke.

Figure 11-1*b* shows a steam-engine indicator diagram. The steam delivers work to the piston during the power stroke and takes back part of this work during the exhaust stroke. In Fig. 11-1*c* the shaded area all the way down to the atmospheric-pressure line represents the work done on the piston during the working stroke. In Fig. 11-1*d* the black area is the work returned during the exhaust stroke; so this area is the net or useful work per working stroke.

Perhaps a simpler way to look at it is to consider that the average height of the diagram from the top line to the bottom line repre-

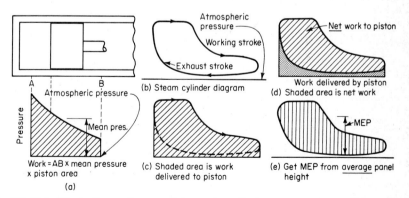

FIG. 11-1 The indicator diagram of the engine tells the operator the conditions of cylinder assembly and the indicated horsepower of the engine.

sents the net useful pressure. This is merely the average pressure on the working stroke minus the average pressure on the exhaust stroke and is called the *mean effective pressure* (MEP).

To get the MEP either use a planimeter or figure the average height of a lot of narrow strips as shown in Fig. 11-1e. Then the indicated horsepower for each piston face in the engine will be

$$\text{ihp} = \frac{PLAN}{33,000}$$

where $P = MEP$
L = length of stroke, *ft*
A = net area of piston face, in. (subtract area of rod in case of crank end)
N = number of working strokes per min

PROBLEM: Calculate the indicated horsepower of a simple double-acting steam engine with the following data.

Piston diameter = 10 in.
Rod diameter = 2 in.
Stroke = 12 in.
Speed = 350 rpm
Head-end MEP = 42 psi
Crank-end MEP = 43 psi

SOLUTION:

Head-end area = 87.5 sq in.
Rod area = 3.1 sq in.
Crank-end area = 84.4 sq in.
Stroke = 1 ft

$$\text{Head-end ihp} = \frac{42 \times 1 \times 87.5 \times 350}{33,000} = 38.9 \text{ hp}$$

$$\text{Crank-end ihp} = \frac{43 \times 1 \times 84.4 \times 350}{33,000} = 38.5 \text{ hp}$$

Total ihp = 38.9 + 38.5 = 77.4 hp   *Ans.*

These operations are ordinarily written as a formula, like this

$$\text{hp} = \frac{PLAN}{33,000}$$

This formula is simply an abbreviated statement of the following rule: indicated horsepower (figured separately for each end) = mean effective pressure × stroke (in feet) × area of piston (in square inches) × working strokes per minute ÷ 33,000.

FIGURING THE FACTOR

Note that the formula

$$\text{ihp} = \frac{PLAN}{33,000}$$

can be written

$$\text{ihp} = \frac{LA}{33,000} \times P \times N$$

Since $LA/33,000$ never changes for a given end of a given engine, we can figure it out once and for all and call it the *factor*. Thus we figure the indicated horsepower of either end as the product of its factor by the mean effective pressure and the revolutions per minute.

Here's how to work out factors for a simple double-acting engine of 15-in. bore, 16-in. stroke, and $2\frac{1}{2}$-in. piston rod (remember that the area of a circle is its diameter squared times 0.7854).

$$\text{Area of head end} = 15^2 \times 0.7854 = 176.5 \text{ sq in.}$$
$$\text{Area of piston rod} = 2.5^2 \times 0.78 = \underline{4.9 \text{ sq in.}}$$
$$\text{Area of crank end (difference)} = 171.6 \text{ sq in.}$$

$$\text{Stroke} = \frac{16}{12} = 1.333 \text{ ft}$$

$$\text{Head-end factor} = \frac{LA}{33,000} = \frac{1.333 \times 176.5}{33,000} = 0.00713$$

$$\text{Crank-end factor} = \frac{LA}{33,000} = \frac{1.333 \times 171.6}{33,000} = 0.00693$$

To be systematic, rule up a form (Table 11-1), enter the data, and compute across, left to right as shown. In the first line (head end) we divide 1.21 by 3.83 to get 0.316 and then multiply 0.316 by 80 to get 25.3; now multiply 25.3 by 225 and then by 0.00713 to get the head-end ihp = 40.6. Follow the same course for the

TABLE 11-1 Form for Figuring ihp

| End, head or crank | Area, sq in. | Indicator diagram | | | P (mean effective pressure) | N, (rpm) | Factor | ihp (PN × factor) |
		Length, in.	Average height, in.	Scale of spring, lb per in.				
Head	1.21	3.83	0.316	80	25.3	225	0.00713	40.6
Crank	1.24	3.83	0.324	80	25.9	225	0.00693	40.4
Total								81.0

214

crank end to get 40.4 ihp. Then add the two for a total of 81.0 ihp of engine. *Ans.*

MEASURING BRAKE HORSEPOWER

The indicated horsepower (ihp) of a reciprocating engine is the power delivered by the steam (or gas, in case of an oil or gas engine) to the working end or ends of the piston. Brake horsepower is the power actually delivered by the whole engine to the connected load, which may be generator, belt, or brake.

We call it brake horsepower because it is sometimes conveniently measured by a prony brake. The brake horsepower (bhp) of an engine is always less than the ihp by the total of various friction losses of the engine. Generally the bhp runs from 80 to 90% of the ihp, which is just another way of saying that the mechanical efficiency runs from 80 to 90%.

Fig. 11-2 shows a very simple prony brake, a double loop of rope running around a pulley or flywheel, with a threaded hook and nut to tighten the rope. The frame holding the ends of the rope bears directly on platform scales. To operate, tighten the nut to put the desired load on the engine and then balance the scales. Measure the engine speed. The radius of action of the force is measured to the centerline of the rope. No other data are necessary.

The radius is measured to the center of the rope rather than to the rim of the wheel because the brake acts as if the rim of the wheel were tangent to the centerline of the rope, that is, to the line

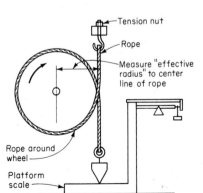

FIG. 11-2 Prony brake measures brake horsepower.

through which the force is transmitted vertically to the scales. This distance is called the *effective radius* or the lever arm.

The scale reading can then be looked upon as a force dragging on this imaginary wheel. When a body is moved against a force, the work done, in foot-pounds, is simply the number of feet traveled multiplied by the force in pounds.

To make this clear, let's assume a brake test in which the wheel diameter is 26 in., rope diameter 1 in., engine speed 165 rpm, and the force on the scales 128 lb. Then the wheel radius is 13 in. Adding half the rope diameter, we get 13.5 in. effective radius. Divide this by 12 to get the radius in feet: $13.5 \div 12 = 1.125$ effective radius.

The circumference of any circle is 2 × radius × 3.1416 so the effective circumference of the pulley will be $2 \times 1.125 \times 3.1416 = 7.0686$, say 7.07.

The engine is turning 165 rpm, so the distance traveled in 1 min is $165 \times 7.07 = 1166.55$ ft. Call it 1166 ft. The force measured by the scales is 128 lb, so the work done in 1 min is $1166 \times 128 = 149.248$ ft-lb. Call this 149,200 for simplicity.

To turn this into horsepower is easy, since 1 hp is defined as the production of work at the rate of 33,000 ft-lb per min. All we have to do is divide the actual foot-pounds delivered per minute by 33,000, giving us $149,200 \div 33,000 = 4,52$ hp. This, obviously, is a very small engine, suited to the simple type of brake employed.

We worked through the foregoing example step by step for clearness. In practice it will save time to use a formula. This formula can be developed exactly as this problem was solved:

Bhp = effective radius, ft × 2 × 3.1416 × rpm × force, all divided by 33,000. This comes down to

$$bhp = \frac{(r/12) \times 2 \times 3.1416 \, NF}{33,000}$$

$$= \frac{rNF}{63,025}$$

where r = effective radius, in.
       N = rpm
       F = force

or $$bhp = \frac{rNF}{63,000}$$

for all practical purposes.

Remember that in *this* formula we must use the effective radius *in inches*. For a check, let's apply the formula to the problem already worked out. Then bhp = 13.5 × 165 × 128 ÷ 63,000 = 4.52 hp *Ans.*

SOME TYPICAL HORSEPOWER CALCULATIONS _____

1. HORSEPOWER OF A DIESEL ENGINE _____

This can be calculated from indicator cards or in the shop from mechanical and electrical brake tests from which the brake horsepower is calculated. The brake mean effective pressure (BMEP) ranges from 63 to 68 psi in 2-cycle engines and from 70 to 85 in 4-cycle units.

$$\text{Thermal efficiency of diesel} = \frac{\text{work done, Btu}}{\text{Btu in fuel}}$$

$$= \frac{\text{work, ft-lb}}{\text{Btu} \times 778 \text{ ft-lb}}$$

$$= \text{about } 33\% \quad \textit{Ans.}$$

Mechanical efficiency is 70 to 87%. Consumption of fuel having a low heat value of not less than 18,500 Btu averages 0.37 to 0.40 lb per bhp per hr for a well-designed diesel. Low fuel consumption is one of the big advantages of diesel engines.

2. HORSEPOWER CONSTANT OF ENGINE _____

PROBLEM: Calculate the horsepower constant (hpc) of an engine having a 22½-in.-diameter cylinder and 42-in. stroke; the piston rod is 3 in. in diameter, and the engine runs 85 rpm.

SOLUTION: The horsepower constant for each end of the cylinder is the number of indicated horsepower developed by 1 lb mean effective pressure (MEP), and therefore to express horsepower constant, the usual formula

$$\text{hp} = \frac{PLAN}{33,000}$$

becomes

$$\text{hpc} = \frac{1LAN}{33,000}$$

By substitution, the horsepower constant for the head end of a $22\frac{1}{2} \times 42$-in. engine running 85 rpm is found to be

$$\text{hpc} = \frac{1[^{42}/_{12}(22\frac{1}{2} \times 22\frac{1}{2})(0.7854 \times 85)]}{33,000}$$

$$= 3.584 \text{ hp per lb MEP for head end}$$

Allowing for a 3-in.-diameter piston rod, the horsepower constant of the crank end is found by

$$\text{hpc} = \frac{([^{42}/_{12}(22\frac{1}{2} \times 22\frac{1}{2}) - (3 \times 3)](0.7854 \times 85)}{33,000}$$

$$= 3.52 \text{ hp per lb MEP for crank end}$$

The hpc for use with the average of the MEPs of both ends would be

$$3.584 + 3.52 = 7.104 \text{ hp per lb av. MEP both ends.} \quad Ans.$$

3. HEAT EQUIVALENT TO HORSEPOWER HOUR _____

PROBLEM: Calculate the heat units that are equivalent to 1 hp-hr acting for 1 hr.

SOLUTION: Laboratory experiments have shown that taking 1 Btu as the mean heat required to increase the temperature of 1 lb of water per °F between 32 and 212°F gives

$$1 \text{ mean Btu} = 778.26 \text{ standard ft-lb}$$

This quantity is called the *mechanical equivalent* of 1 heat unit. For practical computation, it is usually taken as 778 ft-lb. Because 1 hp = 33,000 ft-lb per min, acting for 1 hr it is

$$33,000 \times 60 = 1,980,000 \text{ ft-lb}$$

Thus $1,980,000 \div 778 = 2545$ Btu is equivalent to 1 hp acting for 1 hr. *Ans.*

4. HORSEPOWER OF GASOLINE ENGINE _____

PROBLEM: Calculate the horsepower expected from a four-cylinder gasoline engine having 6-in.-diameter cylinders and 6-in. stroke and operating at 500 rpm.

SOLUTION: Engines of this type are usually rated at 1000 ft piston speed, and horsepower is calculated by the formula

$$\text{hp} = \frac{D^2 \times \text{no. of cylinders}}{2.5}$$

Since the engine has four 6-in. cylinders, at 1000 ft piston speed (which with a 6-in. stroke is equivalent to 1000 rpm)

$$\text{hp} = \frac{36 \times 4}{2.5} = 57.6$$

Thus at 500 rpm the engine would be rated at

$$\frac{57.6 \times 500}{1000} = 28.8 \text{ hp} \quad \textit{Ans.}$$

5. PERCENTAGE OF FUEL ENERGY REALIZED BY ENGINE _____

PROBLEM: An engine uses 25 lb of steam per ihp-hr, and the evaporative economy of the boiler, under the operating conditions, is 8 lb of water per pound of coal. Assuming that the heat value of the coal is 10,000 Btu per lb, calculate the percentage of energy contained in the coal that is realized by the engine.

SOLUTION: Fuel consumption is

$$\frac{25}{8} = 3.125 \text{ lb of coal per hp-hr}$$

Then as 1 hp-hr = 33,000 × 60 = 1,980,000 ft-lb, 1,980,000 ÷ 3.125 = 633,600 ft-lb will be realized per pound of the coal.

Since 1 Btu = 778.26 ft-lb, if the coal contains 10,000 Btu per lb, the energy in a pound of the coal is 7,782,600 ft-lb. Thus the energy realized by the engine per pound of coal used amounts to

$$\frac{633,600 \times 100}{7,782,600} = 8.14\% \quad \textit{Ans.}$$

6. AVERAGE TANGENTIAL PRESSURE ON CRANKPIN _____

PROBLEM: Calculate the average tangential pressure on the crankpin of a 14 × 20 in. engine where the MEP is 40 psi.

SOLUTION: Neglecting the reduction of piston displacement from the presence of the piston rod, the average total pressure acting on the piston would be 14 × 14 × 0.7854 × 40 = 6157.5 lb. Thus with a 20-in. stroke, the work performed per revolution would be

$$6157.5 \times 20 \times 2 = 246,300 \text{ in.-lb}$$

Without allowance for loss from friction, the same amount of work would be transmitted per revolution to the crankpin. In one revolution the length of path described by the crankpin center would be

$$20 \times 3.1416 = 62.832 \text{ in.}$$

Thus the average tangential pressure would be

$$\frac{246,300}{62.832} = 3920 \text{ lb} \quad Ans.$$

7. POWER INCREASE BY OPERATING CONDENSING _____

PROBLEM: What would the increase in power of a 12 × 18 in. steam engine running 200 rpm noncondensing be if it were operated condensing with a 26-in. vacuum?

SOLUTION: A 26-in. vacuum is a pressure of 26 × 0.491 = 12.76 psi less than atmospheric pressure. If the back pressure when operating noncondensing is 2 psi above atmospheric pressure, the reduction of back pressure from operating condensing would be 2 + 12.76 = 14.76 psi. Then the power would be increased

$$\frac{14.76(12 \times 12 \times 0.7854) \times 18 \times 2 \times 200}{12 \times 33,000} = 30.35 \text{ ihp} \quad Ans.$$

NOTE: This calculation holds true for steam turbines also.

8. OPERATING ON REDUCED PRESSURE _____

PROBLEM: A 1500-kW condensing turbine is designed to operate on steam at 350 psi and 600°F. Assume that it is never called on to carry more than 400 kW. Under this load, the pressure on the first-stage nozzles is only about 170 psi. If the plant has no other use for steam above 150 psi, would there be a saving in fuel by reducing boiler pressure to 170 psi?

SOLUTION: Yes, it may help boiler efficiency, but turbine efficiency will not change. The reason is that the throttle acts as a reducing valve to lower the pressure to 170 psi and thus the temperature to 570°F (corresponding temperature from steam tables), but the total heat stays at 1309.4 Btu. If the turbine exhausts to $28^1/_2$ in. of vacuum, the heat available due to adiabatic expansion is 386 Btu, which is 29.5% of the heat in the initial steam.

If steam pressure in the boiler is reduced to provide 170-psi steam, the final steam temperature will probably not be over 600°F. More likely it will be 536.7°F, which is the same superheat as obtained with high-pressure operation. With 170 psi and 600°F steam, the heat content is 1323 Btu, and the heat drop to vacuum at $28^1/_2$ in. is 391 Btu.

Assuming the same turbine efficiency, the result will be a slightly lower steam rate. But the available heat is still 29.5% of the heat in the initial steam, and if the temperature is only 536.7°F, as indicated, the efficiency is 29.1%, which is slightly lower than with high-pressure steam. Before making a change in this case, both the turbine and the boiler manufacturers should be consulted. *Ans.*

9. UTILIZING WASTE HEAT FROM DIESEL TO SAVE FUEL _____

PROBLEM: Show by calculation the savings utilized from using the waste heat (from exhaust and jacket water) of a three-cylinder 12 × 16 in. 135 hp engine if the exhaust is 400°F and the jacket-water outlet is 120°F and the engine runs at about 50% capacity most of time.

SOLUTION: The weight of exhaust gas equals the weight of fuel plus the weight of air, the latter depending on its temperature. As not all of the burned gas escapes, clearance volume can be neglected. Assume that the air temperature at the beginning of compression was 130°F. The volume V in cubic feet per hour is

$$V = \frac{0.7854D^2}{144} \frac{L}{12} \times N \times \frac{\text{rpm}}{2} \times 60$$

where D = cylinder diameter, in.
   L = stroke, in.
   N = number of cylinders
Substituting values gives

$$V = \frac{0.7854 \times 12}{144} \times 12 \times {}^{16}/_{12} \times 3 \times \frac{300}{2} \times 60 = 28{,}274 \text{ cu ft}$$

$$\text{Weight of air} = \frac{PV}{RT}$$

where P = pressure, lb per sq ft = $15 \times 144 = 2160$
   V = 28,270 cu ft per hr
   R = constant = 53.2
   T = absolute temperature = $130 + 460 = 590$
Substituting gives

$$W = \frac{2160 \times 28{,}274}{53.2 \times 590} = 1945.7 \text{ lb}$$

The total weight of exhaust gas is $1945.7 + 30.4 = 1976$ lb.

$$\text{Fuel weight} = 0.45 \times 135 \text{ hp} \times 50\% = 30.4$$

Steam would be generated in an exhaust-gas boiler in which exhaust enters at 400°F and leaves at least 40°F higher than the temperature of steam generated. Assume the steam pressure to be 5 psig. Temperature at this pressure is 228°F, so the leaving-gas temperature is $228 + 40 = 268$°F. Then the heat absorbed from the exhaust by the boiler will be

$$H = W(t_1 - t_2)c$$

where W = weight of exhaust gas = 1976
   t_1 = 400°F
   t_2 = 268°F
   c = specific heat (assume 0.24).
Substituting gives

$$H = 1976 \times (400 - 268) \times 0.24 = 62{,}600 \text{ Btu}$$

As steam at 5 psig has a heat content of 1156 Btu, the heat required to change 1 lb of water at 120°F into steam at 5 psig will be

$$1156 - 120.32 = 1068 \text{ Btu}$$

The amount of steam generated will be

$$\frac{62,600}{1068} = 60 \text{ lb per hr}$$

If the average cost of producing 1000 lb of steam is \$2, then 60 lb of steam per hr is worth only 12 cents. The waste-heat boiler needed may cost about \$5000, so it would require \$5000/\$0.12 = 41,667 operating hours to pay for the waste-heat boiler. *Ans.*

SUGGESTED READING

Elonka, Stephen M.: Standard Plant Operators' Manual," McGraw-Hill Book Company, New York, 1975.

Elonka, Stephen M., and Joseph F. Robinson: "Standard Plant Operators' Questions and Answers," vols. I and II, McGraw-Hill Book Company, New York, 1959.

12

REFRIGERATION AND AIR CONDITIONING

Unlike yesterday, when refrigeration was used mainly to produce ice, today it quick-freezes food and cools living spaces. The operator must often apply and maintain both refrigeration and heating equipment, which has also come to mean air conditioning. Here we present 13 typical calculations, including rating, cooling water, brine required, cooling capacity, and specific heat.

SOME TYPICAL REFRIGERATION CALCULATIONS _____

1. RATING REFRIGERATING MACHINES _____

PROBLEM: Calculate the Btu rating of a 20-ton refrigerating machine.

SOLUTION: A 20-ton refrigerating machine is one that produces a refrigerating effect at a rate equal to the melting of 20 tons of ice per 24 hr. In melting, 1 lb of ice requires a quantity of heat known as the *latent heat of fusion,* which amounts to 144 Btu. Thus 20 tons (2000 lb) of ice would absorb

$$20 \times 2000 \times 144 = 5{,}760{,}000 \text{ Btu} \quad Ans.$$

NOTE that 1 ton of refrigeration is equivalent to the expenditure of negative heat (absorption of heat) at the rate of

$$2000 \times 144 \text{ Btu} = 288,000 \text{ Btu per 24 hr}$$

288,000 Btu being the amount of heat required to melt 1 ton of ice from and at 32°F.

2. REFRIGERATION PRODUCED FROM BRINE COIL _____

PROBLEM: Consider a calcium chloride brine coil in a refrigerator system operating under the following conditions:

Average incoming temperature of brine = 23°F
Average outgoing temperature of brine = 24.75°F
Range in brine temperature = 1.75°F
Brine passing through coils in 24 hr = 857.00 cu ft
Specific gravity of brine = 1.16
Specific heat of brine = 0.83
Calculate the amount of refrigeration produced.

SOLUTION: The heat absorbed per 24 hr would be given by the formula

$$H = W(t_2 - t_1)c$$

where H = Btu absorbed per 24 hr
W = weight of brine passing through coils in 24 hr
t_2 = final temperature of brine
t_1 = initial temperature of brine
c = specific heat of brine

Start with the specific gravity of brine, which is 1.16. Then take the weight of 1 cu ft of water as 62.3 lb. That would make the weight per cubic foot equal to

$$1.16 \times 62.3 = 72.268 \text{ lb}$$

And as 857 cu ft passes through the coils in 24 hr, the value of W in the formula would be

$$857 \times 72.268 = 61,934 \text{ lb}$$

As the brine has a final temperature of 24.75°F and an initial temperature of 23°F, the term $t_2 - t_1$ would be equal to $24.75 - 23 = 1.75$°F. Since c is 0.83, by substitution the formula becomes

$$H = 61{,}934 \times 1.75 \times 0.83 = 89{,}959 \text{ Btu per 24 hr}$$

The unit of refrigeration is the number of Btu that must be abstracted from 1 ton of water at 32°F to produce 1 ton (2000 lb) of ice of the same temperature. Since the latent heat of ice is 144 Btu, which means that 144 Btu must be withdrawn from 1 lb of water at 32°F to produce 1 lb of ice at 32°F, the unit of refrigeration (called 1 ton of refrigeration) is equal to the removal of

$$2000 \times 144 = 288{,}000 \text{ Btu}$$

Thus for removal of 89,959 Btu in 24 hr the refrigeration produced in that time is

$$\frac{89{,}959}{288{,}000} = 0.31 \text{ ton} \quad Ans.$$

3. QUANTITY OF COOLING WATER FOR AMMONIA PLANT _____

PROBLEM: Give the formula for estimating cooling water needed for condensing in an ammonia plant.

SOLUTION: Gallons of water required to be pumped through the condenser can be obtained by the formula

$$g = \frac{(H - q)W}{(t_1 - t_2)8.33}$$

where g = water, gpm
   H = total heat in 1 lb of ammonia entering condenser, Btu
   q = heat of liquid ammonia leaving condenser, Btu
   W = ammonia circulated, lb per min
   t_1 = temperature of entering water, °F
   t_2 = temperature of exit water, °F

NOTE: Values of H, which consists of the latent heat of vaporization of the ammonia at the condenser pressure plus the superheat, can be obtained from a table of properties of ammonia. If the heat of superheat is not shown, it can be calculated by multiplying the difference between the actual ammonia temperature and the boiling temperature at the condenser pressure by 0.63. *Ans.*

4. TEMPERATURE THROUGH COOLING COILS _____

PROBLEM: A submerged 2-in.-pipe coil 1440 ft long is inside a reservoir of 500,000 gal of 56°F water. Water at 120°F is pumped through the coils at a rate of 70 gpm. Water passes through the reservoir at 1300 gpm. Calculate the final temperature obtained from pumping water through the cooling coils shown in Fig. 12-1.

SOLUTION: Here the rate of cooling depends on one *unknown* condition, the character of circulation of the reservoir water *over* the exterior of the 2-in.-pipe coil. For example, if the coil is submerged in the *swiftest* current of the water passing through the reservoir, the cooling will be considerably faster and a lower temperature will be obtained than if the coil were submerged in a part of the reservoir where the water is nearly stagnant.

Using tables from a refrigeration handbook, we can calculate that water pumped through a continuous or single 2-in.-pipe coil at the rate of 70 gpm (583 lb per min) would have a velocity of about 458 ft per min and would pass through 1440 ft of pipe in 3.14 min.

For a velocity of 50 ft per min of the reservoir water surrounding the coil, there would be transfer of about 10 Btu per hr, or 0.166 Btu per min per square foot of surface per degree mean difference of temperature.

If we use t as the final temperature, the mean temperature is

$$\frac{120 + t}{2}$$

and the mean temperature difference is

$$\frac{120 + t}{2} - 56$$

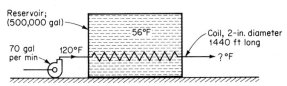

FIG. 12-1   The unknown quantity here is the character of circulation of reservoir water over the exterior of the heating coils.

The cooling surface of 1440 linear ft of 2-in. pipe is

$$\frac{1440}{1.61} = \text{about 900 sq ft}$$

The Btu transferred in the 3.14 min required for the water to transverse the full length of the coil would be

$$3.14 \times 0.166 \times 900 \, \frac{120 + t}{2} - 56 = (120 - t) \times 583$$

for which the final temperature $t = 83°F$. *Ans.*

5. SUCTION PRESSURE AND CAPACITY _____

PROBLEM: Show by computation how suction pressure can determine the compressor capacity in a refrigeration plant.

SOLUTION: First, a gas or vapor has weight. We know that in a steam turbine the steam condensed can easily be weighed, and we also know that it requires 5 to 30 lb of steam to produce 1 hp for 1 hr in some turbines.

Similiarly air has weight because we know that the atmosphere presses down with a weight of 14.7 psi. Each pound of refrigerant (ammonia, for example) evaporated will occupy a certain volume, depending on the pressure (Table 12-1).

Thus if the coil pressure is 0 psig, each pound of ammonia evaporated will fill 17.99 cu ft of space. At 20 psig, each pound has a volume of 7.99 cu ft, so the compressor must handle more cubic

**TABLE 12-1 Volume of
1 lb of Ammonia Vapor at
Selected Pressures**

Pressure, psig	Volume, cu ft
200	1.40
150	1.81
100	2.57
30	5.30
20	7.99
10	10.96
0	17.99

feet of ammonia at low suction pressures. This means that the compressor capacity determines the suction pressure possible in a refrigeration plant. *Ans.*

6. BRINE REQUIRED IN SYSTEM

PROBLEM: Compute the amount of brine circulated per minute to provide 1 ton of refrigeration with a 5°F range in temperature.

SOLUTION: The brine required for a given condition can be calculated as follows: The *heat capacity* of a certain volume of brine depends on the product of the density (specific gravity) and its specific heat (heat units required to raise 1 lb 1°F) and the allowed temperature rise.

EXAMPLE: The cooling effect of 100 gal of brine in raising 4°F would be

$$\underset{\substack{\text{temp.}\\\text{range}}}{4} \times \underset{\text{no. gal}}{100} \times \underset{\text{weight gal}}{8\tfrac{1}{3}} \times \underset{\text{sp. gr.}}{1.2} \times \underset{\substack{\text{sp. heat}\\\text{brine}}}{0.7} = 2788 \text{ Btu}$$

where 1.2 is assumed for the specific gravity and 0.7 for the specific heat of the brine (these values change with each concentration of brine solution).

If it is required to find the *amount* of brine per minute necessary to provide 1 ton of refrigeration with a 5°F range (remembering that 200 Btu per min = 1 ton of refrigeration)

$$200 = \text{no gal} \times 8^1/_3 \times 1.2 \times 0.7$$

Then
$$\text{gal} = \frac{200}{8^1/_3 \times 1.2 \times 0.7 \times 4} = 7.14 \text{ gpm} \quad \textit{Ans.}$$

7. CONDENSER FOR EVAPORATOR

PROBLEM: Consider a triple-effect evaporator that produces 60 tons of distilled water daily. The first-effect pressure is 5 psig, and condenser vacuum is 26 in. The condensing surface is 5 sq ft per pound of steam. A rotary vacuum pump has a 5-hp motor, and a centrifugal pump handles condensed water. Condensate from drums flows to the condenser for deaeration and cooling. Plans are to place three more effects in series and increase steam pressure to 40 psig in order to increase capacity to 100 or 120 tons (about double). Must a larger condenser and vacuum pump be installed if plans are to add another stand of atmospheric cooling coils for the added distilled water?

SOLUTION: To double output by adding three effects requires that the same temperature drop per effect be maintained. With three effects, working from 5 psig to 26 in. of vacuum, the temperature drop is 102°F, or 34°F per effect.

On the new basis, it would have to be 204°F (still 34°F per effect). Then by increasing initial steam temperature to 287°F (40 psig), average temperature difference in each effect would be 27°F. But as only 27°F is available, the total output will be about

$$\frac{27}{34} \times 240{,}000 \text{ lb} = 190{,}000 \text{ lb per day} = 95 \text{ tons}$$

By increasing initial pressure to 40 psig, the temperature drop is increased to 162°F. To pull this up to 204°F requires raising initial pressure to about 85 psig *or* increasing the vacuum to about 29 in. In this case going to 85 psig initial pressure might be the most practical. NOTE: In this problem the condenser handles heat produced by a three-effect evaporator as well as heat flashing from condensate drained from other parts of the system. Under the proposed arrangement, the condenser will handle *less* vapor from the six-effect evaporator plus a *large* amount of heat flashing from increased condensate production. Thus, the total heat load on the condenser will be slightly increased. Even though a slight decrease in vacuum occurs, the existing condenser and vacuum pump should be ample. *Ans.*

8. CAPACITY FOR COOLING AIR _____

PROBLEM: Calculate the refrigeration capacity required to cool 1000 cu ft of air per min from 80 to 40°F. Also find the number of square feet of pipe surface required for the cooling coils.

SOLUTION: In 1000 cu ft of air at 80°F handled per minute, the weight of dry air would be 1000 ÷ 13.6 = 73.5 lb. Then assuming the specific heat at constant pressure to be 0.24, cooling air from 80 to 40°F would require the removal of 73.5 × 0.24 × (80 − 40) = 705.6 Btu.

In addition, each cubic foot of air contains some water vapor. If the humidity is 100%, each cubic foot would contain as much vapor as contained in a cubic foot of dry saturated steam at 80°F and at the pressure of 1.029 in. Hg, at which temperature and pressure the density is 0.00157 lb per cu ft. Thus 1000 cu ft of air saturated with water vapor would contain

$$1000 \times 0.00157 = 1.57 \text{ lb of moisture}$$

If the air is cooled to 40°F without change of pressure, the volume would decrease in the ratio of the absolute temperatures or inversely as 460 + 80 to 460 + 40, making the volume when cooled

$$1000 \frac{460 + 40}{460 + 80} = \text{about 926 cu ft}$$

At 40°F, 1 cu ft of water vapor would weigh 0.00041 lb. Thus the quantity of water vapor that could be held in suspension in 926 cu ft of air at 40°F would be 926 × 0.00041 = 0.38 lb and of the original moisture 1.57 − 0.38 = 1.19 lb, which must be cooled and deposited as water at 40°F.

The latent heat of the original vapor (at 80°F and pressure of 1.029 in. Hg) is 1046.7 Btu. Then condensing the 1.19 lb before reducing its temperature would require

$$1.19 \times 1046.7 = 1245.6 \text{ Btu}$$

Thus to cool the condensate from 80 to 40°F would require

$$1.19 \times (80 - 40) = 47.6 \text{ Btu}$$

or, for the vapor condensed out, there would have to be removal of

$$1266.5 + 47.6 = 1314.1 \text{ Btu}$$

Assuming that the specific heat of superheated steam is 0.5, to cool the 0.38 lb of vapor from 80 to 40°F would require

$$0.38 \times (80 - 40) \times 0.5 = 7.6 \text{ Btu}$$

Thus the total heat to be removed would be 705.6 Btu from the air plus the 1314.1 Btu from moisture condensed to water plus the 7.6 Btu for cooling the remaining moisture, or 2028 Btu. Since 1 ton of refrigeration per 24 hr is the removal of heat at the rate of 200 Btu per minute, cooling 1000 cu ft of air per min under the conditions stated, would require

$$\frac{2028}{200} = \text{about 10 tons refrigerating capacity} \quad Ans.$$

If the air is to be forced across the cooling coil at considerable velocity, the heat transmitted per square foot of surface per degree temperature difference per hour will be between 5 and 20 Btu, depending on the velocity. If we assume 40°F exit temperature of the air and 30°F ammonia temperature in the coil, there would be a difference of

$$\frac{80 + 40}{2} - 30 = 30°F$$

Allowing transfer of 10 Btu per sq ft of coil surface per hr, the coil surface required would be

$$\frac{2028 \times 60}{30 \times 10} = 405 \text{ sq ft}$$

If 1¼-in pipe (0.43 sq ft per 1 ft of length) is used, the coil must contain

$$405 \div 0.43 = 942 \text{ ft of } 1^1/_4\text{-in. pipe} \quad Ans.$$

9. POWER SAVED FROM COOLER WATER

PROBLEM: Assume an ammonia compressor operating under a back pressure of 20 psig in the ammonia suction line and average pressure on the compressor of 185 psig. The temperature of the cooling water through the ammonia condenser is 80°F. Calculate the saving of power for driving the compressor if cooling water of 54°F is used instead of 80°F.

SOLUTION: The best way to solve this problem is to use a Mollier heat chart (see Chap. 4). First, assume that the liquid ammonia is at 96°F, which is the boiling temperature of 200 psia (185 psig). In this condition, we learn from the chart that each pound of ammonia has in it 150 Btu measured from −40°F.

On evaporating in the evaporator coils at 20 psig (35 psia), each pound of dry saturated ammonia vapor contains 614 Btu, which means that 464 Btu has been absorbed from the coils. After compression from 35 to 200 psia, each pound contains 722 Btu, indicating that 108 Btu of work has been done for each 464 Btu of refrigeration. Putting it another way, for each Btu of refrigeration with 80°F water, 0.23 of Btu work is required.

If the cooling water is lowered from 80 to 54°F and the same temperature difference of 16°F between water and ammonia in the condenser is assumed, the liquefying temperature of the ammonia in the condenser will be 70°F, which corresponds to 127 psia.

We also learn from the tables that 1 lb of liquid ammonia at 127 psia contains 120 Btu, so after going through the expansion valve and evaporating at 35 psia, it contains 614 Btu, which means that 494 Btu has been picked up from the coils. After compression back to a discharge pressure of 125 psia, each pound of ammonia vapor contains 691 Btu. This means that $691 - 614 = 77$ Btu has been added by compression, to do 494 Btu of refrigeration.

Thus we see that each Btu of refrigeration with the cooler water requires only 0.15 Btu of work. The work required per ton of refrigeration with the low-temperature water will therefore be 15/23 of that required with the high-temperature water. But the amount of fuel saved per hour depends also upon the efficiency of the driving unit. With the lower-temperature cooling water, power (whether steam, diesel, or electric) consumption would be about 15/23 of that required under the high-temperature water. *Ans.*

10. AMMONIA IN BRINE

PROBLEM: Consider a brine tank having an ammonia leak, which causes a 2-oz sample from the tank to turn pink when 3 drops of phenolphthalein test solution is added. Can the exact amount of ammonia in the brine be calculated?

SOLUTION: First, it is more important to *stop* any leak than to determine the amount of ammonia present. In this case, one must be certain that the phenolphthalein color change is *caused* by ammonia and not just by possible alkalinity of the brine.

The best indicator is Nessler's solution. Several drops added to a brine sample turn *yellow* if a trace of ammonia is present and *brown* if there is any quantity of ammonia in the brine.

An alternate test can be made with litmus paper. Fill a drinking glass half full of brine and add a little caustic soda. Allow time for the soda to dissolve, then cover the glass with a strip of glass to the underside of which is fastened a strip of litmus paper. If ammonia is present, the paper will turn pink in 4 or 5 min from the fumes. Warming the sample will hasten the action.

A rough check of the amount present can be made by performing the same test on known mixtures until a similar reaction time is obtained. The simplest way to determine the exact amount of ammonia present is to send a sample to a testing laboratory. The determination can be made by titrating a weighed sample of the brine solution against one-tenth normal sulfuric acid solution, which can be purchased from any laboratory supplies.

Methyl orange is used as the end-point indicator since it changes from yellow (alkaline) to deep orange (acid) at the transition point. If A is the milliliters of acid used in titration and B the weight in grams of the sample, the percent ammonia equals

$$\frac{A \times 0.017 \times 100}{B}$$

NOTE: If the result is wanted in ounces per gallon, multiply the percent of ammonia by 1.33 and by the density of the brine solution. *Ans.*

11. LINEAR FEET OF PIPE NEEDED

PROBLEM: Find the linear feet of $1\frac{1}{4}$-in. direct-refrigerating coils required to keep a cold-storage room at 30°F if the refrigeration loss is 7000 Btu per hr. The temperature of the brine is 10°F entering the coils and 20°F leaving . The average is 15°F.

SOLUTION: The heat-transfer coefficient of 1.5 Btu per sq ft per hr per °F is usual for this piping (from reference books).

Sq ft refrigeration area

$$= \frac{\text{Btu loss}}{1.5(\text{temp. outside pipe} - \text{temp. inside pipe})}$$

$$= \frac{7000}{1.5(30 - 15)} = 311 \text{ sq ft refrigeration area needed}$$

Circumference of $1\frac{1}{4}$-in. pipe = 5.2

Thus a 1-ft length has an area of $5.2 \times 12 = 62.4$ sq in., or 0.43 sq ft. Then 311/0.43 = 723 linear ft of 1¼-in. pipe is needed.   *Ans.*

NOTE: In calculating the linear feet of pipe required for direct-cooling systems where the pipe surface is exposed to the air of the room to be cooled, usually a transmission allowance of not over 30 Btu per sq ft per hr may be assumed for a temperature difference of from 15 to 20°F.

12. COOLING FOR COLD-STORAGE ROOM

PROBLEM: How many Btu of refrigeration will be required for a cold-storage room of 40 × 50 × 12 ft to keep it at a temperature of 35°F when outside the temperature is 70°F?

SOLUTION: To find the Btu to be withdrawn from a cold-storage room to maintain constant temperature, multiply the sum of the area of the walls, floor, and ceiling in square feet by the estimated leakage through the insulation, opening of doors, etc. (about 30%, or 3 in formula given here) by the number of degrees of temperature the room is lowered. Dividing the heat units to be withdrawn by the Btu per ton refrigeration, which may be taken at 288,000 (latent heat of ice 144 × 2000 lb), gives the tons of refrigeration required. Thus

$$\text{Area of wall} = (40 + 40 + 50 + 50) \times 12 = 2160$$
$$\text{Area of floor and ceiling} = (40 \times 50 \times 2) = \underline{4000}$$
$$\text{Total} \qquad\qquad\qquad\qquad\qquad 6160 \text{ sq ft}$$
$$\text{Temperature outside} = 70°F$$
$$\text{Temperature inside} = \underline{35°F}$$
$$35°F \text{ difference}$$

NOTE: An empirical formula is to allow 1 ton of refrigeration to 2000 cu ft of space for small installations and about 2200 cu ft for larger ones.

The formula is

$$H = 3 \times A \times (T - t)$$

where H = refrigeration required, Btu

A = area of floor, walls, and ceiling, sq ft

T = temperature of adjoining compartments or outside air, °F

t = temperature to be maintained in cold-storage room, °F

3 = constant for leakage of heat through walls

Substituting gives

$$3 \times 6160 \times (70 - 35) = 646,800 \text{ Btu}$$

Since 1 ton of refrigeration = 288,000 Btu, to reduce Btu to tons

$$H = \frac{646,000}{288,000} = 2.24 \text{ tons} \quad Ans.$$

13. REFRIGERATION FOR STORED GOODS

PROBLEM: How much refrigeration is required to cool 25,000 lb of lean beef from a temperature of 95 to 35°F?

SOLUTION: Here we multiply the weight of the goods by their specific heats (see Table 12-2) and the product by the difference between ordinary heat of the stored goods and temperature of the storage room.

TABLE 12-2   Specific Heat and Latent Heat of Various Food Products

Substance	Composition		Specific heat above freezing in heat units	Specific heat below freezing in heat units	Latent heat of freezing in heat units
	Water	Solids			
Lean beef	72	28	0.77	0.41	2
Fat beef	51	49	0.60	0.34	72
Veal	63	37	0.70	0.39	90
Fat pork	39	61	0.51	0.30	55
Eggs	70	30	0.76	0.40	100
Potatoes	74	26	0.80	0.42	105
Cabbage	91	9	0.93	0.48	129
Carrots	83	17	0.87	0.45	118
Cream	59.25	30.75	0.68	0.38	84
Milk	87.50	12.50	0.90	0.47	124
Oysters	80.38	19.62	0.84	0.44	114
Whitefish	78	22	0.82	0.43	111
Eels	62.07	37.93	0.69	0.38	88
Lobster	76.62	23.38	0.81	0.42	108
Pigeon	72.40	27.60	0.78	0.41	102
Chicken	73.70	26.30	0.80	0.42	105

* The specific heat of a substance is the ratio of the heat required to raise the temperature of a certain weight of the substance 1°F to that required to raise the temperature of the same weight of water 1°F. As the specific heat is not constant at all temperatures, it is generally assumed that it is determined by raising the temperature from 62 to 63°F. For most substances it is practically constant for temperatures up to 212°F.

$$H = W \times S \times (T - t)$$

where H = refrigeration required, Btu
W = weight of stored goods, lb
S = specific heat of stored goods
T = temperature of goods when placed in storage, °F
t = temperature of cold-storage room, °F

For this problem, we learn that for lean beef above the freezing point, specific heat is 0.77. The difference in temperature between 95 and 35°F is 60°F. Substituting these values in the formula gives

$$25,000 \times 0.77 \times 60 = 1,155,000 \text{ Btu}$$

Then $\qquad H = \dfrac{1,155,000}{288,000} = 4.01 \text{ tons} \quad Ans.$

NOTE that Btu per ton of refrigeration = 288,000.

SUGGESTED READING

Elonka, Stephen M., and Quaid W. Minich: "Standard Refrigeration and Air Conditioning Questions and Answers," McGraw-Hill Book Company, New York, 1973. (Has 45 calculations.)
Elonka, Stephen M., and Joseph F. Robinson: "Standard Plant Operators' Questions and Answers," vols. I and II, McGraw-Hill Book Company, New York, 1959.

13
ELECTRICITY

Today electrical equipment has replaced the older steam equipment in many plants. Thus operators in modern building and industrial plants, including power generation and marine plants, must be familiar with the new equipment under their care. Here we cover some practical calculations that often must be made, including resistance heating, current taken by induction motors, rating of ac generators, and size of conductors.

SOME TYPICAL ELECTRICAL CALCULATIONS ————————

1. HEATING WATER ————————————————————————————

PROBLEM: Assume that 25 kW of 3-phase electrical power at 220 V and 60 cycles is available at *no* cost. Calculate the amount of water which can be heated per hour to temperatures ranging from 120 to 200°F.

SOLUTION: First, when 1 kW is totally expended in heat, it produces 3415 Btu per hr. (See Table 10-1, Chap 10.) Therefore, 25 kW will produce

$$25 \times 3415 = 85,375 \text{ Btu per hr}$$

If no heat were lost, this would raise the temperature of 1000 lb of water through 85.4°F in 1 hr, or 500 lb through twice the number of degrees.

If such a heater is well insulated, heat losses should not go over 10%. Then about 457 lb of water can be heated per hr from 32 to 200°F or 873 lb from 32 to 120°F.   *Ans.*

2. CHANGING VOLTAGE OF AN ALTERNATOR

PROBLEM: What voltage can be obtained by connecting the winding 2-parallel star, series delta, and 2-parallel delta of a 6600-V 3-phase 60-cycle alternator operating at 3600 rpm with a 36-coil winding connected series star?

SOLUTION: Since the machine generates 6600 V when connected series star, it will develop one-half of 6600 when connected 2-parallel star, or

$$\frac{6600}{2} = 3300 \text{ V} \quad Ans.$$

When connected series delta, the voltage will be that of the series star connection divided by 1.732, or

$$\frac{6600}{1.732} = 3810 \text{ V} \quad Ans.$$

With a 2-parallel delta connection, the volts will be one-half that obtained with a series-delta connection, or

$$\frac{3810}{2} = 1905 \text{ V} \quad Ans.$$

NOTE: It may be possible in this case to change the speed, excitation, and winding pitch of this machine to obtain a standard 2200 or 2300 V, but before trying to do so, it is best to consult the manufacturer.

3. AC VOLTAGE ON ROTARY CONVERTER

PROBLEM: Calculate the required ac voltage at the collector rings of a 6-phase rotary converter if the dc voltage is 250 V.

SOLUTION: The value of the voltage at the collector rings of a 6-phase rotary converter to give 250 V at the commutator will depend upon how the converter is connected to the transformers.

EXAMPLE: In double delta the voltage at the collector rings will be the dc voltage times 0.612, or

$$250 \times 0.612 = 153 \text{ V} \quad Ans.$$

If a diametrical connection is used, the ac volts equal the dc volts times 0.707, or

$$250 \times 0.707 = 176 \text{ V} \quad Ans.$$

A third arrangement is the 6-phase connection, in which the ac volts are equal to the dc volts times 0.354, or

$$250 \times 0.354 = 88 \text{ V} \quad Ans.$$

NOTE: These voltages are theoretical values, because clearly in practice the voltages will probably be about 5 to 10 V higher. Also, the connection generally used is the diametrical arrangement, as it allows using the highest ac voltage at the collector rings. *Ans.*

4. CURRENT TAKEN BY AN INDUCTION MOTOR _____

PROBLEM: Calculate the full-load current of a 25-hp 3-phase 60-cycle 220-V induction motor and explain how the current taken by an induction motor is calculated.

SOLUTION: The current per terminal taken by an induction motor usually can be found on the nameplate of the machine. If not, the following formulas give values close enough for practical purposes.

For single-phase motors the full-load current per terminal is

$$\text{Amperes} = \frac{\text{horsepower} \times 1000}{\text{volts}}$$

For four-wire 2-phase motors

$$\text{Amperes per terminal} = \frac{\text{horsepower} \times 1000}{\text{volts} \times 2}$$

For three-wire operation the current in the outside wires is the same as for a four-wire circuit, but the current in the center leg is equal to the outside-leg amperes times 1.414. For a 3-phase motor

$$\text{Amperes per terminal} = \frac{\text{horsepower} \times 1000}{\text{volts} \times 1.732}$$

Thus in the above problem it equals

$$\frac{25 \times 1000}{220 \times 1.732} = 65.6 \text{ A} \quad \textit{Ans.}$$

5. ELECTRICAL INPUT TO DEVELOP 15 bhp

PROBLEM: Will an electric-driven pump that requires 15 hp when driven by a 20-hp motor consume 20 hp, or will it consume 15 hp?

SOLUTION: Actual or brake horsepower developed by the motor will be the number of horsepower required by the pump, regardless of the rated capacity of the motor. Clearly, the amount of electric power absorbed by the motor depends on the efficiency of the motor when developing 15 bhp. A 20-hp motor developing 15 bhp would have an efficiency of about 80%, thus requiring an electrical input of

$$\frac{15}{0.8} = 18.75 \text{ electric hp}$$

or

$$18.75 \times 746 = 13,987.5 \text{ W} \quad \textit{Ans.}$$

6. SIZE OF SYNCHRONOUS MOTOR

PROBLEM: Assume a plant with a maximum load of about 325 kW, with power factor around 0.72. If 78 hp load is to be added, calculate the size of the synchronous motor needed to drive the combined load and to raise the power factor to 0.90.

SOLUTION: Synchronous motors usually are rated in kilovolt-amperes; therefore in this problem the motor will be so rated. The additional mechanical load on the motor will be 78 hp, or

$$\frac{78 \times 746}{1000} = 58 \text{ kW}$$

This makes the total kilowatt load equal to

$$325 + 58 = 383$$

The kilovoltampere load equals kilowatts divided by the power factor. Thus in the first case kVA = $325 \div 0.72 = 452$, and in the second, kVA = $383 \div 0.90 = 426$.

The wattless component WC = $\sqrt{kVA^2 - kW}$; then with present load

$$WC = \sqrt{452^2 - 325^2} = 314$$

and with the synchronous motor added

$$WC' = \sqrt{426^2 - 383^2} = 186 \text{ kVA}$$

Here the difference between WC and WC', or $314 - 186 = 128$ kVA, represents the leading wattless component that must be supplied by the synchronous motor, in addition to doing 58 kW of mechanical work.

Then the total motor capacity required is equal to the square root of the sum of the squares of the two loads, or

$$\sqrt{128^2 + 58^2} = 140 \text{ kVA}$$

and the power factor of the motor equals kilowatts divided by kilovoltamperes = $58 \div 140 = 0.41$.

Thus we see a 140-kVA synchronous motor operating at 0.41 power factor which will do 78 hp of mechanical work and raise the power factor of the total load to 0.90. Also the kilovoltampere load on the generators will be reduced from 452 to 426 kVA. Additionally, under the new condition, the voltage regulation will also be improved. *Ans.*

7. RATING OF AC GENERATORS

PROBLEM: Calculate (1) the kilowatt rating of a 550-V 300-A 3-phase alternator at 0.80 power factor and (2) the machine's kilowatt rating at a power factor of 1.

SOLUTION: (1) At 0.80 power factor, the kilowatt rating = $550 \times 300 \times 1.732 \times 0.80 \div 1000 = 228.62$. This means that at 80% power factor the alternator can supply only a 228.62 kW load. *Ans.*

(2) At a power factor of 1 the alternator has a kilowatt rating equal to volts × amperes × 1.732 × power factor ÷ 1000 = $550 \times 300 \times 1.732 \times 1 \div 1000 = 285.78$. This means that this

machine when operated at a power factor of 1 can supply a load of 285.78 kW. *Ans.*

8. SIZE OF CONDUCTORS

PROBLEM: (1) Calculate the size of the conductors required to transmit 1600 hp at 0.75 power factor 15 miles with a loss of 7% of the power generated in the line. The circuit is 3-phase with 11,000 V at the generator and has conductors spaced 36 in. apart. (2) Calculate the required percent of regulation.

SOLUTION: (1) With 11,000 V at the generator, the voltage to neutral of a 3-phase Y circuit will be

$$\frac{11,000}{1.732} = 6350$$

Assuming 15% regulation, the volts E to neutral at the receiver end of the line will be

$$\frac{6350}{1.15} = 5520$$

Watts $W = \text{hp} \times 746 = 1600 \times 746 = 1,193,600$

The current I (per wire) when the power factor is 0.75 is

$$I = \frac{W}{3 \times E \times \text{PF}} = \frac{1,193,600}{3 \times 5520 \times 0.75} = 96 \text{ A}$$

Allowing the loss in the line to be 7% of power generated, the watts loss per wire is

$$W_n = \frac{W}{3} \times \frac{0.07}{0.93} = \frac{1,193,600}{3} \times \frac{0.07}{0.93} = 29,947$$

$$\text{Resistance per wire} = \frac{W_n}{I^2} = \frac{29,947}{96 \times 96} = 3.25 \ \Omega$$

and the resistance per mile is

$$\frac{3.25}{15} = 0.217 \ \Omega$$

NOTE: Resistance is in ohms, shown as Ω.

The nearest standard wire is a 250,000–cir mil conductor, which has a resistance of 0.2253 Ω, making the total resistance of one wire equal

$$0.2253 \times 15 = 3.38 \; \Omega$$

With conductors spaced 36 in. apart, the inductive reactance in ohms (at 60 cycles) per mile of single 250,000-cir mil conductor is 0.626, making a total of

$$0.626 \times 15 = 9.39 \; \Omega \quad Ans.$$

(2) When the receiver voltage E is known, the generator voltage E_g is found from the formula

$$E_g = \sqrt{(E \cos \theta + IR)^2 + (E \sin \theta + IX)^2}$$

where R = resistance, Ω
X = reactive ohms of one conductor
θ = angle corresponding to power factor in circuit

For a power factor of 75%, cos θ = 0.75 and sin θ = 0.66. Then

$$E_g = \sqrt{\begin{array}{l}(5520 \times 0.75 + 96 \times 3.38)^2 \\ \qquad\qquad + (5520 \times 0.66 + 96 \times 9.39)^2\end{array}}$$

$$= 6370$$

$$\text{Percent regulation} = \frac{E_g - E}{E} \times 100$$

$$= \frac{6350 - 5520}{5520} \times 100 = 15\%$$

NOTE: This value is close enough for all practical purposes. Since there is no direct method of making these calculations, a certain percent regulation must be assumed and the calculation made as shown. If this does not come close enough, another value must be assumed and the calculation made again.   *Ans.*

9. HORSEPOWER REQUIRED TO DRIVE PUMP _____

PROBLEM: Consider a 3000-gpm pump on the 385-ft level in a mine shaft. Calculate the size of motor required to meet these conditions.

SOLUTION: Using the formula

$$\text{hp (theoretical)} = \frac{\text{gpm} \times 8.33H}{33,000E}$$

where H = head, ft
         E = efficiency of pump (assume 80%)
         8.33 = weight per U.S. gal water, lb

gives $\text{hp} = \dfrac{\text{gpm} \times H}{3960E} = \dfrac{3000 \times 385}{3960 \times 0.80} = 364\text{-hp motor}$ *Ans.*

(Use next standard size motor higher.) NOTE: The head on the pump in such problems is not the vertical distance from its level to the point of discharge but the vertical distance between source of supply and point of discharge plus friction, entrance, and exit losses, which is called *total dynamic head.* Losses must be calculated in terms of feet of head and added to static head. Losses are influenced by shape of intake, size of suction and discharge pipes, number of bends, valves, and other fittings, etc. To be precise, this total figure should be H in the formula (which it obviously is not here). Pump efficiency can be obtained from characteristic curves supplied by each manufacturer.

SUGGESTED READING

Elonka, Stephen M., and Julian L. Bernstein: "Standard Electronics Questions and Answers," vols. I and II, McGraw-Hill Book Company, New York, 1964. (Has 88 calculations and formulas.)

Moore, Arthur H., and Stephen M. Elonka: "Electrical Systems and Equipment for Industry," Van Nostrand Reinhold Company, New York, 1972. (Has over 200 calculations and formulas.)

14

METRIC UNITS AND CONVERSION FACTORS

This compilation of conversion factors represents working-tool information that is otherwise usually scattered broadly throughout technical literature. The primary emphasis has been placed on the multiplication factors involved in converting the fundamental electrical and magnetic units.[1]

However, because practicing engineers often have to work with data from other branches of engineering, frequently used conversion factors for the following basic types of units are also included:

area	linear acceleration
angles	linear velocity
angular acceleration	mass
angular velocity	power
flow of water	pressure
force	temperature
heat and energy	volume
length	weight

The customary units of weight and mass are avoirdupois unless designated otherwise.

[1] Since the Cgs (centimeter-gram-second) Electromagnetic System of units, and the Cgs Electrostatic System of units are almost solely confined to theoretical work, no effort was made to incorporate them into the listings. However, an abbreviated table of their relationships to the Practical System of units appears on the last page.

TO CONVERT	INTO	MULTIPLY BY

A

acres	sq feet	43,560.0
"	sq meters	4,047.
"	sq miles	1.562×10^{-3}
"	sq yards	4,840.
acre-feet	cu feet	43,560.0
" "	gallons	3.259×10^5
amperes/sq cm	amps/sq in.	6.452
" " "	amps/sq meter	10^4
amperes/sq in.	amps/sq cm	0.1550
" " "	amps/sq meter	1,550.0
amperes/sq meter	amps/sq cm	10^{-4}
" " "	amps/sq in.	6.452×10^{-4}
ampere-hours	coulombs	3,600.0
" "	faradays	0.03731
ampere-turns	gilberts	1.257
ampere-turns/cm	amp-turns/in.	2.540
" " "	amp-turns/meter	100.0
" " "	gilberts/cm	1.257
ampere-turns/in.	amp-turns/cm	0.3937
" " "	amp-turns/meter	39.37
" " "	gilberts/cm	0.4950
ampere-turns/meter	amp-turns/cm	0.01
" " "	amp-turns/in.	0.0254
" " "	gilberts/cm	0.01257
ares	acres	0.02471
"	sq meters	100.0
atmospheres	cms of mercury	76.0
"	ft of water (at 4°C)	33.90
"	in. of mercury (at 0°C)	29.92
"	kgs/sq cm	1.0333
"	kgs/sq meter	10,332.
"	pounds/sq in.	14.70
"	tons/sq ft	1.058

B

barrels (oil)	gallons (oil)	42.0
bars	atmospheres	0.9869
"	dynes/sq cm	10^6
"	kgs/sq meter	1.020×10^4
"	pounds/sq ft	2,089.
"	pounds/sq in.	14.50
Btu	ergs	1.0550×10^{10}
"	foot-lbs	778.3
"	gram-calories	252.0
"	kilocalories	0.252

TO CONVERT	INTO	MULTIPLY BY
Btu	horsepower-hrs	3.931×10^{-4}
"	joules	1,054.8
"	kilogram-calories	0.2520
"	kilogram-meters	107.5
"	kilowatt-hrs	2.928×10^{-4}
Btu/hr	foot-pounds/sec	0.2162
" "	gram-cal/sec	0.0700
" "	horsepower-hrs	3.929×10^{-4}
" "	watts	0.2931
Btu/min	foot-lbs/sec	12.96
" "	horsepower	0.02356
" "	kilowatts	0.01757
" "	watts	17.57
Btu/sq ft/min	watts/sq in.	0.1221
bushels	cu ft	1.2445
"	cu in.	2,150.4
"	cu meters	0.03524
"	liters	35.24
"	pecks	4.0
"	pints (dry)	64.0
"	quarts (dry)	32.0

C

centares (centiares)	sq meters	1.0
Centigrade	Fahrenheit	$(C° \times 9/5) + 32$
centigrams	grams	0.01
centiliters	liters	0.01
centimeters	feet	3.281×10^{-2}
"	inches	0.3937
"	kilometers	10^{-5}
"	meters	0.01
"	miles	6.214×10^{-6}
"	millimeters	10.0
"	mils	393.7
"	yards	1.094×10^{-2}
centimeter-dynes	cm-grams	1.020×10^{-3}
" "	meter-kgs	1.020×10^{-8}
" "	pound-feet	7.376×10^{-8}
centimeter-grams	cm-dynes	980.7
" "	meter-kgs	10^{-5}
" "	pound-feet	7.233×10^{-5}
centimeters of mercury	atmospheres	0.01316
" " "	feet of water	0.4461
" " "	kgs/sq meter	136.0
" " "	pounds/sq ft	27.85

TO CONVERT	INTO	MULTIPLY BY
centimeters of mercury	pounds/sq in.	0.1934
centimeters/sec	feet/min	1.9685
" "	feet/sec	0.03281
" "	kilometers/hr	0.036
" "	knots	0.0194
" "	meters/min	0.6
" "	miles/hr	0.02237
" "	miles/min	3.728×10^{-4}
centimeters/sec/sec	feet/sec/sec	0.03281
" " "	kms/hr/sec	0.036
" " "	meters/sec/sec	0.01
" " "	miles/hr/sec	0.02237
circular mils	sq cms	5.067×10^{-6}
" "	sq mils	0.7854
" "	sq inches	7.854×10^{-7}
coulombs	faradays	1.036×10^{-5}
coulombs/sq cm	coulombs/sq in.	64.52
" " "	coulombs/sq meter	10^4
coulombs/sq in.	coulombs/sq cm	0.1550
" " "	coulombs/sq meter	1,550.
coulombs/sq meter	coulombs/sq cm	10^{-4}
" " "	coulombs/sq in.	6.452×10^{-4}
cubic centimeters	cu feet	3.531×10^{-5}
" "	cu inches	0.06102
" "	cu meters	10^{-6}
" "	cu yards	1.308×10^{-6}
" "	gallons (U.S. liq.)	2.642×10^{-4}
" "	liters	0.001
" "	pints (U.S. liq.)	2.113×10^{-3}
" "	quarts (U.S. liq.)	1.057×10^{-3}
cubic feet	bushels (dry)	0.8036
" "	cu cms	28,320.0
" "	cu inches	1,728.0
" "	cu meters	0.02832
" "	cu yards	0.03704
" "	gallons (U.S. liq.)	7.48052
" "	liters	28.32
" "	pints (U.S. liq.)	59.84
" "	quarts (U.S. liq.)	29.92
cubic feet/min	cu cms/sec	472.0
" " "	gallons/sec	0.1247
" " "	liters/sec	0.4720
" " "	pounds of water/min	62.43
cubic feet/sec	million gals/day	0.646317
" " "	gallons/min	448.831
cubic inches	cu cms	16.39
" "	cu feet	5.787×10^{-4}

TO CONVERT	INTO	MULTIPLY BY
cubic inches	cu meters	1.639×10^{-5}
" "	cu yards	2.143×10^{-5}
" "	gallons (U.S. liq.)	4.329×10^{-3}
" "	liters	0.01639
" "	mil-feet	1.061×10^{5}
" "	pints (U.S. liq.)	0.03463
" "	quarts (U.S. liq.)	0.01732
cubic meters	bushels (dry)	28.38
" "	cu cms	10^{6}
" "	cu feet	35.31
" "	cu inches	61,023.0
" "	cu yards	1.308
" "	gallons (U.S. liq.)	264.2
" "	liters	1,000.0
" "	pints (U.S. liq.)	2,113.0
" "	quarts (U.S. liq.)	1,057.
cubic yards	cu cms	7.646×10^{5}
" "	cu feet	27.0
" "	cu inches	46,656.0
" "	cu meters	0.7646
" "	gallons (U.S. liq.)	202.0
" "	liters	764.6
" "	pints (U.S. liq.)	1,615.9
" "	quarts (U.S. liq.)	807.9
cubic yards/min	cubic ft/sec	0.45
" " "	gallons/sec	3.367
" " "	liters/sec	12.74

D

days	hours	24.0
"	minutes	1,440.0
"	seconds	86,400.0
decigrams	grams	0.1
deciliters	liters	0.1
decimeters	meters	0.1
degrees (angle)	minutes	60.0
" "	quadrants	0.01111
" "	radians	0.01745
" "	seconds	3,600.0
degrees/sec	radians/sec	0.01745
" "	revolutions/min	0.1667
" "	revolutions/sec	2.778×10^{-3}
dekagrams	grams	10.0
dekaliters	liters	10.0
dekameters	meters	10.0

TO CONVERT	INTO	MULTIPLY BY
drams	grams	1.7718
"	grains	27.3437
"	ounces	0.0625
dynes	grams	1.020×10^{-3}
"	joules/cm	10^{-7}
"	joules/meter (newtons)	10^{-5}
"	kilograms	1.020×10^{-6}
"	poundals	7.233×10^{-5}
"	pounds	2.248×10^{-6}
dynes/sq cm	bars	10^{-6}

E

TO CONVERT	INTO	MULTIPLY BY
ergs	Btu	9.480×10^{-11}
"	dyne-centimeters	1.0
"	foot-pounds	7.367×10^{-8}
"	gram-calories	0.2389×10^{-7}
"	gram-cms	1.020×10^{-3}
"	horsepower-hrs	3.7250×10^{-14}
"	joules	10^{-7}
"	kg-calories	2.389×10^{-11}
"	kg-meters	1.020×10^{-8}
"	kilowatt-hrs	0.2778×10^{-13}
"	watt-hours	0.2778×10^{-10}
ergs/sec	Btu/min	$5,688 \times 10^{-9}$
" "	ft-lbs/min	4.427×10^{-6}
" "	ft-lbs/sec	7.3756×10^{-8}
" "	horsepower	1.341×10^{-10}
" "	kg-calories/min	1.433×10^{-9}
" "	kilowatts	10^{-10}

F

TO CONVERT	INTO	MULTIPLY BY
farads	microfarads	10^6
faradays	ampere-hours	26.80
"	coulombs	9.649×10^4
fathoms	feet	6.0
feet	centimeters	30.48
"	kilometers	3.048×10^{-4}
"	meters	0.3048
"	miles (naut.)	1.645×10^{-4}
"	miles (stat.)	1.894×10^{-4}
"	millimeters	304.8
"	mils	1.2×10^4
feet of water	atmospheres	0.02950

TO CONVERT	INTO	MULTIPLY BY
feet of water	in. of mercury	0.8826
" " "	kgs/sq cm	0.03048
" " "	kgs/sq meter	304.8
" " "	pounds/sq ft	62.43
" " "	pounds/sq in.	0.4335
feet/min	cms/sec	0.5080
" "	feet/sec	0.01667
" "	kms/hr	0.01829
" "	meters/min	0.3048
" "	miles/hr	0.01136
feet/sec	cms/sec	30.48
" "	kms/hr	1.097
" "	knots	0.5921
" "	meters/min	18.29
" "	miles/hr	0.6818
" "	miles/min	0.01136
feet/sec/sec	cms/sec/sec	30.48
" " "	kms/hr/sec	1.097
" " "	meters/sec/sec	0.3048
" " "	miles/hr/sec	0.6818
feet/100 feet	per cent grade	1.0
foot-pounds	Btu	1.286×10^{-3}
" "	ergs	1.356×10^{7}
" "	gram-calories	0.3238
" "	hp-hrs	5.050×10^{-7}
" "	joules	1.356
" "	kg-calories	3.24×10^{-4}
" "	kg-meters	0.1383
" "	kilowatt-hrs	3.766×10^{-7}
foot-pounds/min	Btu/min	1.286×10^{-3}
" " "	foot-pounds/sec	0.01667
" " "	horsepower	3.030×10^{-5}
" " "	kg-calories/min	3.24×10^{-4}
" " "	kilowatts	2.260×10^{-5}
foot-pounds/sec	Btu/hr	4.6263
" " "	Btu/min	0.07717
" " "	horsepower	1.818×10^{-3}
" " "	kg-calories/min	0.01945
" " "	kilowatts	1.356×10^{-3}
furlongs	rods	40.0
"	feet	660.0

G

gallons	cu cms	3,785.0
"	cu feet	0.1337
"	cu inches	231.0

TO CONVERT	INTO	MULTIPLY BY
gallons	cu meters	3.785×10^{-3}
"	cu yards	4.951×10^{-3}
"	liters	3.785
"	pints	8.0
"	quarts	4.0
gallons (liq. Br. Imp.)	gallons (U.S. liq.)	1.20095
gallons (U.S.)	gallons (Imp.)	0.83267
gallons of water	pounds of water	8.3453
gallons/min	cu ft/sec	2.228×10^{-3}
" "	liters/sec	0.06308
" "	cu ft/hr	8.0208
gausses	lines/sq in.	6.452
"	webers/sq cm	10^{-8}
"	webers/sq in.	6.452×10^{-8}
"	webers/sq meter	10^{-4}
gilberts	ampere-turns	0.7958
gilberts/cm	amp-turns/cm	0.7958
" "	amp-turns/in	2.021
" "	amp-turns/meter	79.58
gills	liters	0.1183
"	pints (liq.)	0.25
gin	martinis (dry)	$20g + 1v$
grains (troy)	grains (avdp)	1.0
" "	grams	0.06480
" "	ounces (avdp)	2.0833×10^{-3}
" "	pennyweight (troy)	0.04167
grains/U.S. gal	parts/million	17.118
" " "	pounds/million gal	142.86
grains/Imp. gal	parts/million	14.286
grams	dynes	980.7
"	grains	15.43
"	joules/cm	9.807×10^{-5}
"	joules/meter (newtons)	9.807×10^{-3}
"	kilograms	0.001
"	milligrams	1,000.
"	ounces (avdp)	0.03527
"	ounces (troy)	0.03215
"	poundals	0.07093
"	pounds	2.205×10^{-3}
grams/cm	pounds/inch	5.600×10^{-3}
grams/cu cm	pounds/cu ft	62.43
" " "	pounds/cu in.	0.03613
" " "	pounds/mil-foot	3.405×10^{-7}
grams/liter	grains/gal	58.417
" "	pounds/1,000 gal	8.345
" "	pounds/cu ft	0.062427
" "	parts/million	1,000.0

TO CONVERT	INTO	MULTIPLY BY
grams/sq cm	pounds/sq ft	2.0481
gram-calories	Btu	3.9683×10^{-3}
" "	ergs	4.1868×10^{7}
" "	foot-pounds	3.0880
" "	horsepower-hrs	1.5596×10^{-6}
" "	kilowatt-hrs	1.1630×10^{-6}
" "	watt-hrs	1.1630×10^{-3}
gram-calories/sec	Btu/hr	14.286
gram-centimeters	Btu	9.297×10^{-8}
" "	ergs	980.7
" "	joules	9.807×10^{-5}
" "	kg-cal	2.343×10^{-8}
" "	kg-meters	10^{-5}

H

TO CONVERT	INTO	MULTIPLY BY
hectares	acres	2.471
"	sq feet	1.076×10^{5}
hectograms	grams	100.0
hectoliters	liters	100.0
hectometers	meters	100.0
hectowatts	watts	100.0
henries	millihenries	1,000.0
horsepower	Btu/min	42.44
"	foot-lbs/min	33,000.
"	foot-lbs/sec	550.0
horsepower (metric) (542.5 ft lb/sec)	horsepower (550 ft lb/sec)	0.9863
horsepower (550 ft lb/sec)	horsepower (metric) (542.5 ft lb/sec)	1.014
horsepower	kg-calories/min	10.68
"	kilowatts	0.7457
"	watts	745.7
horsepower (boiler)	Btu/hr	33.479
" "	kilowatts	9.803
horsepower-hrs	Btu	2,547.
" "	ergs	2.6845×10^{13}
" "	foot-lbs	1.98×10^{6}
" "	gram-calories	641,190.
" "	joules	2.684×10^{6}
" "	kg-calories	641.1
" "	kg-meters	2.737×10^{5}
" "	kilowatt-hrs	0.7457
hours	days	4.167×10^{-2}
"	minutes	60.0
"	seconds	3,600.0

TO CONVERT	INTO	MULTIPLY BY
hours	weeks	5.952×10^{-3}

I

inches	centimeters	2.540
"	feet	8.333×10^{-2}
"	meters	2.540×10^{-2}
"	miles	1.578×10^{-5}
"	millimeters	25.40
"	mils	1,000.0
"	yards	2.778×10^{-2}
Inches of mercury	atmospheres	3.342×10^{-2}
" " "	feet of water	1.133
" " "	kgs/sq cm	3.453×10^{-2}
" " "	kgs/sq meter	345.3
" " "	pounds/sq ft	70.73
" " "	pounds/sq in.	0.4912
inches of water (at 4°C)	atmospheres	2.458×10^{-3}
" " " "	inches of mercury	7.355×10^{-2}
" " " "	kgs/sq cm	2.540×10^{-3}
" " " "	ounces/sq in.	0.5781
" " " "	pounds/sq ft	5.204
" " " "	pounds/sq in.	3.613×10^{-2}

J

joules	Btu	9.480×10^{-4}
"	ergs	10^7
"	foot-pounds	0.7376
"	kg-calories	2.389×10^{-4}
"	kg-meters	0.1020
"	watt-hrs	2.778×10^{-4}
joules/cm	grams	1.020×10^4
" "	dynes	10^7
" "	joules/meter (newtons)	100.0
" "	poundals	723.3
" "	pounds	22.48

K

kilograms	dynes	980,665.
"	grams	1,000.0
"	joules/cm	0.09807
"	joules/meter (newtons)	9.807

TO CONVERT	INTO	MULTIPLY BY
kilograms	poundals	70.93
"	pounds	2.205
"	tons (long)	9.842×10^{-4}
"	tons (short)	1.102×10^{-3}
kilograms/cu meter	grams/cu cm	0.001
" " "	pounds/cu ft	0.06243
" " "	pounds/cu in.	3.613×10^{-5}
" " "	pounds/mil-foot	3.405×10^{-10}
kilograms/meter	pounds/ft	0.6720
kilograms/sq cm	atmospheres	0.9678
" " "	feet of water	32.81
" " "	inches of mercury	28.96
" " "	pounds/sq ft	2,048.
" " "	pounds/sq in.	14.22
kilograms/sq meter	atmospheres	9.678×10^{-5}
" " "	bars	98.07×10^{-6}
" " "	feet of water	3.281×10^{-3}
" " "	inches of mercury	2.896×10^{-3}
" " "	pounds/sq ft	0.2048
" " "	pounds/sq in.	1.422×10^{-3}
kilograms/sq mm	kgs/sq meter	10^6
kilogram-calories	Btu	3.968
" "	foot-pounds	3,088.
" "	hp-hrs	1.560×10^{-3}
" "	joules	4,186.
" "	kg-meters	426.9
" "	kilojoules	4.186
" "	kilowatt-hrs	1.163×10^{-3}
kilogram meters	Btu	9.294×10^{-3}
" "	ergs	9.804×10^7
" "	foot-pounds	7.233
" "	joules	9.804
" "	kg-calories	2.342×10^{-3}
" "	kilowatt-hrs	2.723×10^{-6}
kilolines	maxwells	1,000.0
kiloliters	liters	1,000.0
kilometers	centimeters	10^5
"	feet	3,281.
"	inches	3.937×10^4
"	meters	1,000.0
"	miles	0.6214
"	millimeters	10^6
"	yards	1,094.
kilometers/hr	cms/sec	27.78
" "	feet/min	54.68
" "	feet/sec	0.9113
" "	knots	0.5396

TO CONVERT	INTO	MULTIPLY BY
kilometers/hr	meters/min	16.67
" "	miles/hr	0.6214
kilometers/hr/sec	cms/sec/sec	27.78
" " "	ft/sec/sec	0.9113
" " "	meters/sec/sec	0.2778
" " "	miles/hr/sec	0.6214
kilowatts	Btu/min	56.92
"	foot-lbs/min	4.426×10^4
"	foot-lbs/sec	737.6
"	horsepower	1.341
"	kg-calories/min	14.34
"	watts	1,000.0
kilowatt-hrs	Btu	3,413.
" "	ergs	3.600×10^{13}
" "	foot-lbs	2.655×10^6
" "	gram-calories	859,850.
" "	horsepower-hrs	1.341
" "	joules	3.6×10^6
" "	kg-calories	859.85
" "	kg-meters	3.671×10^5
" "	pounds of water evaporated from and at 212° F.	3.53
" "	pounds of water raised from 62° to 212° F.	22.75
knots	feet/hr	6,080.
"	kilometers/hr	1.8532
"	nautical miles/hr	1.0
"	statute miles/hr	1.151
"	yards/hr	2,027.
"	feet/sec	1.689

L

league	miles (approx.)	3.0
lines/sq cm	gausses	1.0
lines/sq in.	gausses	0.1550
lines/sq in.	webers/sq cm	1.550×10^{-9}
" " "	webers/sq in.	10^{-8}
" " "	webers/sq meter	1.550×10^{-5}
links (engineer's)	inches	12.0
links (surveyor's)	inches	7.92
liters	bushels (U.S. dry)	0.02838
"	cu cm	1,000.0
"	cu feet	0.03531
"	cu inches	61.02

TO CONVERT	INTO	MULTIPLY BY
liters	cu meters	0.001
"	cu yards	1.308×10^{-3}
"	gallons (U.S. liq.)	0.2642
"	pints (U.S. liq.)	2.113
"	quarts (U.S. liq.)	1.057
liters/min	cu ft/sec	5.886×10^{-4}
" "	gals/sec	4.403×10^{-3}
lumens/sq ft	foot-candles	1.0
lux	foot-candles	0.0929

M

TO CONVERT	INTO	MULTIPLY BY
maxwells	kilolines	0.001
"	webers	10^{-8}
megalines	maxwells	10^{6}
megohms	microhms	10^{12}
"	ohms	10^{6}
meters	centimeters	100.0
"	feet	3.281
"	inches	39.37
"	kilometers	0.001
"	miles (naut.)	5.396×10^{-4}
"	miles (stat.)	6.214×10^{-4}
"	millimeters	1,000.0
"	yards	1.094
"	varas	1.179
meters/min	cms/sec	1.667
" "	feet/min	3.281
" "	feet/sec	0.05468
" "	kms/hr	0.06
" "	knots	0.03238
" "	miles/hr	0.03728
meters/sec	feet/min	196.8
" "	feet/sec	3.281
" "	kilometers/hr	3.6
" "	kilometers/min	0.06
" "	miles/hr	2.237
" "	miles/min	0.03728
meters/sec/sec	cms/sec/sec	100.0
" " "	ft/sec/sec	3.281
" " "	kms/hr/sec	3.6
" " "	miles/hr/sec	2.237
meter-kilograms	cm-dynes	9.807×10^{7}
" "	cm-grams	10^{5}
" "	pound-feet	7.233
microfarad	farads	10^{-6}

TO CONVERT	INTO	MULTIPLY BY
micrograms	grams	10^{-6}
microhms	megohms	10^{-12}
"	ohms	10^{-6}
microliters	liters	10^{-6}
miles (naut.)	feet	6,076.103
" "	kilometers	1.852
" "	meters	1,852.
" "	miles (statute)	1.1508
" "	yards	2,025.4
miles (statute)	centimeters	1.609×10^5
" "	feet	5,280.
" "	inches	6.336×10^4
" "	kilometers	1.609
" "	meters	1,609.
" "	miles (naut.)	0.8689
" "	yards	1,760.
miles/hr	cms/sec	44.70
" "	feet/min	88.
" "	feet/sec	1.467
" "	kms/hr	1.609
" "	kms/min	0.02682
" "	knots	0.8684
" "	meters/min	26.82
" "	miles/min	0.01667
miles/hr/sec	cms/sec/sec	44.70
" " "	feet/sec/sec	1.467
" " "	kms/hr/sec	1.609
" " "	meters/sec/sec	0.4470
miles/min	cms/sec	2,682.
" "	feet/sec	88.
" "	kms/min	1.609
" "	miles (naut.)/min	0.8684
" "	miles/hr	60.0
mil-feet	cu inches	9.425×10^{-6}
milliers	kilograms	1,000.
milligrams	grams	0.001
milligrams/liter	parts/million	1.0
millihenries	henries	0.001
milliliters	liters	0.001
millimeters	centimeters	0.1
"	feet	3.281×10^{-3}
"	inches	0.03937
"	kilometers	10^{-6}
"	meters	0.001
"	miles	6.214×10^{-7}
"	mils	39.37
"	yards	1.094×10^{-3}

TO CONVERT	INTO	MULTIPLY BY
million gals/day	cu ft/sec	1.54723
mils	centimeters	2.540×10^{-3}
"	feet	8.333×10^{-5}
"	inches	0.001
"	kilometers	2.540×10^{-8}
"	yards	2.778×10^{-5}
miner's inches	cu ft/min	1.5
minutes (angles)	degrees	0.01667
" "	quadrants	1.852×10^{-4}
" "	radians	2.909×10^{-4}
" "	seconds	60.0
myriagrams	kilograms	10.0
myriameters	kilometers	10.0
myriawatts	kilowatts	10.0

N

nepers	decibels	8.686

O

TO CONVERT	INTO	MULTIPLY BY
ohms	megohms	10^{-6}
ohms	microhms	10^{6}
ounces	drams	16.0
"	grains	437.5
"	grams	28.349527
"	pounds	0.0625
"	ounces (troy)	0.9115
"	tons (long)	2.790×10^{-5}
"	tons (metric)	2.835×10^{-5}
ounces (fluid)	cu inches	1.805
" "	liters	0.02957
ounces (troy)	grains	480.0
" "	grams	31.103481
" "	ounces (avdp.)	1.09714
" "	pennyweights (troy)	20.0
" "	pounds (troy)	0.08333
ounces/sq in.	pounds/sq in.	0.0625

P

parts/million	grains/U.S. gal	0.0584
" "	grains/Imp. gal	0.07016
" "	pounds/million gal	8.345

TO CONVERT	INTO	MULTIPLY BY
pennyweights (troy)	grains	24.0
" "	ounces (troy)	0.05
" "	grams	1.55517
" "	pounds (troy)	4.1667×10^{-3}
pints (dry)	cu inches	33.60
pints (liq.)	cu cms.	473.2
" "	cu feet	0.01671
" "	cu inches	28.87
" "	cu meters	4.732×10^{-4}
" "	cu yards	6.189×10^{-4}
" "	gallons	0.125
" "	liters	0.4732
" "	quarts (liq.)	0.5
poundals	dynes	13,826.
"	grams	14.10
"	joules/cm	1.383×10^{-3}
"	joules/meter (newtons)	0.1383
"	kilograms	0.01410
"	pounds	0.03108
pounds	drams	256.
"	dynes	44.4823×10^4
"	grains	7,000.
"	grams	453.5924
"	joules/cm	0.04448
"	joules/meter (newtons)	4.448
"	kilograms	0.4536
"	ounces	16.0
"	ounces (troy)	14.5833
"	poundals	32.17
"	pounds (troy)	1.21528
"	tons (short)	0.0005
pounds (troy)	grains	5,760.
" "	grams	373.24177
" "	ounces (avdp.)	13.1657
" "	ounces (troy)	12.0
" "	pennyweights (troy)	240.0
" "	pounds (avdp.)	0.822857
" "	tons (long)	3.6735×10^{-4}
" "	tons (metric)	3.7324×10^{-4}
" "	tons (short)	4.1143×10^{-4}
pounds of water	cu feet	0.01602
" " "	cu inches	27.68
" " "	gallons	0.1198
pounds of water/min	cu ft/sec	2.670×10^{-4}
pound-feet	cm-dynes	1.356×10^7
" "	cm-grams	13,825.
" "	meter-kgs	0.1383

TO CONVERT	INTO	MULTIPLY BY
pounds/cu ft	grams/cu cm	0.01602
" " "	kgs/cu meter	16.02
" " "	pounds/cu in.	5.787×10^{-4}
" " "	pounds/mil-foot	5.456×10^{-9}
pounds/cu in.	gms/cu cm	27.68
" " "	kgs/cu meter	2.768×10^4
" " "	pounds/cu ft	1,728.
" " "	pounds/mil-foot	9.425×10^{-6}
pounds/ft	kgs/meter	1.488
pounds/in.	gms/cm	178.6
pounds/mil-foot	gms/cu cm	2.306×10^6
pounds/sq ft	atmospheres	4.725×10^{-4}
" " "	feet of water	0.01602
" " "	inches of mercury	0.01414
" " "	kgs/sq meter	4.882
" " "	pounds/sq in.	6.944×10^{-3}
pounds/sq in.	atmospheres	0.06804
" " "	feet of water	2.307
" " "	inches of mercury	2.036
" " "	kgs/sq meter	703.1
" " "	pounds/sq ft	144.0

Q

TO CONVERT	INTO	MULTIPLY BY
quadrants (angle)	degrees	90.0
" "	minutes	5,400.0
" "	radians	1.571
" "	seconds	3.24×10^5
quarts (dry)	cu inches	67.20
quarts (liq.)	cu cms	946.4
" "	cu feet	0.03342
" "	cu inches	57.75
" "	cu meters	9.464×10^{-4}
" "	cu yards	1.238×10^{-3}
" "	gallons	0.25
" "	liters	0.9463

R

TO CONVERT	INTO	MULTIPLY BY
radians	degrees	57.30
"	minutes	3,438.
"	quadrants	0.6366
"	seconds	2.063×10^5
radians/sec	degrees/sec	57.30
" "	revolutions/min	9.549

TO CONVERT	INTO	MULTIPLY BY
radians/sec	revolutions/sec	0.1592
radians/sec/sec	revs/min/min	573.0
" " "	revs/min/sec	9.549
" " "	revs/sec/sec	0.1592
revolutions	degrees	360.0
"	quadrants	4.0
"	radians	6.283
revolutions/min	degrees/sec	6.0
" "	radians/sec	0.1047
" "	revs/sec	0.01667
revolutions/min/min	radians/sec/sec	1.745×10^{-3}
" " "	revs/min/sec	0.01667
" " "	revs/sec/sec	2.778×10^{-4}
revolutions/sec	degrees/sec	360.0
" "	radians/sec	6.283
" "	revs/min	60.0
revolutions/sec/sec	radians/sec/sec	6.283
" " "	revs/min/min	3,600.0
" " "	revs/min/sec	60.0
rods	feet	16.5

S

seconds (angle)	degrees	2.778×10^{-4}
" "	minutes	0.01667
" "	quadrants	3.087×10^{-6}
" "	radians	4.848×10^{-6}
square centimeters	circular mils	1.973×10^{5}
" "	sq feet	1.076×10^{-3}
" "	sq inches	0.1550
" "	sq meters	0.0001
" "	sq miles	3.861×10^{-11}
" "	sq millimeters	100.0
" "	sq yards	1.196×10^{-4}
square feet	acres	2.296×10^{-5}
" "	circular mils	1.833×10^{8}
" "	sq cms	929.0
" "	sq inches	144.0
" "	sq meters	0.09290
" "	sq miles	3.587×10^{-8}
" "	sq millimeters	9.290×10^{4}
" "	sq yards	0.1111
square inches	circular mils	1.273×10^{6}
" "	sq cms	6.452
" "	sq feet	6.944×10^{-3}
" "	sq millimeters	645.2

TO CONVERT	INTO	MULTIPLY BY
square inches	sq mils	10^6
" "	sq yards	7.716×10^{-4}
square kilometers	acres	247.1
" "	sq cms	10^{10}
" "	sq ft	10.76×10^6
" "	sq inches	1.550×10^9
" "	sq meters	10^6
" "	sq miles	0.3861
" "	sq yards	1.196×10^6
square meters	acres	2.471×10^{-4}
" "	sq cms	10^4
" "	sq feet	10.76
" "	sq inches	1,550.
" "	sq miles	3.861×10^{-7}
" "	sq millimeters	10^6
" "	sq yards	1.196
square miles	acres	640.0
" "	sq feet	27.88×10^6
" "	sq kms	2.590
" "	sq meters	2.590×10^6
" "	sq yards	3.098×10^6
square millimeters	circular mils	1,973.
" "	sq cms	0.01
" "	sq feet	1.076×10^{-5}
" "	sq inches	1.550×10^{-3}
square mils	circular mils	1.273
" "	sq cms	6.452×10^{-6}
" "	sq inches	10^{-6}
square yards	acres	2.066×10^{-4}
" "	sq cms	8,361.
" "	sq feet	9.0
" "	sq inches	1,296.
" "	sq meters	0.8361
" "	sq miles	3.228×10^{-7}
" "	sq millimeters	8.361×10^5

T

temperature (°C) +273	absolute temperature (°C)	1.0
temperature (°C) +17.78	temperature (°F)	1.8
temperature (°F) +460	absolute temperature (°F)	1.0
temperature (°F) − 32	temperature (°C)	5/9
tons (long)	kilograms	1,016.

TO CONVERT	INTO	MULTIPLY BY
tons (long)	pounds	2,240.
" "	tons (short)	1.120
tons (metric)	kilograms	1,000.
" "	pounds	2,205.
tons (short)	kilograms	907.1848
" "	ounces	32,000.
" "	ounces (troy)	29,166.66
" "	pounds	2,000.
" "	pounds (troy)	2,430.56
" "	tons (long)	0.89287
" "	tons (metric)	0.9078
tons (short)/sq ft	kgs/sq meter	9,765.
" " " "	pounds/sq in.	2,000.
tons of water/24 hrs	pounds of water/hr	83.333
" " " " "	gallons/min	0.16643
" " " " "	cu ft/hr	1.3349

W

watts	Btu/hr	3.413
"	Btu/min	0.05688
"	ergs/sec	10^7
"	foot-lbs/min	44.27
"	foot-lbs/sec	0.7378
"	horsepower	1.341×10^{-3}
"	horsepower (metric)	1.360×10^{-3}
"	kg-calories/min	0.01433
"	kilowatts	0.001
watt-hours	Btu	3.413
" "	ergs	3.60×10^{10}
" "	foot-pounds	2,656.
" "	gram-calories	859.85
" "	horsepower-hrs	1.341×10^{-3}
" "	kilogram-calories	0.8598
" "	kilogram-meters	367.2
" "	kilowatt-hrs	0.001
webers	maxwells	10^8
"	kilolines	10^5
webers/sq in.	gausses	1.550×10^7
" " "	lines/sq in.	10^8
" " "	webers/sq cm	0.1550
" " "	webers/sq meter	1,550.
webers/sq meter	gausses	10^4
" " "	lines/sq in.	6.452×10^4
" " "	webers/sq cm	10^{-4}
" " "	webers/sq in.	6.452×10^{-4}

TO CONVERT	INTO	MULTIPLY BY
	Y	
yards	centimeters	91.44
"	feet	3.0
"	inches	36.0
"	kilometers	9.144×10^{-4}
"	meters	0.9144
"	miles (naut.)	4.937×10^{-4}
"	miles (stat.)	5.682×10^{-4}
"	millimeters	914.4

NEW METRIC UNIT PREFIXES

The National Bureau of Standards scientists have decided to follow the recommendations of the International Committee on Weights and Measures to use new prefixes for denoting multiples and sub-multiples of metric units.

The International Committee adopted the prefixes at its meeting in Paris in the fall of 1958.

Prefixes to be used by the Bureau of Standards are listed in the October, 1959, issue of NBS's Technical News Bulletin.

In addition to the numerical prefixes already in common use, the Committee expanded the list by adding the four prefixes marked with an asterisk. Thus, for example, 10^{-12} farad is to be called 1 picofarad . . . replacing the designation "1 micromicrofarad," which some engineers have been using.

Multiples	Prefixes	Multiples	Prefixes
10^{12}	tera-*	10^{-1}	deci-
10^{9}	giga-*	10^{-2}	centi-
10^{6}	mega-	10^{-3}	milli-
10^{4}	myria-	10^{-6}	micro-
10^{3}	kilo-	10^{-9}	nano-*
10^{2}	hekto-	10^{-12}	pico-*
10	deka-		

* (tēr′a, jī′ga, nā′no, pī′co).

METRIC CONVERSION TABLE _____

The convenient table on page 268 provides a fast and easy means of conversion from one metric notation to another, including the newly designated units mentioned above. The value labeled "Unit" represents the basic units of measurement, such as ohms, watts, amperes, grams, etc. First, locate the original or given value in the left-hand column. Follow this line horizontally to the vertical column headed by the prefix of the desired value. The figure and arrow at this intersection represent the direction in which the decimal point should be moved and the number of places to move it.

EXAMPLE Convert 0.15 kilowatts to watts. Starting at the "Kilo-" box in the left-hand column, move horizontally to the column headed by "Unit" (since **watt** is a basic unit of measurement), and read 3→. Thus 0.15 kilowatts is the equivalent of 150 watts.

EXAMPLE Convert 4,500 kilocycles to megacycles, read in the box horizontal to "Kilo-" and under "Mega-" the notation ←3, which means a shift of the decimal point three places to the left. Thus, 4,500 kilocycles is the equivalent of 4.5 megacycles.

METRIC CONVERSION TABLE

ORIGINAL VALUE	DESIRED VALUE													
	Tera-	Giga-	Mega-	Myria-	Kilo-	Hekto-	Deka-	Units	Deci-	Centi-	Milli-	Micro-	Nano-	Pico-
Tera-		3↑	6↑	8↑	9↑	10↑	11↑	12↑	13↑	14↑	15↑	18↑	21↑	24↑
Giga-	↓3		3↑	5↑	6↑	7↑	8↑	9↑	10↑	11↑	12↑	15↑	18↑	21↑
Mega-	↓6	↓3		2↑	3↑	4↑	5↑	6↑	7↑	8↑	9↑	12↑	15↑	18↑
Myria-	↓8	↓5	↓2		1↑	2↑	3↑	4↑	5↑	6↑	7↑	10↑	13↑	16↑
Kilo-	↓9	↓6	↓3	↓1		1↑	2↑	3↑	4↑	5↑	6↑	9↑	12↑	15↑
Hekto-	↓10	↓7	↓4	↓2	↓1		1↑	2↑	3↑	4↑	5↑	8↑	11↑	14↑
Deka-	↓11	↓8	↓5	↓3	↓2	↓1		1↑	2↑	3↑	4↑	7↑	10↑	13↑
Units	↓12	↓9	↓6	↓4	↓3	↓2	↓1		1↑	2↑	3↑	6↑	9↑	12↑
Deci-	↓13	↓10	↓7	↓5	↓4	↓3	↓2	↓1		1↑	2↑	5↑	8↑	11↑
Centi-	↓14	↓11	↓8	↓6	↓5	↓4	↓3	↓2	↓1		1↑	4↑	7↑	10↑
Milli-	↓15	↓12	↓9	↓7	↓6	↓5	↓4	↓3	↓2	↓1		3↑	6↑	9↑
Micro-	↓18	↓15	↓12	↓10	↓9	↓8	↓7	↓6	↓5	↓4	↓3		3↑	6↑
Nano-	↓21	↓18	↓15	↓13	↓12	↓11	↓10	↓9	↓8	↓7	↓6	↓3		3↑
Pico-	↓24	↓21	↓18	↓16	↓15	↓14	↓13	↓12	↓11	↓10	↓9	↓6	↓3	

	Practical Unit	Cgs Electromagnetic Unit	Cgs Electrostatic Unit
Emf	volt = 10^8 abvolts volt = 3.3×10^{-3} statvolt	abvolt = 10^{-8} volt abvolt = 3.3×10^{-11} statvolt	statvolt = 300 volts (approx.) statvolt = 3×10^{10} abvolts
Resistance	ohm = 10^9 abohms ohm = 1.1×10^{-12} statohm	abohm = 10^{-9} ohm abohm = 1.1×10^{-21} statohm	statohm = 9×10^{11} ohms statohm = 9×10^{20} abohms
Current	ampere = 10^{-1} abampere ampere = 3×10^9 statamperes	abampere = 10 amperes abampere = 3×10^{10} statamperes	statampere = 3.3×10^{-10} ampere statampere = 3.3×10^{-11} abampere
Quantity	coulomb = 10^{-1} abcoulomb coulomb = 3×10^9 statcoulombs	abcoulomb = 10 coulombs abcoulomb = 3×10^{10} statcoulombs	statcoulomb = 3.3×10^{-10} coulomb statcoulomb = 3.3×10^{-11} abcoulomb
Capacitance	farad = 10^{-9} abfarad farad = 9×10^{11} statfarads	abfarad = 10^9 farads abfarad = 9×10^{20} statfarads	statfarad = 1.1×10^{-12} farad statfarad = 1.1×10^{-21} abfarad
Inductance	henry = 10^9 abhenries henry = 1.1×10^{-12} stathenry	abhenry = 10^{-9} henry abhenry = 1.1×10^{21} stathenries	stathenry = 9×10^{11} henries stathenry = 9×10^{20} abhenries
Energy	joule = 10^7 ergs	erg = 10^{-7} joule	erg = 10^{-7} joule
Power	watt = $\dfrac{10^7 \text{ ergs}}{\text{sec}}$	erg = $\dfrac{10^{-7} \text{ watt}}{\text{sec}}$	erg = $\dfrac{10^{-7} \text{ watt}}{\text{sec}}$

APPENDIX

MEASUREMENTS ⸻

LENGTH

12 inches	=	1 foot
3 feet	=	1 yard
5,280 feet	=	1 statute mile
6,080 feet	=	1 nautical mile
1 mil	=	0.001 inch

AREA

144 square inches	=	1 square foot
9 square feet	=	1 square yard
Cross-sectional area in circular mils	=	Square of diameter in mils

VOLUME

1,728 cubic inches	=	1 cubic foot
27 cubic feet	=	1 cubic yard

WEIGHT

16 ounces	=	1 pound
2,000 pounds	=	1 short ton
2,240 pounds	=	1 long ton

CIRCULAR MEASURE

60 seconds	=	1 minute
60 minutes	=	1 degree
360 degrees	=	1 circle
90 degrees	=	1 right angle
$11\frac{1}{4}$ degrees	=	1 point on the compass

TIME

60 seconds	=	1 minute
60 minutes	=	1 hour
24 hours	=	1 day
365 days	=	1 year

CONVERSION FACTORS

Atmosphere (standard)	=	29.92 inches of mercury
Atmosphere (standard)	=	14.7 pounds per square inch
1 horsepower	=	746 watts
1 horsepower	=	33,000 foot-pounds of work per minute
1 British thermal unit	=	778 foot-pounds
1 cubic foot	=	7.48 gallons
1 gallon	=	231 cubic inches
1 cubic foot of fresh water	=	62.5 pounds
1 cubic foot of salt water	=	64 pounds
1 foot of head of water	=	0.434 pounds per square inch
1 inch of head of mercury	=	0.491 pounds per square inch
1 gallon of fresh water		8.33 pounds
1 barrel (oil)	=	42 gallons
1 long ton of fresh water	=	36 cubic feet
1 long ton of salt water	=	35 cubic feet
1 ounce (avoirdupois)	=	437.5 grains

THERM-HOUR CONVERSION FACTORS

1 therm-hour = 100,000 Btu per hour.

1 brake horsepower = 2544 Btu per hour

1 brake horsepower = $\dfrac{2544}{100,000} = 0.02544$ therm-hour

1 therm-hour = $\dfrac{100,000}{2544} = 39.3082$ brake horsepower (40 hp is close enough)

1 therm-hour = $\dfrac{100,000}{33,475} = 2.9873$ boiler horsepower (3 hp is close enough)

EXAMPLE: How many therm-hours in a 100-hp engine?
ANSWER: $100 \times 0.02544 = 2.544$ therm-hours

BOILER HORSEPOWER

1 boiler hp	=	33,475 Btu per hour
	=	34.5 lb steam per hour at 212°F
	=	139 sq ft EDR (equivalent direct radiation)
1 EDR	=	240 Btu per hour
1 kW	=	3413 Btu per hour

WEIGHT OF WATER AT 62°F

1 cu in.	=	0.0361 lb (of water)
1 cu ft	=	62.355 lb
1 gal	=	8.3391 lb (8⅓ close enough)

MISCELLANEOUS DATA _____

3413 British thermal units (Btu)	=	1 kilowatt-hour (kW-hr)
1,000 watts	=	1 kilowatt (kW)
1.341 horsepower (hp)	=	1 kilowatt
2,545 Btu	=	1 horsepower-hour (hp-hr)
0.746 kilowatt	=	1 hp
1 micron	=	one millionth of a meter (unit of length)

GLOSSARY

ABSOLUTE HUMIDITY: The weight of water vapor in a unit volume. Commonly expressed as grains per cubic foot (7000 grains = 1 lb).

ABSOLUTE PRESSURE: The sum of the gage reading and the atmospheric pressure. When the gage is open to atmosphere, it reads zero. At sea level, the atmospheric pressure commonly used is 14.7 psi. This atmospheric value decreases with elevation. For example, at 2000 ft the pressure is 13,664 psi; at 10,000 ft, only 10.1 psi; and at 16,000 ft, it is down to 7.7 psi.

ABSOLUTE TEMPERATURE: The temperature as read on the Fahrenheit scale plus 460. Specifically, the observed temperature plus 459.67°F. On the centigrade (Celsius) scale, the observed temperature plus 273.15°C.

ABSOLUTE ZERO: A temperature of 460°F below zero on the Fahrenheit scale. Specifically, a temperature of -459.67°F, or -273.15°C. At absolute zero, there is no molecular motion; thus no heat is generated.

ADIABATIC EXPANSION: The expansion when no heat is added to, or taken from, a substance or system undergoing a process. Steam expanded behind the piston of a steam engine after the point of cutoff approaches adiabatic expansion.

AIR CONDITIONING: Usually the control within a structure of atmosphere, including temperature, humidity, and motion. It may also include control of distribution, pressure, dust, bacteria, odors, toxic gases, and ionization.

AIR-FUEL RATIO: The amount of air, in cubic feet or pounds, being furnished for combustion per cubic foot or per pound of fuel. For example, 12 lb of air per 1 lb of coal is a 12-to-1 ratio and gives near perfect combustion.

AMBIENT TEMPERATURE: The temperature of air in an enclosure. Example: ambient air temperature in a power plant may be 98°F.

ANALYSIS, PROXIMATE: An analysis of solid fuel which is used to find the percentages of moisture, volatile matter, fixed carbon, and ash per unit weight of the sample. For example, a proximate analysis of a coal might show the sample to contain 3% moisture, 10% volatile matter, 78% fixed carbon, and 9% ash.

ANALYSIS, ULTIMATE: A chemical analysis of a fuel which determines the percentage of the chemical constituents in percent of the weight of the unit sample. An ultimate analysis determines the percentages of sulfur, hydrogen, carbon, nitrogen, oxygen, and ash. The ultimate analysis is required to determine a heat balance and the efficiency of the combustion.

BAROMETRIC PRESSURE: The atmospheric pressure as indicated by a barometer, calibrated in inches of mercury (in. Hg). At sea level, the normal barometric pressure is accepted as 30 in. Hg., although the exact pressure under the standard conditions of 70°F air temperature and 60% relative humidity is 29.921 in. Hg.

BRITISH THERMAL UNIT: A unit of heat energy. It is defined as the quantity of heat required to raise the temperature of 1 lb of water 1°F, and abbreviated as Btu.

CALORIE: The unit of heat energy required to raise the temperature of 1 gram of water from 0° to 1°C. It is approximately equal to the amount of heat required to heat 1 gram of water 1 degree Celsius at a constant atmospheric pressure. One calorie is the equivalent of 0.003968 Btu.

CALORIFIC VALUE: The heat value of a fuel, expressed in either Btu per pound or calories. For example, 1 lb = 453.58 grams (approximately).

CELSIUS (formerly) CENTIGRADE: The temperature scale on which the melting and freezing points of ice are rated as zero and the boiling point of water is 100, all at atmospheric pressure. The absolute temperature on the Celsius scale is −273.15; thus on this scale water boils at 373.15°C absolute. To convert Celsius to Fahrenheit temperatures, multiply the Celsius reading by $9/5$ and add 32. Thus the boiling point of water in Fahrenheit degrees, is 100°C × $9/5$ + 32 = 212°F. By reversing this procedure, Fahrenheit temperatures may be converted to their Celsius scale values: (212 − 32) × $5/9$ = 180 × $5/9$ = 100°C.

CONDUCTION, THERMAL: The rate of heat flow through unit area of a nonmoving body, of given size and shape, per unit temperature difference. Heat is conducted through the metal in the shell and tubes of a boiler. Substances differ widely in their ability to conduct heat. For example, metals are usually good conductors; soot and boiler scale are very poor conductors.

CONDUCTIVITY: The rate of heat flow through a homogeneous material, expressed in Btu per hour per square foot, per degree Fahrenheit of temperature difference.

CONVECTION: The movement of a fluid set up by a combination of differences in density and the force of gravity. Example: In a vertical tank, water warmed at the bottom will rise and displace the cooler water at the top. The cooler water then sinks to the bottom, in accordance with the convective laws. Gravity and warm-air heating systems operate similarly.

DEGREE DAY: The number of heating degree days for each calendar day is the difference in degrees between the mean temperature for that day and 65°F. A mean for the day of 50°F represents $65 - 50 = 15$ degree days. The temperature of 65°F is the dividing temperature between heat needed and not needed.

DEW POINT: (1) The air temperature at which any reduction of the ambient temperature would produce some condensation of the air's water-vapor content. (2) The temperature at which a vapor liquefies is called its dew point.

DRY STEAM: Steam that has a temperature consonant with its pressure and contains no more than $1/2$ of 1% moisture.

EFFICIENCY: The efficiency of any equipment is the output divided by the input. In boiler operation, efficiency is the ratio of the energy fed to the boiler to the energy obtained from the boiler. For example, a pound of coal with a calorific value of 14,000 Btu per lb is burned under a steam boiler to produce 11,000 Btu per hr in steam output. The efficiency of output to input is 11,000 divided by 14,000 equals about 80% efficiency. Other forms of efficiency apply to transmission of power, generation of power, etc.

ENTHALPY: A term used instead of *total heat,* or *heat content.* Enthalpy is expressed in Btu per lb.

EXCESS AIR: Combustion of fuel is primarily the combining of combustible substances of the fuel with oxygen of the air. A fuel requires a definite amount of oxygen, which is obtained from air, to effect complete combustion. Amount of air used in excess of amount needed is known as excess air. While excess air is necessary to effect complete combustion, too much air causes a decrease in efficiency.

FIRE POINT: The lowest temperature at which oil will emit enough vapor to burn continuously when ignited.

FLASH POINT: The temperature at which sufficient vapor is emitted from oil to produce a momentary flame when ignited.

GRAVITY, SPECIFIC: The ratio of the gravity of a given substance and volume to the gravity of a standard substance at the same volume and at a standard temperature. For liquids, the standard substance and temperature is water at 39.2°F, which is the point of water's greatest density. For gases, the standard substance is air, at the same temperature as the gas under consideration. The specific gravity of solids, especially woods, is referred to water, which is 1.

HEAT, LATENT: The heat, in Btu, required for a material to change its state, such as ice to water and water to water vapor (steam).

HEAT, SENSIBLE: An amount of heat that changes the temperature of a material but does not change its form.

HEAT, SPECIFIC: The amount of heat absorbed or relinquished by a unit of a substance, resulting in a temperature change of 1°F. The common unit is the pound, and the unit expressing heat is the Btu for liquids and solids. The specific heat of water is 1; of air, 0.24.

ISOTHERMIC: The description of a condition of change accomplished at constant temperature.

KELVIN: The temperature scale on which lowest possible temperature, designated as *zero*, is 273.15 degrees below the zero on the Celsius scale. To convert from Celsius to Kelvin temperatures (C to K), add 273.15 to the Celsius reading. Thus the boiling point of water in the atmosphere, which is 100°C, becomes 373.15°K.

LOAD FACTOR: The ratio of the average load during a given period and the normal maximum, or full capacity, load rating of the unit under consideration. Applicable also to the complete system.

MEAN INDICATED PRESSURE: In engine technology, the average net pressure per square inch acting on the piston during the power stroke. It is determined by the use of an indicator while the engine is operating.

MECHANICAL EQUIVALENT OF HEAT: The amount of mechanical energy equal to one unit of heat. One Btu = 778.2 ft-lb of mechanical energy.

MERCURY COLUMN: A column of mercury used to measure pressure. One inch of mercury at 62°F equals 0.4897 psi and is the equivalent of a water column 13.57 in. high. At 32°F the inch of mercury exerts a pressure of 0.49112 psi.

MICRON: A unit of length, which is a thousandth of one millimeter, or a millionth of a meter.

pH, or pH VALUE: A term for the hydrogen ion concentration in water, which denotes whether the water is acid, alkaline, or neutral. A pH value of 8 or more indicates a condition of alkalinity; 6 or less, acidity. A pH of 7 means the water is neutral, neither alkaline nor acid. The hydrogen ions are counted in their concentrations on the basis of grams per liter.

RADIATION: The transmission of heat without the use of a material carrier, such as the heat traveling through a vacuum, which the Earth receives from the sun, or electromagnetic waves, which raise the temperature of a cooler surface when absorbed.

RADIATION, EQUIVALENT DIRECT (EDR): The amount of heat assumed to be delivered by one square foot of direct radiation under standard conditions of 215°F steam temperature and 70°F ambient, or 240 Btu.

REFRIGERATION (ONE TON): (1) The standard ton of refrigeration represents the absorption of 288,000 Btu per 24 hr, or 12,000 Btu in 1 hr. (2) The amount of heat that must be removed from 1 ton (2000 lb) of water to convert the water into ice. Since the latent heat of freezing is 144 Btu per lb, this figure is obviously 288,000 Btu.

RELATIVE HUMIDITY: The weight of water vapor present in air (gas) expressed as a percentage of the maximum weight of water vapor possible in the considered air (gas) at the given temperature and pressure. Relative humidity is represented by curved lines on the psychrometric chart.

SUPERHEAT: A term used for steam, or any other gas, that is a measure of the increase of temperature for these gases [which normally have a pressure characteristic of their temperature (see Steam Tables)] when the temperatures are higher than is normal for the existing pressure.

THERM: A unit of heat having a value of 100,000 Btu. Commonly used in gas-combustion studies. 1 therm-hour = 100,000 Btu per hr.

VISCOSITY: The characteristic of fluids that causes them to resist a change shape (flow). Generally expressed in terms of Seconds Saybolt Universal, or Seconds Saybolt Furol. In both cases, seconds represent the time required by a given liquid to pass through a standard orifice at a temperature of 100°F for the Universal, and 122°F for the Furol.

INDEX

Addition, 1
  fast method of, 2
  of fractions, 12
  mental, 3
Air:
  compressed, weight of, 191
  cooling, capacity for, 230
Air conditioning (*see* Refriger-
    ation)
Alternator, changing voltage
    of, 239
Ammonia in brine, 233
Ammonia leak, 233
Ammonia plant, 226
  brine required for, 229
  cooling water for, 226
Ammonia vapor, volume of, at
    selected pressures, table,
    228
Angle, right, 58

Approximate division, 30
Approximations, 27
Areas, 45
  of circles, 45, 51, 52, 57
  of irregular shapes, 49, 55
  of triangles, 56

Balancing, 96
Baumé degrees, 154, 155
Beams, strength of, 65–72
  bending moment, 65, 67,
    70, 71
  cantilever, 69
  safety, 70
  section modulus, 70
  simple, 68
    formula for, 69
  unit stress, 70
Bell cranks, 87, 97